D1045251

THE CHURCH THAT STAYED

WRITTEN BY JOHN ROBERT SMITH

THE LIFE AND TIMES OF
CENTRAL PRESBYTERIAN CHURCH
IN THE HEART OF ATLANTA, 1858-1978

THE CHURCH THAT STAYED

JOHN ROBERT SMITH

WRITTEN BY
JOHN ROBERT SMITH
PUBLISHED BY
**THE ATLANTA
HISTORICAL SOCIETY**

LIBRARY OF CONGRESS
CATALOG CARD NO.: 79-52840
PRODUCED BY
AMPERSAND STUDIOS
PRINTED IN THE UNITED
STATES OF AMERICA

THE CHURCH THAT STAYED

CONTENTS

This book is dedicated to all those who, under God, have helped keep Central "central" throughout the first 120 years of its history, and to all who will carry that ministry forward in the decades to come.

AUTHOR'S FOREWORD

Throughout all my years as director of the Urban Church Department of the Presbyterian Church, U.S., I never came across another church anywhere quite like the Central Presbyterian Church in Atlanta. Not only was it managing to stay in its downtown location with strength, but it was also continuing to serve its changing downtown area with unchanging compassion and real style.

I was acquainted in my work with many great and committed congregations, both within and beyond the bounds of our denomination, all earnestly striving for the same goals, but most of them not quite making it. How then account for Central Church? How was it achieving a meaningful ministry in an area where so many churches fail?

The answer, I was sure, could never be encapsulated in any how-to-do-it essay about Central or any other congregation. Really helpful answers could derive only from a full and honest and openly recounted history. Unfortunately, written institutional histories of that type are rare. In the case of churches, they are almost non-existent. Consequently, many helpful lessons that congregations could learn from each other go unlearned. The successes and the honest failures within the histories of our churches continue not to be communicated. That, to my mind, is a great pity.

Therefore, when after my retirement the Atlanta Historical Society asked me to carry out the historical research out of which this publication has grown, I accepted the opportunity most eagerly.

The Atlanta Historical Society is preserving on behalf of Central Presbyterian Church all the existing official records of that church. Also preserved within the same archives are the records which Dr. Stuart R. Oglesby carefully maintained throughout the forty-seven year period he was associated with this church as pastor or pastor emeritus.

It was within these extensive holdings of Dr. Oglesby and of Central Church itself that my research was primarily carried forward, with the official Minutes of Session being a major source of data in compiling the Central story. Newspaper and periodical files throughout the 120-year history of the church plus, of course, files of the congregations own *Weekly* publication provided additional excellent historical resources. Another source of information was the published histories of Atlanta, especially Mr. Franklin M. Garrett's *Atlanta and Its Environs*, and the unpublished manuscripts of certain dissertations dealing with Atlanta history. Particularly exciting, as well, were the facts and opinions contained in the diaries and letters of various citizens of early Atlanta, ensconced in the archives. Most of all, though, it was the remembered oral history of Centralites themselves that most vividly brought the Central story to life to me.

These Centralites, invariably, are modest about Central's accomplishments as a downtown church. They feel that their best efforts have never measured up to the size of the opportunities for ministry which God has given them. Their pleasure in the publication of this history arises not from wanting others to suppose that Central is doing such a great work, but rather from a hope that other congregations, learning from the Central story, may tender more faithful witness in whatever situation God has placed them.

Central's church history committee, assembled under the energetic leadership of Mrs. Harry L. (Margaret) Carlisle, did yeoman service throughout in searching out hidden nuggets and in keeping the project on course. Our debt to all of the following committee members is gratefully acknowledged:

Mrs. Harry L. (Margaret) Carlisle, Chairman

Dr. Fred Bellinger
Mr. Roy T. Greene
Dr. Douglas G. MacRae
Mrs. F.W. (Maud) Nardin
Col. Stuart R. Oglesby III
Miss Patsy A. Wiggins
Miss Dorothy Woods
Mr. V. Jack Yarbrough
Mrs. V. Jack Yarbrough

Special gratitude and appreciation are due committee members V. Jack Yarbrough, Douglas MacRae and Stuart R. Oglesby, III, who served at the request of the chairman as a special editorial group. The value of the advice and leadership of this small group would indeed be hard to over-estimate.

In a spirit typical of Central Church, a small army of members who are not even part of the church history committee gave their time and skills most helpfully on behalf of this undertaking. Their contributions were greatly needed and appreciated.

Credit for the many excellent historical pictures enhancing this volume must go to the Atlanta Historical Society. Also gratefully acknowledged are some additional pictures furnished by members and friends of Central and used in the closing chapter.

The amount of money required for getting a book such as this into production is huge indeed. It is only because of certain exceedingly generous gifts, from both Centralites and individual sources, that the publication has been accomplished. To these liberal donors I express the gratitude of all.

This entire project could hardly have begun to develop without the catalytic influence and role of the Atlanta Historical Society, under whose aegis this history is being published. Very special accolades must go to Miss Patsy A. Wiggins, the Society's able and effective Director of Acquisitions. Her encouragement and wise counsel have been simply tremendous throughout. She, Mrs. Carlisle, and Col. Oglesby have my very special thanks.

The Church That Stayed has no pretensions of being the complete story of this church. That story has heights and depths as many and varied as the names in Chapter Eight. In no way could all become incorporated in one slim volume. My hope for this volume is rather that it serve as a framework sturdy enough to gather about it more more and more of the Central story — especially that part of the story which is still in Central's future.

John Robert Smith

Atlanta, Georgia 1979

Atlanta's earliest Presbyterians joined with the earliest Baptists and Methodists in an ecumenical sharing of this little log building erected in 1847. Here the pioneering Atlanta Presbyterian Church was organized on January 8, 1848, and here continued to worship until its own building was completed three years later.

THE CHURCH THAT STAYED

Chapter I
The Beginnings (1858 — 1869)

In the providence of God and in the wisdom of man, the Central Presbyterian Church first launched into life in Atlanta, Georgia, directly across Washington Street from City Hall in the year 1858.

A more intimidating year and place for establishing a new, thirty-nine member congregation would be hard even to imagine. War clouds, big and ominous in the year of Central's beginning, already warned of the mighty storm to come.

And once the war came, the full force and brunt of it was going to center over Atlanta. Though one of the youngest of all Georgia towns, Atlanta had already emerged as the transportation crossroads of the South and those steel rails which made it a burgeoning terminus would soon become lightning rods attracting the deadliest bolts that war could hurl.

The point within Atlanta where the coming conflict would center was City Hall itself. This Williamsburg-like building, occupying the very site where the Georgia State Capitol now stands, seemed destined to attract more than its share of the sights and sounds of war. It and the fledgling Presbyterian congregation, which had bought its land just across the street, shared a time and place distinctly hazardous to their health.

Perhaps this shared hazard caused City Hall to cooperate helpfully in getting its new little neighbor underway. Since no building stood on the site which Central Presbyterian Church had purchased for its use, Mayor Luther J. Glenn and the City Council invited the new congregation to make City Hall its place of meeting until its own building could be erected.

Thus it came about that it was in the ample common room of Atlanta's City Hall that the people of Central Church first gathered as a congregation to worship God. And there they continued to worship and grow during the months their own tall-spired building was taking shape across the street:

Central's handsomely columned first building, completed early in 1860, survived the Civil War and served almost a quarter of a century before being replaced by the present sanctuary.

The Beginnings (1858-1869)

> The spire on Central Presbyterian Church has assumed its proportions and height. Unlike a great many spires we have seen, it is well proportioned and presents a taking appearance. It cannot be a great while before that congregation is permitted to occupy its house, which promises to be an ornament to the city, and speaks well for the liberality of the people who built it.
>
> (*Georgia Temperance Crusader,* August 5, 1859)

It cannot be supposed though that Central's emergence as Atlanta's thirteenth church generated more than modest interest throughout the city. Like the adolescent it then was, Atlanta was rapidly growing. The beginning of Central Presbyterian represented but one among many exciting happenings of the time in this growing little city. During the one year of 1858, no less than nineteen substantial new brick buildings were added to Atlanta's downtown area. At the corner of Courtland and Auburn Avenue, the "Calico House" residence finally stood completed in all its wildly-colored 'glory' and became Atlanta's conversation piece of the year. At about the same time, at the nearby corner of Courtland and Ellis Streets, the new building which was to house Atlanta's pioneering College For Women got finishing touches and many admiring glances. Even more admiring were glances the young ladies of Atlanta had for the uniforms displayed by members of the Gate City Old Guard, founded that year as one of the most prestigious and Southern of all the military organizations of the region. Old Guard uniforms were proudly evident a year later for the Atlanta speech of Stephen Douglas, the Democratic candidate for President running against a Republican candidate named Abraham Lincoln. Background music for all these happenings was the crescendo of car-loaded goods and finished products pounding in across shiny steel rails from all directions to converge at this new terminal spot.

Converging also upon this terminal spot were people — many of them from all directions. They came in increasing numbers to stake their future with that of this exciting young city. During the five-year period prior to Central's organization as a Church, Atlanta had doubled in population.

Growing even more rapidly during the same years was the membership roll of Atlanta Presbyterian Church. This church, which occupied a modest red brick building on Marietta Street, was the parent Presbyterian congregation of the city of Atlanta.

But for reasons not fully disclosed, the parent congregation soon became a sharply divided church family. By the middle of 1857, the difference of opinion between the two factions became serious enough to require presbytery intervention. The minutes of the June 25, 1857 meeting of Flint River Presbytery (superseded after the Civil War by

The pioneering Atlanta Presbyterian Church, of which Central's founding members were a part, worshiped in this Marietta Street building until early in 1858 when the membership became re-formed into two new congregations — Central and First. In 1858, Pastor John E. DuBose moved from here to the same Tallahassee church that the Rev. P.C. Enniss was to serve more than a century later.

the Presbytery of Atlanta) remain tantalizingly silent as to what the specific contentions within the membership were really about. They focus instead on the action the presbytery was being asked to deal with: the resignation or not of Pastor John E. DuBose. Part of the Atlanta Presbyterian Church membership demanded a dissolution of the pastoral relationship while the other group of members (they were later to form into Central Church) just as strongly opposed this action.

Presbytery decided against dissolving the pastoral connection on the grounds that the departure of Dr. DuBose would have no bearing at all on the rift that was there. But, declared presbytery, . . . "in view of the prevailing differences of opinion in the Atlanta Church on matters not involving any vital principle of doctrine or church polity, and yet threatening to disturb, if not destroy the peace and prosperity of the church, it be and hereby is directed that the said congregation divide and constitute two distinct congregations."

This June 25, 1857 ruling of Flint River Presbytery was promptly appealed to the next higher court, the Synod. It was early in 1858 before presbytery once again could come to grips with the Atlanta Church rift. At its February 10th meeting, a group of "some forty" Atlanta Church members (later to be formed into Central Church) came petitioning the presbytery to divide the total membership into two new and separate congregations. The remaining members, larger in number, came with a counter-petition urging presbytery not to do so.

The presbytery once again ruled in favor of the smaller "Central" contingent and on February 11, 1858 ordered that the parent Atlanta Presbyterian Church be immediately divided into two new congregations.

In ordering this division, the Flint River Presbytery stipulated only that the membership group within the Atlanta Presbyterian Church which was to take its new life in the old building should become known as First Presbyterian Church, while the membership group, planning to move and begin its new life at a new site to be purchased on the then fashionable Washington Street, should be named Second Presbyterian Church.

But the name "Second" was strongly resisted by the Presbyterians moving to City Hall Square. It was felt, perhaps, that "second" connoted a degree of inferiority not at all in keeping with Atlanta's new spirit of derring-do. Certainly it was not in keeping with the spirit of the people who were establishing their new church which would be, they felt, at the very heart and center of Atlanta's activity. They wanted to name their church, not Second, but "Central."

The presbytery quickly agreed to the name and completed arrangements for organizing the two new churches. Central Presbyterian Church became officially established on February 14, 1858. Exactly one week later the sister congregation, Atlanta's First Presbyterian Church, came officially into being. Out of the old original Atlanta Presbyterian Church had grown two new congregations.

Early in 1858 when Central Church was just starting its ministry, the threat of war was already full-grown. There is no evidence, though, that the congregation was in the least intimidated by that threat. Like the prophet Jeremiah who, wars or not, bought his field, so Central, wars or not, set about building its first sanctuary. The completed structure emerged on the Atlanta scene as any thing but tentative or uncertain. Its soaring walls were solidly brick, its Corinthian columns stood bold as exclamation points, and its steeple topped all the others Atlanta could offer. The Centralites who gathered there for their first service on March 4, 1860, were as proud as they were undaunted.

Daily Intelligencer & Examiner.

ATLANTA,

SUNDAY, FEBRUARY 14, 1858.

☞ The Daily Intelligencer & Examiner is delivered every morning to Subscribers in all parts of Atlanta, at $6, per annum in advance.

The Weekly paper is issued every Thursday and sent out by the mails of that day.

☞ For Latest News SEE THIRD PAGE.

☞ Rev. J. L ROGERS will preach in the Presbyterian Church on to-day, at the usual morning hour, 10 o'clock.

Flint River Presbytery at its recent meeting, having constituted two new Churches out of the old Presbyterian Church, that portion who petitioned the Presbytery for a division of the Church, will be *organized* at 3 o'clock this afternoon, in the same hoeus.

A full attendance of members and pew-holders, and the public generally, is respectfully requested.

This from the *Daily Intelligencer* and *Examiner* on the very day of Central's beginning gives notice of the 3:00 P.M. meeting at which Central became officially organized as a church. The same Atlanta newspaper on the following Saturday carried the additional notice: "The other branch of the church (First) will organize tomorrow we learn."

Well before it had a building of its own, however, this enterprising congregation was already operating a seminary for the girls and young ladies of Atlanta, as attested by an advertisement in the August 13, 1862 issue of *The Daily Intelligencer*:

> CENTRAL FEMALE SEMINARY
> Washington Street, Atlanta, Ga.
>
> The exercises of this School will be resumed on Monday, August 19.
>
> Rooms, large and well furnished. Grateful for the very liberal patronage received during the past three years, they hope to merit a continuance and increase of the school, as they have greatly increased their facilities and means of advancing their pupils.
>
> For terms, please see Circular, or call at Lecture Rooms, New Central Presbyterian, opposite City Hall.

The hilltop location of the new Central Presbyterian Church, opposite City Hall, was in those pre-war days as delightful a spot as could be found in all Atlanta:

> Capitol Square was City Hall square then, for Milledgeville was still the capitol of Georgia. The softly rolling green square was substantially fenced with stout wooden posts and pointed palings bearing, at intervals, signs threatening a $100 fine to anybody who posted bills or tampered with the fence itself. At the corners, Atlanta's new gas lamp posts with their square lanterns were the pride of the town, for the new gas works had been only recently installed, and near each post was a stout stone pillar to keep runaway horses or careless drivers from crashing a vehicle into the lamp post and breaking the main that supplied it.
>
> The graceful red brick building which was the City Hall and the first meeting place of the Central Presbyterian congregation, was crowned with a white wooden cupola which gave the place an air of a Virginia provencial town. Wiry little oak saplings, each protected by a wooden framework, were set out on the dirt sidewalks where they were to grow into the great old oak trees which still shade Washington Street and Capitol Square. And on four sides of the square stood the fine ante-bellum mansions of Atlanta's pioneers. (*The Atlanta Journal*, May 9, 1937)

That idyllically-described world of 1860 gave little hint of the fateful decade which 1860 introduced. It was a decade which thrust upon young Atlanta-town days as unbelievable as any through which a city and its people have ever tried to exist. The town's burgeoning economy ground to a halt. Its currency inflated to the point of uselessness. Its public halls became hospitals crowded with the war-wounded and dying. Its daily news was of the ever-nearer encroachment of invading armies bent on Atlanta's destruction. Its sounds

The Rev. John E. DuBose
Atlanta Presbyterian Church
Pastor 1854 - 1858

The Rev. J.L. Rogers
Central Pastor 1859 - 1863

The Rev. Robert Q. Mallard
Central Pastor 1863 - 1866
General Assembly Moderator
1896

The Rev. Rufus K. Porter
Central Pastor 1867 - 1869

became the endless explosions of enemy shells, lofted into Atlanta's streets and houses from nearby vantage points. Its sights became that of occupying forces coming and claiming Atlanta as a prize of war.

The stores which had been the busy heart of Atlanta's economy were looted bare. The railroads which had made this a terminal spot were rendered largely unusable. The civilian population which had chosen Atlanta as its home was told on order of General Sherman to go and take up residence, as best it could, somewhere else. And all the homes and buildings which had been the visible aspect of Atlanta were, unless an exception was ordered, systematically burned into charred ruins, which had to be raised or continue stunned and all but lifeless.

And what of Central Church? What of the fledgling congregation which had so enthusiastically dedicated its first building at the very onset of that fateful Atlanta decade? It is only through outside sources of information that we can piece together any semblance of an answer. For, as fortune would have it, Central's own official records of its life as a congregation from its beginnings up through 1869 suffered the same fate as Atlanta itself. They were destroyed. The fire which in 1869 brought destruction to the house of Moses Cole destroyed also the church records which had been put there for safekeeping. The experience of years of war and reconstruction had persuaded Mr. Cole, as Central's Clerk of Session, that the records would be more safely preserved in his house than in the usually unprotected church building.

But destroyed they were. Enough non-church sources of information survived destruction to enable the piecing together of glimpses, at least, of what Centralites were doing and seeing and thinking during that first decade.

We know, for one thing, that Central, though young and still unsturdy, spurned the relative safety of a neutral sideline position as to secession and plunged brashly into Southern waters. When Atlanta staged its huge celebration to cheer South Carolina's secession in 1860, there to lead the prayers for this heady event was the Rev. J. L. Rogers, Central's first pastor. And when on January 2, 1861, there was a city and county-wide election to determine whether secessionists or moderates from Atlanta would go to the State convention in Milledgeville which was to decide Georgia's secession stance, not only did the secessionists win, but the secessionist who got more votes by far than any of the rest was Dr. Joseph P. Logan, one of Central's two original elders. This same elder from Central was a Georgia delegate to the Southern Congress held in Montgomery, Alabama, for the setting up of a Confederacy.

This carefully researched painting by historian-artist Wilbur G. Kurtz depicts Atlanta just before its destruction in 1864. Superimposed numbers indicate (1) Central Presbyterian Church (2) City Hall (3) St. Phillips Episcopal Church (4) Immaculate Conception Church (5) Trinity Methodist Church (6) Second Baptist Church (7) the John Neal house.

We know also that early in 1863 when Dr. Rogers left and Central called its second pastor, the Rev. R. Q. Mallard, he too soon caught the Southern fever and was not at his job long before he followed the men of his congregation into action and joined up with the fighting forces of the Confederacy. Soon he became a prisoner of war, and it was well after the hostilities had ended before he was permitted to return to his flock at Central. Thus Central Presbyterians, or as many of them as survived the war or the expulsion order, were utterly without pastoral leadership during that most devastating of times.

The war years were made particularly devastating for Centralites as they observed the increasingly voracious appetite which the war had for Central's manpower. The demand, which at the outset was for all men between 18 and 35, was gradually expanded until even the sixty-year olds were being thrown into battle. To make the point more vividly, muster which followed each new call-up always took place at the spot where Central had a grandstand seat — on the neighboring lawns of City Hall.

Another known fact out of these hazy years is that when Sherman's forces began to move in from the north and the west in late 1864 to take what was by then a defenseless Atlanta, it was the deep-toned bell in Central's tower that warned the endangered city with peals so vigorously rung that the bell became hopelessly cracked and remained so the rest of its days.

But Central's involvement was not ended. When General William T. Sherman entered the conquered city, claiming his prize and establishing his headquarters, the headquarters he chose was practically on Central's doorstep. For the General claimed for his private use the elegant Neal house which shared Washington Street with Central on the corner where Atlanta's present City Hall now stands. The realities of war could hardly have been closer for Central than during those early fall days of 1864.

The John Neal mansion, Southwest corner of Washington and Mitchell Streets, where General Sherman established his 1864 headquarters and which in 1870 became home for Oglethorpe University and later for Girls High School, can be seen in the foreground of this 1860 photograph. In the near background is Second Baptist Church with Central beyond.

General Sherman's proximity had at least one positive consequence. When by his order the torch was set to the rest of Atlanta, the one notably spared section was that occupied by the churches and buildings in the vicinity of City Hall. Or, to put it more correctly, those churches and buildings in the vicinity of the Neal house were spared. For the General was much too prudent a man to endanger his own lush quarters needlessly by random sparks which would be ejected by the burning down of Immaculate Conception or Second Baptist or St. Philips Episcopal or Trinity Methodist or the City Hall or Central Presbyterian. So it was that Central's building, though battered and badly used, survived at least the first stage of occupation.

Central's immunity from flames, however, probably would have expired when Sherman left the Neal house to take up his march to the sea had not Immaculate Conception's Father O'Reilly shown Irish spunk in protecting his own church and manse. Part of the December 7, 1864, report which General W. P. Howard made to Governor Joseph E. Brown concerning the post-occupation state of Atlanta, tells that story:

> Second Baptist, Second (sic) Presbyterian, Trinity and Catholic churches are safe, all attributable to Father O'Reilly who refused to give up his parsonage to Yankee officers who were looking for fine houses for quarters, and there being a large number of Catholic soldiers in the Yankee army who volunteered to protect the Catholic church and parsonage, and would not allow any adjacent house or church to be fired that would endanger them.

If Central's building was left standing, not much else in its life was. War, small-pox, loss of pastor, economic chaos, and citizen expulsion had all left their marks. Now, on the lawns and streets about Central were the camps of the conquerers. The space was crowded roof to roof with the temporary quarters erected for their use. And the massive slaughter-house operations providing meats for the Federal forces were in Central Church itself — in ground floor rooms which had been the Sunday School area:

> The beautiful new church building seemed ruined — its bell damaged, its basement blood-splattered and reeking, and its upper story sanctuary strewn with all the debris of an army of occupation. (*The Atlanta Journal*, May 9, 1937)

The plight of the city of Atlanta itself was no better. In his valedictory address to the City Council upon finishing his term at the end of 1865, Mayor Calhoun, a Central member, painted a poignant picture of the destitution in which General Sherman had left the city:

This monument erected in front of Atlanta's present City Hall commemorates the brave part played by Father O'Reilly.

The Federal troops occupying City Hall Square in the Fall of 1864 filled Central's "frontyard" to the brim, and commandeered its Sunday School rooms for their slaughter-house operations. The cupolaed City Hall had served as Central's meeting place from 1858 till 1860.

The rainbow-colored *Calico House.*

> There was not a dollar in the City Treasury. We had to bury the dead on credit and could not raise funds to remove the filth and litter from the streets. The wells, pumps and cisterns were all out of order. We had no prison or market house. Half of our citizens were still in exile. Those who returned had no money and their houses generally destroyed and all their stock and personal property gone.
>
> Our destitute and suffering situation was known to the world, but no friendly voice was heard on our behalf, and no kind hand ministered to our needs.
>
> (*The Daily Intelligencer*, January 10, 1866)

But *Surgens, Resurgens*. Both the city and its thirteenth church somehow survived — with spirit. When the first Confederate Memorial Day was observed in Atlanta in 1866, the provisional authorities stipulated that no speeches were to be made; but an Atlanta newspaper reported the next day with great satisfaction that Pastor Robert Q. Mallard of the Central Presbyterian Church, who had been appointed to lead the observance, managed to make a speech anyway, so eloquent and fervent and stirring was the masterful prayer he delivered for the occasion.

The spirited congregation was not only surviving but also growing. By 1870, when extant church records take up Central's story again, the membership had inched its way back up and the church had enjoyed the services of Rev. Rufus K. Porter, its first post-war pastor.

Chapter 2
Trouble In The Ranks (1870 — 1883)

The Civil War finally ended — but not Atlanta's trauma. Demoralization and moral confusion occupied the city as pervadingly as had Sherman's soldiers. In 1868, schoolteacher Elizabeth Sterchi observed in letters to friends that Atlanta had become thronged with people "of most savage tastes, given to fighting, murdering, stealing, quarreling, begging, swearing, and drinking. It does seem to me that the devil himself had taken hold of this place."

She might have added that the devil was encountering strong resistance at Central Presbyterian Church — at churches everywhere, in fact. For a religious revival of great power had swept in among fighting forces, North and South, during the final months of the war. The revival became a veritable spiritual force which immediately moved into contention against the prevailing moral permissiveness already engulfing the armies.

Throughout the final year of the war, an all-out moral struggle was being waged. It pitted the forces of moral degeneration, which already held the field, against a new challenger — religious fervor. The ensuing battle, as it moved forward among the soldiers, grew into a vigorous war within the war — on both sides of the Mason-Dixon Line.

By the end of 1865, the armed conflict had ended, but not the moral struggle. For more than another decade it continued, unabated. By the year 1870, the crest had been reached. The Atlanta of that year was in all respects a city of contrasts. Still dominated by the feckless "reconstruction" government which had been imposed upon it, the city enjoyed no system of public education and its public streets were so deep in mud that "Mud City" became a commonly-used description, and funeral processions trying to move down Hunter Street often became hopelessly bogged in the miry mess.

Fostering a very different image, however, was the "other" Atlanta of 1870. That year the Presbyterian-related Oglethorpe University of Baldwin County was re-established in the John Neal mansion, Central's near neighbor. This giant step forward in the city's educational fortunes came about largely through the efforts of Central member Lemuel P. Grant, who was the great railroad pioneer of Georgia and the donor for whom Atlanta's Grant Park became named.

Meanwhile, Col. Grant and another Central member, Dr. Joseph P. Logan, were among civic leaders pressing to get a worthy system of public schooling established for the city, and both men were named to Atlanta's first Board of Education formed in 1872. Matriculation was now clearly outdoing Mud in the lively battle between the two contrasting faces of Atlanta.

Even more lively, however, was the battle waged during the early 1870's between the entrenched forces of Right and Wrong. The Atlanta of that period took on the aspect of some hugely-staged Morality Play. On one side of this drama were the devilish doings observed by Miss Sterchi. On the opposing side were churches like Central, vigorously doing battle against the degenerative forces of evil which lay all about and even within.

It was the 'within' part of this battle against evil that would become an almost fatal engagement for Central Church.

Religious revival during the war meant a revival of church growth after the war. The same Central Church which in 1864 had become decimated almost to the point of extinction was by 1870 a healthy and growing congregation of 186 communicants.

This new congregation was considerably different from the "all-alike" people who comprised Central's earlier little family. For like Atlanta itself, the church's post-war congregation had become excitingly heterogeneous. A review of the sessional records of the period shows that Central's new members were coming from all areas of the nation — from the North and West, as well as from the South. More significant than where they came from, however, was that they came with new varieties of views as to what was acceptable behavior. Attitudes of many different shadings were now represented among the good people of the Central Congregation. Some of them, almost inevitably, would become caught in the crossfire of the Church's battle against 'wrong'.

To speak of the battle of the 1870's in Atlanta as a morality play is not to minimize the seriousness of the conflict. Nor is it to suggest that the tide of battle could have been turned by a church which was less than militant and unequivocal in its fighting stance. The opposition had to be met head-on. Out of a collision-course conflict of that nature, excesses were sure to grow.

The collision would have been somewhat less crunching at Central had the congregation chosen a man of blander qualities to become its second post-war leader. The Rev. J. T. Leftwich was not a bland man. Brilliant, handsome, and enormously talented, he was a natural to attract people to himself and to Central. Among those attracted was

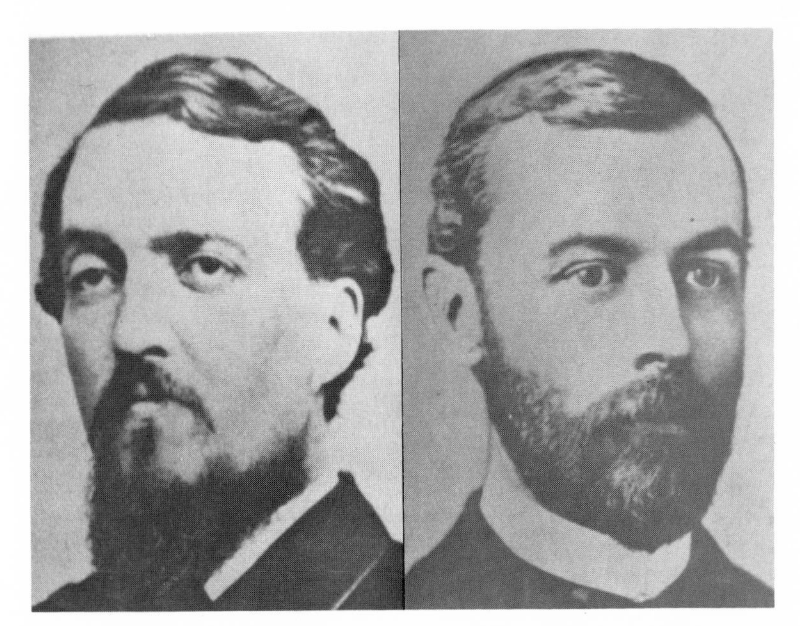

The Rev. J. T. Leftwich
Central Pastor 1869-1879

The Rev. William E. Boggs
Central Pastor 1880-1882
General Assembly Moderator
1909

Principal John Isham of the Crew Street School in Atlanta, whose journal, faithfully recounting his doings between 1868 and 1881, is still preserved. Though a non-Presbyterian when Dr. Leftwich first arrived on the Atlanta scene, he became an avid follower, attending every service without exception, summarizing in his journal the sermons he heard Dr. Leftwich preach, and pronouncing each the most "powerful" he had ever heard.

Besides being a powerful preacher, Dr. Leftwich was also as strong and remorseless and dominating a warrior for righteousness as ever led a church Session into battle. The times being what they were, it was this last-named trait that brought upon Central those particular problems from which it was long to suffer.

The problems were already underway when Central's oldest surviving official records pick up the story of them in the middle of 1870. They reflect that within the first year of Dr. Leftwich's arrival at Central, there was a rash of resignations among various leadership groups within the church — all for reasons undisclosed. Resignations included the whole Board of Deacons, the Chorister, the Sunday School Superintendent, and the entire Session.

In the case of the Session, however, the congregation proved stubborn. After hearing the elders explain why they wished to quit, the congregation responded to their resignation request by saying that if the delinquencies of certain members were indeed as bad as claimed by the new pastor, the Session should deal with the problem without delay. Thus, instead of letting the elders resign, the congregation of Central Church ordered them to "resume with quickened zeal your abdicated rulership in this church."

A less militant minister would not have heard in the congregation's mandate quite the marching orders heard by Dr. Leftwich. He had perceived, perhaps rightly, that the times required bold and even harsh disciplines. And he perceived, perhaps wrongly, that harsh and relentless disciplines were precisely what the congregation was asking for. At any rate, the pastor marched determinedly against evil with his sword unsheathed, and, being a leader of great power, his Session followed. Thus, gradually at first, but increasingly, there began to unfold a kind of reign of terror of pastor and Session over people which, before being brought to an end more than a decade later, had all but spelled the ruin of Atlanta's Central Presbyterian Church.

The Session's beginning efforts at expressing its authority bear little resemblance to a reign of terror. There was nothing remotely ruinous to Central's welfare in those first tests by the Session of its disciplinary powers. Those first tests were simply for the purpose of bringing back into line those members who had fallen into the practice of "habitually absenting themselves from the public worship and ordinances of the church." Delinquent members were warned to resume those duties required by the church or suffer the disciplines that would have to be imposed.

And the warnings seemed to work. Almost without exception, the Session was able to report in its minutes precisely the response it had sought. Greater faithfulness to churchly duties was promised by those who had become careless of them. Under the mere threat of punishment the backsliders returned chastened to their accustomed pews.

Encouraged by these early successes, the Session became ready to try its hand at applying discipline for a more grievous error — even if committed by one of their own members. Into such a grievous error had fallen a recently elected ruling elder. This spirited young Atlanta business leader had joined Central in 1866, and before long was elected to the Session. But by 1872, he had evidently fallen upon stressful times for he took to drinking a bit and was even reported to have been seen publicly drunk on Whitehall Street and Pryor Street and elsewhere.

When the Moderator confronted the young elder with these rumors, he readily acknowledged to him and to the rest of the Session

Central was diligently disciplining erring members and Atlanta was busy growing when this 1875 photograph was taken from Whitehall Street. Central's spire (1) can be seen in the background between City Hall (2) on one side and the newly-completed Immaculate Conception Church (3) on the other side.

the public state of intoxication of which he had been accused, but claimed that it was all due to his having considerably overdone his physician's advice "to partake of a measure of ardent spirits for reasons of health." He thereupon expressed deep remorse and begged forgiveness at the hands of his fellow elders. But his fellow-elders were reluctant to bestow their forgiveness so cheaply. They demanded, instead, a much fuller explanation than so far given of the sins into which he had fallen.

So, a few days later there came from him to the Session a long letter explaining in painful details the errors which had overtaken him, again repenting and begging to be forgiven. The Session, after pondering the letter, decided that to forgive would be a weakness on its part. So instead of forgiveness, the accused elder got a citation ordering him to come to trial on a day appointed by the Session and there be confronted by witnesses. The defendant continued his pleas for pardon, but the Session was adamant. They would hold court in the

Lecture Hall of Central Church beginning on December 5th, 1872, and would then render judgment after hearing all the witnesses against him and whatever defense he could muster for himself.

The trial came off as scheduled. The pastor was the prosecutor. He and the rest of the Session were judge and jury together. It was no surprise, therefore, that at trial's end several days later, the Session was ready and waiting with its "guilty as charged" verdict. But then, in a burst of leniency, the Session declared itself willing to withhold the discipline of excommunication provided the accused make full and public confession of his sins and make public pledges of his reformation before the whole congregation on the next Sabbath morning. This he did and his name remained among Central's members, but no longer as a ruling elder.

This downfall of the young elder at the hands of the Session in late 1872 began a decade of increasingly harsh judgments by pastor and Session against Central's erring members. A cynic might conclude that pastor and Session, having tasted something of the allurements of power exercised over other people, became addicted to that taste. A kinder and perhaps not less accurate assessment, however, would be that a strong and determined pastor and Session recognized also that only by the application of harsh discipline could standards of righteousness be maintained decently and in order.

At any rate, the Session of Central Church became in those years a virtually full-time court of law. At the same December 5th court session which brought about the downfall of the young elder, the Session also quickly excommunicated a Sunday School officer who had been prodded into a duel, and started proceedings against a third member charged by his pastor with having engaged in the "constant practice of buying tickets in the so-called Georgia State Lottery." In such fashion, at meeting after meeting, there were accusations by the pastor, followed by citations by the Session summoning erring members to stand trial. Citations went alike to unwed mothers and to women who had journeyed to Savannah on Sabbath excursion trips. They were issued alike for men who sold liquor, and for men caught drinking it. In each case there were trials, and endless pages of court proceedings filled with legal language and the verbatim testimony of many witnesses as recorded by court stenographers employed for the occasion.

In the Session's trials, acquitals never resulted; forgiveness was never bestowed. So unforgiving was the pastor and his Session in those days that one of the accused members who later moved to Kentucky was refused a letter of transfer so that he could join another church there. But the Presbytery of Atlanta (formed out of the old Flint River Presbytery) finding that the man had no charges against him and was a member in good and regular standing, sent down an order to the Session that the requested letter of transfer be forwarded immediately. This the Session reluctantly agreed to do — by a split vote.

It is not to be supposed though that the Presbytery of Atlanta was itself entirely blameless as a contributing factor in the increasingly harsh sway that the Session of Central Church now held over its erring members. A pastoral letter, which the Presbytery sent out early in 1877 to be required reading in every one of its congregations, urged the severest sort of resistance to and punishment for "all violations of the law of the church in reference to worldly amusements such as card playing, theater going and dancing."

If the Session of Central Church had needed any outside encouragement in pursuing its crusade against sinners within its ranks, the Presbytery's own strong urging would have provided it. So pity the poor deacon of Central Church who, late in the Christmas season of that same year in which Presbytery sent out its pastoral letter, was discovered to have permitted dancing to take place at a party he gave for his daughter and her teenage friends. The pastor and Session, armed with this information, pounced on their discovered sinner as upon a bone tossed out to be devoured.

Dr. Leftwich, always ready, leaped to the attack with his charge against his deacon and with his already prepared resolution for the Session to adopt:

> Whereas it is reported by common fame that Mr. Frank E. Block, a member and Deacon of this church, has been guilty of violating the law of the church in reference to worldly amusements in this: First, that the said Frank E. Block did on or about the 27th of December last past gave an entertainment in his residence on McDonough Street in this city at which dancing was permitted and encouraged. Second, that the said Frank E. Block by his own act in thus encouraging a violation of the law of the church, has tempted other and younger members of the church to sin. Therefore be it resolved that the church be directed to issue citations requiring the said Frank E. Block to appear before the Session on Monday, January 27th 1878 at 4:00 P.M. in the Lecture Room to answer in reference to these matters.

In response to the adopted resolution, the trial of Deacon Block began. The pastor, in his chosen role of prosecutor, had ready a huge sheath of questions which he proceeded to fire at the accused. Mr. Block, at first, carefully answered each query. But as the trial progressed, Dr. Leftwich's questioning was with such increasing belligerency that a member of the Session finally interrupted to enter and have recorded in the minutes his official protest. The Moderator, however, simply overruled the protest and continued as before. This same pattern was evidently planned to continue during the second day of the trial. But overnight, Mr. Block had prepared a long and carefully worded defense (later printed and distributed in booklet form) which would stand, he said, as the only answer he intended to give to any additional questions the prosecutor might put to him. Then he added: "The manner in which I was interrogated on yesterday was so unpleasant and disagreeable that I decline to answer any further questions. Know this though, that I did not intend the little dance at my house to be either 'lascivious' or 'promiscuous,' and flatly deny that it was so."

The absence of answers did not in the least deter the pastor-prosecutor who propounded his almost endless array of prepared questions until all were asked and the trial completed. First on his feet as the trial ended was the Clerk of Session, holding in his hand a resolution which Dr. Leftwich had prepared for the Session to adopt. It was a long, accusatory document recounting the defendant's sins in great detail, but it was in the last paragraph that the Elders learned how they were expected to vote:

> It is therefore declared as the sense of this Session that the said Frank E. Block be suspended from all the privileges of church membership until he shall give evidence of repentance for this offense and make promise of reformation for the future. The Moderator is requested to announce this action of the Session at the regular forenoon service next Sabbath.

As the Clerk finished his reading, two other elders immediately offered milder substitutes for the motion already made. But it was a lost cause; the Moderator's resolution prevailed.

When the verdict was read to the Congregation on the next Sunday morning it was met by a new kind of quiet anger. A spontaneous sort of protest movement began to mount, led by Attorney Henry P. Farrow. The protest took the tongue-in-cheek pattern of letters to the Session in which scores of Central members writing to the Session, accused themselves of crimes at least as bad, they said, as those of Mr. Block. They accused themselves and each other of having played bridge or backgammon on such-and-such dates, or of having gone to theatrical performances on such-and-such dates. Therefore they demanded that the Session now summons them and all such sinners to trial with a view to having them excommunicated. With almost half the membership demanding and waiting to be tried and excommunicated, the Session was thrown into an unanticipated quandary. But the ever resourceful Moderator then recalled that Mr. Block, immediately after

DEFENCE OF F. E. BLOCK.

ATLANTA, GA., February 8, 1878.

To the Session of the Central Presbyterian Church:

DEAR BRETHREN—In answer to the charge contained in your citation of January 7th, 1878—

"Whereas it is reported by common fame that Mr. Frank E. Block, a member and Deacon of this church, has been guilty of violating the laws of this church, in reference to worldly amusements, in this, that, 1st, The said F. E. Block did, on or about the 27th of December last past, give an entertainment, at his residence, on McDonough street, in this city, at which dancing was permitted and encouraged; 2nd, That the said F. E. Block, by his own act, in thus encouraging a violation of the laws of the church, has tempted other and younger members of the church to sin"—

I beg leave to make the following defense:

I was reared by religious parents,, my mother a member, and my father a constant attendant,of a Presbyterian church, until its dissolution with that denomination, and afterwards in the same church with the same pastor in the Congregational denomination. I think careful attention was paid by my parents to my moral training. I was a constant attendant of the Sabbath-school. My evenings were spent at home, unless by special permission; but that home was made attractive to me by the quiet enjoyment of fireside amusements—dancing among the rest. I was taught that dancing was not only proper, but a *desirable* amusement, when indulged in at the proper time, with proper persons, and preferable to boisterous games, many of them in which kissing was the prominent feature. I attended parties given by church members, and, without exception, the chief amusement was dancing. A few months since, my mother and sister came from a distant State to visit me. They received polite attentions from my friends here, and, shortly before their return, I gave my sister a party, and, as you state, "dancing was permitted." But I deny that it was a

Page 1 of Deacon Frank Block's 18 page defense against his pastor's strong effort to excommunicate him for the dance he allowed in his home.

his sentencing by the Session, had written to declare his intention of appealing the action to Presbytery. So, to Mr. Farrow and each of the letter-writers went this notice:

> Inasmuch as Mr. Frank E. Block had given notice of his intention to appeal from a recent decision that this Session made concerning participation on the part of members of the church in certain worldly amusements, it is proper and becoming of this Session to suspend action in reference to offenses of this class until that appeal shall have been acted on by the higher courts of the church.

But Mr. Farrow, for one, had had quite enough. He wrote a long and scathing letter which ended as follows:

> Now brethren of the Session, I do not wish to deceive you and I do not wish you to deceive yourselves. The eyes of the world are upon you. You profess to hold in your hands the keys to the Kingdom of Heaven, personally intrusted to you by our Lord and Savior Jesus Christ. You profess to be able to remit or retain the guilt of sins, to be able by your censure to close against me and others forever the doors of heaven. You have given it out to the world that you intend to purify our church, and that you intend to enforce the laws of God even if the carrying out of your intentions leaves not one stone upon another of our church.
>
> If you persist in inflicting harsh and cruel disciplines as punishment for such indifferent kinds of sins, then take heed lest upon you rest the consequences, in the eyes of man and of God.

The Session was utterly unmoved by Mr. Farrow's warnings or by the incipient little uprisings within the congregation. Such opposition it deemed as nothing compared to its high calling to purify the church from evil ways. So, throughout much of the remainder of 1878, the pastor and Session continued on course. Dr. Leftwich continued to introduce new charges against erring members, and the Session continued to issue new citations. The only hitch in the smooth progress of their way occured in mid-year when pastor and Session undertook to discipline the Bowie sisters. The pretty young teenagers, being accused of dancing, were ordered to come before the Session and in confession and penitence pledge their reformation. So the summoned pair came, seemingly the very soul of innocence, sweetness, light, and repentance. They had come, they said, to make their pledge just as the Session demanded. Which pledge they then offered with words as follows: "We do solemnly promise not ever to dance again, so long as we are members of Central Presbyterian Church. We ask that you immediately issue for us letters of transfer out of Central Presbyterian Church."

Central's earliest sanctuary provided a stately setting for services of corporate worship throughout its first five pastorates, of which that of Dr. Leftwich was by far the longest — and the stormiest.

The pastor-Session combination no doubt suffered a bit of hurt pride at being out-flanked by the Bowie sisters. But they could afford to lose such skirmishes so long as the battles continued to turn out in their favor. Early in November, 1878, however, came the startling word of their defeat in a very big battle indeed. The appeal, which Mr. Block had introduced against the decision of the Session concerning him, had finally been answered. From the Synod of Georgia (and later from the General Assembly itself) came a judicial decision ordering that the Session's action against Mr. Block be completely set aside. This presumption by the Synod to reverse his action so angered Dr. Leftwich that, then and there, he offered his resignation through the Session for congregational action. The Session was stunned by this sudden turn of events — but not the congregation. The majority of the membership knew exactly what to do with the resignation offer; they intended to accept it — and did. By a better than two-to-one margin, the congregation voted to sever the relationship at month's end.

Dr. Leftwich was probably more than a bit surprised at such a show of spunk on the part of the people of his congregation, but he manifestly still had plenty of his own. His sermon to the congregation on next Sunday morning was stubbornly non-repentant. He scorned those who yearned to keep the peace of the church undisturbed. "...Let the ploughshare be driven through the church again and again, if need be," he declared.

The prospect of an early severance of the relation which Dr. Leftwich had so long had with Central, filled certain members with anger. This mood is reflected in John Isham's journal entry of the time:

> ...his departure will be a great and irreparable loss to Central Presbyterian Church, and I do not enjoy the notoriety those have gained who have been the immediate cause of his withdrawal. If they have any sense they must be filled with shame and self-contempt.

It can be assumed that these were not pleasant days at Central Church. The wounds were too deep for superficial healings. Dr. Robert L. Dabney, noted theologian and preacher of the time, came from Richmond to serve as the moderator of the congregational meeting of December 1, 1878, which was to act on Dr. Leftwich's departure. At its conclusion, Dr. Dabney admonished the congregation to consider well the causes of its "present problem," and prayed that the congregation would "not despair."

It is difficult to determine from the records whether, with the departure of Dr. Leftwich, the dominant mood of Central became one of liberation or one of confusion and uncertainty. For the first time in many years, the congregation became free to be itself. But it may have forgotten how. Celebrating their new freedom, some members called for a church-wide season of confession and repentance. But other members, celebrating the same freedom, called instead for action. Some insisted on slow-paced caution before calling another minister; others were for getting on with it immediately. Some were for granting a clean-wiped slate to every Central member with any sort of sessional charge pending against him; others were for maintaining a firm hand where discipline was called for. Some elders wished to resign from the Session; other elders would not permit them to resign. The Session prepared and mailed to each member an earnest plea for harmony and peace — but there was no peace. Central, clearly, had not yet found its way out.

With the help of the Rev. Dr. William Boggs, who followed Dr. Leftwich, Central might have begun finding its way out if two circumstances had been different.

First of all, Dr. Boggs was greatly delayed in beginning his new work at Central. At the very time he had planned on moving to Atlanta, a death-dealing epidemic of yellow fever broke out in Memphis, and he was reluctant to leave his congregation there without pastoral attention

The Calhoun House
A Central family of the mid-1870's poses on the porch of their Washington Street home. Both William L. Calhoun and his father before him served as mayors of Atlanta.

at such a time. The consequent delay lasted many months.

Second, it was during that interval that the Session of Central Church, unbelievably, lapsed back into an old habit. At the urging of one of the elders, it initiated proceedings against a Central Sunday School teacher accused of not paying a certain $200 debt. From the time of that first citation early in 1880, it was to be three torturous years before the trial finally ended and its paralyzing hold on the congregation had finally subsided.

It is difficult even to imagine how horrendously this seemingly simple disciplinary action by the Session got out of hand during the three-year period. Charges produced counter-charges. Witnesses accused other witnesses. The accused became the accuser.

Two hundred and thirty pages of the Session's records and countless days of the Session's time were consumed. The case was heatedly debated at meetings of the Presbytery of Atlanta and at meetings of the Synod of Georgia and, finally, on the floor of the General Assembly itself. The relentless demands of the affair caused

Dr. Boggs to leave Central before completing even two years of ministry, and caused his successor to give serious consideration to quitting after only six months. The case almost became the final peg in Central's coffin.

That's how it was early in 1883, as Central's first quarter century of life finally limped to an end.

If the chief pleasure of the *devil* is to sabotage good things before they can even get started, then Central Church, right up into 1883, must have been his prize show-piece.

But if the chief pleasure of *God* is to work the miracles of his grace on what otherwise had to remain a hopeless mess, then Central, during most of its life since 1883, must stand as one of His favorite case studies of conversion and regeneration.

Central's Centennial Celebration, 1958, the way they conceived the 1880's.

Chapter 3
Turning The Corner (1883-1896)

Central's morale may have suffered considerably during its crisis years, but not its growth, nor its status as a leading congregation of the city. New members in undiminished numbers had continued to join its ranks throughout the long and strong but stormy pastorate of Dr. Leftwich, and during the shorter pastorate of Dr. Boggs.

The church had continued to grow not only in numbers but also in quality. Even in 1883, when internal problems were at crest, the names listed on Central's membership roll could have served as a nucleus, at least, of a *Who's Who in Atlanta* publication of that period.

The congregation also, for all its painful division and discord, was of one strong mind in wanting the corner quickly to get turned toward Central's real and better future. The congregation was also of one mind in sensing that the whether-or-not of Central's corner-turning depended to an almost frightening degree on the new minister, whoever that might be.

It was this awareness which in 1882 sent the Pulpit Committee out, quite literally, on a quest for the best. The search finally ended in Augusta County, Virginia, at the sedate old Tinkling Springs Church where Dr. Givens Brown Strickler was pastor.

Although still a young man, G.B. Strickler had already established his mark as one of the more able ministers to be found in the whole denomination. It was a major victory therefore for the church and for Atlanta when he accepted the congregation's call to come to Central as its new pastor.

That was in the mid-summer of 1882. Although the new pastor arrived on the scene in April of 1883 and at least tentatively began his work at Central, it was to be late February of the following year before he finally became committed to staying. Until then it was touch-and-go as to whether this pastorate could actually develop on any long-term basis. Just to trace the agonizing uncertainties of that almost two-year period is to sense how greatly the future of Central Church rode upon the decision that would finally prevail.

The questions confronting Dr. Strickler during that fateful twenty-two month period were formidable indeed. First came questions as to whether the work he had promised to undertake at Central would be at all suited to his particular temperament and state of health. Then there was the question as to when he could leave Tinkling Springs, inasmuch as a succession of illnesses among his children were causing an embarrassing number of delays in even beginning the work in Atlanta. Finally, after barely beginning his ministry at Central, came questions as to whether he should continue at this Central Church pastorate which was proving so utterly stressful for him or return to Virginia where the famed Union Theological Seminary was offering him a professorship and a life far less hazardous to his health. Thus after being at Central only six months, G.B. Strickler became fully convinced that he could not do his best work there and would therefore request severance of the pastoral relationship so that he could begin the more suitable service being urged upon him by the Seminary.

The people of Central Church did not intend, however, to give up G.B. Strickler without a fight. They loved and appreciated their new leader far too much for that. The paper they adopted on September 16, 1883, left none of these sentiments in doubt:

> Whereas it has come to our knowledge that a strong effort is being made to deprive us of our pastor, we feel compelled by a sense of duty to ourselves and the cause of the Master to enter our solemn protest against such a proceeding. Dr. Strickler having, as we and he believed, come to us under and by divine guidance, and having, as it were, but commenced his work here — yet so successfully that he has already secured the confidence and Christian love of every member of this church, and the admiration and esteem of all others who have enjoyed his ministrations, his removal at this time would be a very great disaster to our church and to the cause of Presbyterianism throughout this section of the state. Such an act would involve consequences to us which we fear to contemplate. One of the least of these would be the abandonment of the creation of a new and enlarged church building.

Then the paper adopted by the congregation ended with a final swipe at its declared rival for its pastor's affections: "We believe the field for usefulness here (at Central) is wider and broader than any position any theological seminary can furnish, and that in the latter position (Dr. Strickler) would in a measure be hiding under a bushel the light God has given him."

With the line of battle between Central and the seminary thus drawn, there was no neutral ground on which Dr. Strickler could stand. He had to chose either to continue the work he had barely begun

The Rev. Givens Brown Strickler
Central Pastor 1883-1896
General Assembly Moderator 1887

or to leave Central and join the faculty at Union. After almost two months of struggle, the die was finally cast — or so it seemed. It was a chilly November 13, 1883 morning when Dr. Strickler, having settled in his own mind what he should do, sat at his desk at the Washington Street manse and wrote to inform the Session about it:

> Not until today have I been able to reach a definite conclusion as to my duty in reference to my appointment to a Professorship in Union Theological Seminary, Virginia. Several weeks ago I informed the Directors of the Seminary that I could not leave this church at once, and declined to go at least until the beginning of the next Session in Sept. 1884 — leaving it an open question whether I would go even then. During the past two weeks I have received a communication from them stating that they and the Faculty of the Seminary and the students will cheerfully wait until that time, if I will consent to come then. In these circumstances, I do not see my way clear to refuse to go.

Dr. Strickler, in his letter of resignation, then continued at length to explain his reasons for wanting to go to the seminary professorship. Not only was it, he felt, a more significant opportunity than that offered by "any single church, however important that church might be," but he had also found the work at Central so stressful that it was almost impossible for him "to sleep on Saturday night before preaching and equally impossible to sleep Sunday night after preaching." He declared this was ruining his uncertain health, and he desired to be permitted to resign from his work at Central Church.

Two Sundays later Dr. Strickler's letter got its reading before the assembled congregation. As the reading ended, the mood within the pews had become one of resignation, tinged with deep feelings of failure. Compliance seemed now inevitable, and growing from it would be an equally inevitable and lasting hurt to the church. In such a situation, it would have been understandable if the congregation had displayed some resentment at being so soon deprived of its minister. However, the resolution adopted that morning by the congregation displayed no resentment toward their young minister now so bent on leaving them, but rather the sincerest expressions of affection and esteem:

> "His short ministry with us has not only been satisfactory but greatly enjoyed and highly profitable. As a pastor he is affable, courteous and unassuming. As a biblical instructor he is profound, clear and logical. In spiritual guidance he presents most cogently the fear and love of God."

But these winsome attributes, missing, perhaps, in some of Central's earlier experiences, made the anticipated departure of Dr. Strickler all the more regrettable. The loss of him, declared the congregation, would be "a great detriment to Central Church, and likewise to Presbyterianism and to religion in general in our State." Nonetheless, because it saw no alternative in sight, the congregation did what it had to do and gave its assent to the requested dissolution of the pastoral relationship between G.B. Strickler and Central Church. It did so, the resolution declared, "only because of the demands of his health and of what seems to him a better serving of the cause of our Master."

Central people on their part were far from convinced that Dr. Strickler could possibly serve the cause of the Master better as a seminary professor than in continuing as their pastor. So, even though Central's assent to his leaving was official, no one there was quite ready yet to grant that all doors were firmly and finally closed. The possibility that there could even yet be an intervention of some kind was a hope that was alive and well among Centralites even though their

Central Church fills the foreground of 1882 picture taken from atop City Hall. Just one year later both buildings were to be in the process of being replaced — City Hall by the new State Capitol, and Central by its new (1885) building.

December 7th resolution was now signed and sealed. Caught up in the spirit of this lingering hope, the ruling elders of the church called themselves together on December 15th for an informal meeting in offices of the State Railroad Commission, of which Elder Campbell Wallace was Commissioner.

After hours of debate back and forth among themselves, a plan was formulated as their final, all-out effort to persuade Dr. Strickler to reconsider and change his decision about leaving. But the pastor, when they approached him — though most gracious — declined absolutely to reconsider. Then, almost as an after-thought, Dr. Strickler observed to his elders that the only possible way his decision to go to the Seminary could be reversed would be for the Atlanta Presbytery itself to rule that it must be reversed.

This patently was not much of a straw for grasping, but grasp it Central did — the Session first, and then the congregation. At a congregational meeting on the first Sunday of 1884, three representatives were elected to plead Central's cause before the Presbytery which would be called together specifically to make a determination between Dr. Strickler, who was asking that his pastoral relation with Central be dissolved, and Central, asking that its pastor's request be

The new Fulton County Court House was dedicated in 1883 just in time to serve as Central's interim meeting place while its new church building was being erected.

refused. To plead Central's cause, the congregation elected a most persuasive trio headed by Col. P.L. Mynatt, an attorney, who was most ably assisted by Major Samuel B. Spencer, another prominent Atlanta attorney and former mayor of the city, and by Jesse W. Rankin, founder of the Lamar and Rankin Drug Company and more recently president of the Metropolitan Street Railway Company. The three men really had their work cut out for them. Should they be unable to persuade presbytery to rule on Central's behalf, the church would be left leaderless, its recovery hopes dashed, and its plans for replacing the existing church building with a far more adequate structure would come to a jolting halt. Also at stake was Central's future capacity to attract outstanding ministers if, by an adverse ruling of presbytery, it were shown to have been unable to keep Dr. Strickler in its service for even one full year. Central's future, depending upon which way the presbytery decided, was clearly in the balance.

No remaining records recount the exact arguments and pleas which Atlanta Presbytery heard on that day of its called meeting. But when all arguments on both sides had been heard and the votes cast and tallied, the presbytery, surprisingly, had denied Dr. Strickler's request. He was to continue as Central's pastor and he did for thirteen years.

With the pastor issue finally and happily settled, Central lost little time in taking its building plans out of the moth balls. Within the space of a few short weeks, bonds were sold, additional land space bought, architectural drawings completed, and contracts entered into for construction of the new building and demolition of the old. Nearby St. Philips Episcopal Church offered its chapel for Central's use during whatever time Central was without a building, and Second Baptist Church likewise sent word that whenever any part of its plant was not being used, the space was at Central's full disposal. Finally, however, it was an invitation to use the large basement rooms of the newly-built Fulton County Courthouse that appealed to Central as the most feasible interim arrangement, and that arrangement was made.

By May 18, 1884, these plans and arrangements had all moved far enough along for the congregation to be called to assemble for a history-making final service in the old Central Church building before its demolition. An appropriate event on that occasion was the reading of a history of the soon-to-be demolished building as prepared by Maj. J.M. Patton, Central's Clerk of Session since 1870 and Treasurer of the State of Georgia:

> This building was first used by the congregation of the Central Presbyterian Church on the 4th of March 1860, and on that day it was dedicated as a house for the worship of Almighty God.
>
> Its first pastor, the Rev. J.R. Rogers, served until February 1863 when he resigned the charge. The pulpit was then filled by the Rev. Dr. Baird of the Cumberland Presbyterian denomination (he was then stationed at this place in service of the Confederate government) until the autumn of that year when the Rev. Robert Q. Mallard of Liberty County, who had been elected pastor, entered upon his duties. In the summer of 1864, the congregation was scattered upon the approach of the Federal Army during the siege and shelling of the city and its subsequent occupation by the Federals. The building was mercifully protected, only one shell having struck it and that a small shot at the base of the spire doing but little damage. It was also shielded from the

> conflagration which laid the greater part of the town in ashes.
>
> Early in the year 1865, the greater part of our people returned to their homes and our pulpit was occupied for several months by the Rev. John S. Wilson, D.D., pastor of the First Presbyterian Church whose building had been rendered unfit for use by the shells of the enemy.
>
> Our own pastor, during that time, was a prisoner of war, having been captured in the neighborhood of Savannah. Upon release Mr. Mallard returned and continued his ministry with us until the latter part of the year 1866 when he received a call and went to the Presbyterian Church of New Orleans.
>
> Early in the year 1867, the Rev. Rufus K. Porter was elected our pastor and continued greatly beloved until he was called to the Temple above in July 1869. Then the Rev. R.C. Ketchence supplied our pulpit until the Rev. J.T. Leftwich was elected pastor. Dr. Leftwich entered upon his duties early in 1870 and continued until January 1879 when he resigned. Dr. R. C. Vaughn and Dr. Jesse J. Robinson supplied our pulpit until December when Dr. William C. Boggs who had been elected pastor in July commenced his labor among us and continued until the autumn of 1882 when he resigned to accept a professorship in Columbia Theological Seminary.
>
> Our present pastor, the Rev. G.B. Strickler, D.D., was elected pastor in 1882 and entered into his duties in 1883. The Church has grown from a membership of 39 to 473. The demand for more room here led our people to the belief that the best interest of the Master's Kingdom, so far as committed to us, require that these sacred halls shall give way to a larger and more spacious edifice. This therefore will be the last service ever held within the halls of dear old Central Church.

Once the final service "within the halls of dear old Central" had ended and the people had filed out of their accustomed pews for the last time, it was to be sixteen long, noisy, and dusty months before they were again back in a building of their own. While it is true that many of the twenty-four years of their life together in the old church building had been less than happy and harmonious, the people of Central must nonetheless have looked upon the dismantlement of their church home with much sadness. But, especially for the founding members, there was still more to be sad about, for getting demolished across the street during exactly the same period was the old City Hall building in which they had first gathered for worship. This double dose of nostalgia with which Central folk witnessed the demise of the old was more than compensated for as they witnessed also the gradual emergence of the new. For, like the new and grander Kimball House Hotel then taking shape out of the charred remains of the old Kimball House in nearby downtown, or like the Georgia State Capitol building about to rise out of that vast excavation scooped where City Hall had stood, Central's own new building was taking on a shape which for at least the next ninety-five years was to be one of Atlanta's more familiar and stablizing sights.

At last, early in the Fall of 1885, came Central's big day. Its new building was finally ready for use and dedication — a day to be remembered. The *Atlanta Constitution* captured the sights and feelings of the day in its next morning's edition:

> Yesterday (October 4, 1885) was a perfect Sunday. The clouds which hung in the heavens for a week had disappeared, and instead of cold rains had come floods of golden sunlight and crisp invigorating air. It was indeed a fitting day for the dedication of the beautiful new Central Presbyterian Church which had just been completed. All other Presbyterian churches in the city were closed so that their pastors and people might participate in the dedication service.
>
> Sitting in the gallery, it was a grand spectacle to see the multitude, composed not only of Presbyterians but also of representatives of every religion and creed in the city, filling every nook and cranny of this magnificent sanctuary.
>
> It is a noble building, an honor to the congregation which erected it and to the city among whose chief ornaments it must be numbered. It is, all in all, perhaps the handsomest and most commodious church in Atlanta. The cost of this church, as it stands complete, is about $50,000.
>
> The rich stained glass windows, the heavy brass gaseliers with their white tapers, the massive and polished woodwork in solid walnut, the luxuriant pews softly upholstered, the bright carpets, and the pervading sense of airy comfort completed the feeling of satisfaction at being present in such a church. Without disparaging any of the elegant temples in the city, it may be said that this is the most beautiful church ever occupied by an Atlanta congregation.
>
> The services throughout were profoundly impressive and the day will be forever memorable in the history of Central Presbyterian Church.

But among Central members themselves there was a notable absence of fanfare surrounding their memorable accomplishment. A brief, one-sentence footnote which Mr. Patton appended to his sessional minutes stands as the only official word among Central's records that its long-sought goal was now a reality. Members, assembling for the first time in their new sanctuary, must have felt an enormous surge of gratitude to God. The prevailing mood seems to have been a strong and solemn determination to accept the second chance which their new building now represented — a chance to get on

Architectural sketch of Central's second and still-serving church building. When dedicated late in 1885 the *Atlanta Constitution* described it as "the most beautiful ever occupied by an Atlanta congregation."

into their new and real future as a church.

The seeds of a "new" Central had never actually been absent. Able rank-and-file members had always been there as an enormous but largely unused reservoir of enlightened leadership waiting and hoping to have its day. The Central congregation, to use a judgment noted in the October 26, 1885 edition of *The Atlanta Evening Capitol*, had always been one "representing the best people of the city." Now, though, there was a new and different spirit evident among them.

Especially notable was the different spirit and attitude with which the Session now dealt with its discipline cases. In contrast to Central's 1873 Session which summarily excommunicated a repentant Sunday School officer who confessed having been prodded into a duel, the new style 1887 Session confronted with a similar situation responded with a new compassion:

> After due consideration, we the Session do receive the confession and repentance as full explanation of Captain Jackson's wrongful connection with the (duelling) event, and cordially urge upon our brother to go forward in the full discharge of all his Christian duties.

The same kind of contrast between the new-style Session and the old, this time involving actions with reference to unwed mothers, becomes evident in the events of July 23, 1893. On that date a well-respected woman member came to inform the Session that her unmarried daughter now had a child, and that she had come to plead that the Session, when it removed her daughter's name from the roll of members, carry out its action as quietly as possible. But the Session did even better. Instead of excommunicating the young, unwed mother for her misdeed, the Session now appointed two of their members as special personal advisors to help both the woman and her mother through their long period of crisis.

Nowhere though is the changed spirit of the Session better exemplified than in the 1892 apology it adopted with reference to its action twenty years earlier in removing from office the young ruling elder charged with public intoxication. The Session, apologizing, expressed deep regret over the intemporate charges it had spread upon its minutes back in 1872, fearing it, "...might make an entirely erroneous impression on anyone now reading it as to the Christian character" of this man who, "...enjoys the unqualified respect and confidence of all his brethern."

Meanwhile, the new spirit so evident in the Session was discernible as well in all other aspects of Central's life. Under the influence of Dr. Strickler's own diligent and effective person-to-person pastoral ministry, the congregation at Central became a more caring congregation. To a degree not previously characteristic of them, the people were ministers to each other — and to others. Outreach was fast becoming the image that came to mind when people thought of Central Church. Missionary outreach, especially in the Atlanta area itself, became a consuming passion of the people of Central. And, undergirding all this newness was a new congregation-wide devotion to prayer. The extent to which prayer groups were becoming a force and a way of life at Central is evidenced by the thrust of this church notice which appeared late in 1885 in an Atlanta newspaper:

> Central Presbyterian Church, Washington Street, Rev. G.B. Strickler, D.D., Pastor. Preaching at 11 A.M. and 7:30 P.M. by

> the pastor. Sunday School at 9:30 A.M., Professor W.W. Lumpkin, Superintendent. *Regular weekly Prayer Meeting on Wednesday evening at 7:30. Young Men's Prayer Meeting on Thursday evening at 7:30. Cottage Prayer Meeting on Friday evening at 7:30.* All persons, strangers and visitors are cordially invited to attend.

By 1888, the Young Men's Prayer Association of Central Church had become an active force for mission outreach within the Atlanta area. Almost a dozen new mission Sunday Schools were launched under its leadership. Most of these continued active for a number of years; many of them became organized into continuing Presbyterian churches. But always, funds and personnel went out unstintedly from Central for the support and leadership of these undertakings. Then, as the time became ripe for the organizing of these mission points into a full-fledged church, a group of Central members would "colonize" to become a nucleus of members for the new church. In two cases, the new chuches originally carried the name of the particular elder of Central who had led out in the development of the church. Wallace Church (for Elder Campbell Wallace) and Rankin Church (for Elder Jesse W. Rankin) are examples. During the thirteen years of Dr. Strickler's ministry, the Session minutes, which in earlier years had been dominated by the trials and convictions of erring members, now became dominated by the activity of mission outreach. The minutes of the Session became alive with references to places and names such as Georgia Avenue, Wallace Chapel, West End, Fair Street, Edgewood, Inman Park, Zion, Pryor Street, Rankin Chapel, The Glassworks, and Reynold Town. In connection with each of these names and places, Central Church was actively engaged in the works of purchasing sites, erecting buildings, supplying leadership, employing ministers, and furnishing members. So close was Central's relationship to these products of its outreach that in the year 1890, Central elder and Sunday School Superintendent, W.W. Lumpkin was the active and official superintendent as well of the Sunday School of five other Presbyterian churches and chapels in Atlanta.

Despite giving up so many of its finest members for the forming of new churches, Central itself was growing at a most healthy pace. Its membership more than doubled, and its stewardship progressed to the point that by 1893, Central was able to designate a full half of its budget for others. The elusive peace and harmony, which the Session had futilely sought in its Pastoral letter just ten years earlier, was now everywhere evident. An Atlanta newspaper of that period reported:

> The congregation is one of the largest in the city and, now that the new Capitol is completed, Central has the best surroundings

Centralites were prominent among the onlookers in this 1885 cornerstone laying event for the new State Capitol being constructed across the street from the church. The Capitol was completed in 1889.

> of any church in the city. The members of Central are much attached to Dr. Strickler, and he well deserves it.

But suddenly into this Utopia came alarming news. In the Atlanta Sunday morning newspapers on May 26, 1895, was a news story, datelined Richmond, reporting that the board of Union Theological Seminary, Central's old nemesis, had officially acted to elect Dr. Strickler to a professorship there. That very day, as soon as the morning service was over and Dr. Strickler had left for the Manse, the elders went into an urgent huddle "to prepare a protest against the action of the Union Theological Seminary of Virginia in trying to take our beloved pastor from us, to ask our pastor to remain with us, and to ask him to decide to do so *now* and let our hearts be at rest."

Then followed a long and earnest resolution very much like the one drawn up under similar circumstances a dozen years earlier, stating to Dr. Strickler how esteemed and needed by Central he was, informing him how much less a ministry than his present one the professorship would be, and entreating him to stay. To this the congregation added its own official resolution, and added to them both, was a third resolution from the official board of neighboring Second Baptist Church, all asking Dr. Strickler please not to leave.

For a full year, Dr. Strickler indeed did not leave. But by mid-1896, it was finally over. Union Seminary had won its long, long tussle. This time, unlike the time twelve years earlier, no ruinous consequences to Central rode upon the decision. For by now Central Presbyterian Church was safely around its corner and was striding into its future. There were huge goals yet to be achieved but Central was firmly and confidently on its way. The Corner had been turned.

Miss Azile Simpson, Church Librarian for over 50 years. Her sister, Miss Belle Simpson, was superintendent of the Beginners Department for over 50 years.

Chapter 4
Equipping The Saints (1896-1908)

Central became a vastly happier and more effective church during the course of its corner-turning years. By 1896, this once divided congregation had not only found its unity, but also its purpose. Central truly had come a long, long way since those days just a dozen years earlier when the sheer uncertainty of its unity and purpose gave G.B. Strickler many anxious moments during the beginning months of his ministry there.

By 1896, not even a vestige of those anxieties still remained to worry Dr. Strickler's successor who came aboard that year. Theron Rice was able to view his call to Central as an exciting and unqualified opportunity, and he accepted it eagerly.

The new hall mark of Central Presbyterian Church was now what had been its chief want — its great unity and vitality. This attracted young Dr. Rice into its leadership. And this continued to attract the long succession of outstanding ministers who have served this congregation ever since.

It's remarkable how similar were Dr. Strickler and Dr. Rice. Each came to Central from a pastorate in Virginia; each upon finishing his work at Central moved on to a professorship at the Union Theological Seminary in Virginia; and each while at Central was a powerful influence for good not only throughout the congregation but also throughout the city and the denomination.

A ruling elder, who greatly admired each of these men under whose pastorate he had served, wrote comparing them in the April 12, 1905 issue of the *Weekly*. To describe Dr. Strickler, he conjured up such superlatives as Pious, Logical, Matchless. But for Dr. Rice, the unnamed ruling elder managed nonetheless to call up the at least equalling adjectives of Masterful, Enthusiastic, Devout. It can be ventured, that if Strickler's matchless logic and piety were the exact leadership qualities Central had required for getting around its corner, then Rice's devout and masterful enthusiasm were the precise leadership qualities which could equip the congregation for the exciting journey that lay ahead.

Already known as a praying congregation during Dr. Strickler's pastorate, Central began under Rice to exhibit that quality in even more pronounced fashion. Every sort of crisis situation, whether within the congregation or in the city or world without, became almost instinctively for the people of Central their summons into gatherings for corporate prayer. When the jolting economic depression in the 1890's threatened to interrupt Central's customarily prompt payments against its indebtedness, a series of church-wide prayer meetings sought the right answers until they were found. When Atlanta became torn by racial strife in the fall of 1906, the congregation repeatedly assembled together in earnest prayers for justice and peace. When the General Assembly of the Presbyterian Church in the United States came to Central for its 1899 meeting, its coming had been prepared by literally months of corporate prayer on its behalf by the people of Central. When the faithful old 1860 pipe organ, then in its second Central sanctuary, began showing signs of terminal illness, the music committee sought and got congregation-wide prayers for the committee's guidance. So did Central's building committee a few years later when a burgeoning Sunday School attendance could no longer be accommodated in the building space then at hand.

A chief reason Central's Sunday School had now out-grown its quarters was the election in 1900 of Mr. John J. Eagan as superintendent of the school. *The Atlanta Constitution* reporting on that event, described Eagan as "one of Atlanta's most successful young business men." Successfulness was unmistakenly the impact of Eagan's mark upon the educational development of Central Church. The same leadership qualities that enabled John J. Eagan's metal company to achieve top ranking, and the same Eagan leadership qualities which later brought Central and Atlanta and indeed the whole Southeast to new levels of concern for the socio-economic needs of all citizens, were now the qualities which led in bringing Central's ministry of education to peak pitch.

Eagan, like Rice himself, was an utterly dedicated evangelist. He saw the educational thrust of Central as affording a prime opportunity for "bringing people to the Lord and enabling them to grow in their faith." His aim therefore from the very outset was for quality education for Central. This meant aiming for better space for the school, good training and a high level of dedication on the part of each teacher, and a growing "commitment to Christ" on the part of each scholar. The three-pronged aim of Eagan's superintendency can be traced in these samplings of what he was writing for his *Weekly* readers between 1900 and 1905. A paragraph from the Dec. 8, 1900 *Weekly* is typical of John Eagan's repeated appeal for more Sunday School space:

The Rev. Theron H. Rice
Central Pastor 1896-1908

> Again last Sabbath did our steadily increasing school show how inadequate and poorly lighted and arranged were its quarters. To continue to grow and improve our school must have both better light and arrangement. This is a crying need which must be dealt with at once. Otherwise we must not only stop organizing new classes, but also say to those teachers now doing such faithful missionary work, cease these efforts.

His emphasis on thoroughly prepared and dedicated teaching is caught up in this item which Mr. Eagan prepared for the *Weekly* of March 16, 1901:

> Other schools may surpass us in beauty of building and convenience of room, and others may surpass us in numbers, but in the devotion of our teachers to their duty I believe ours are second to none. This faithfulness, carried on in humble dependence upon God, will surely bring us the blessing we so earnestly pray for.

The letter which John Eagan wrote to certain Sunday School pupils, and which was printed in the *Weekly* of Nov. 5, 1905, leaves no uncertainty as to what was his prime passion in Christian education:

> Signs indicate God's presence in our school in unusual

> power. Last Sabbath without any fanfare about fifty of your fellow students expressed their desire to lead Christian lives and accept Christ as Savior. Our hope and prayer is that you too will accept Christ as your Savior, now and always.

Sunday School life under John Eagan was also an enormous amount of fun. Issues of the *Weekly* carried enticing accounts of Sunday School entertainment of all kinds: of Sunday School orchestra performances, of Sunday School candy pulls, and of those annual Sunday School picnics which saw Centralites by the hundreds journey en mass by train each June for a day's frolic at places such as Lithia Springs or Powder Springs.

But for all the fun things generated by Eagan and his cohorts, they never once overlooked quality Christian education as the prime reason for the existence of a Sunday School. The benefits which the pupils of that school individually and collectively have gained as participants in that quality indoctrination have lingered across the years. The *Weekly* for the first two decades of this century was virtually a Sunday School newspaper. Each issue was alive with the names of new pupils, the names of pupils who had made the Honor Roll, and the names of pupils who had earned promotion to a higher school level. These all are the very names of those who later were to personify Central's now familiar character and style, and who still exemplify that staunch and well-nurtured faith which even now persists as Central's most basic strength.

The new Sunday School building, which Mr. Eagan had been vigorously pushing for as one of his chief goals, finally got realized. This was the first new space constructed since 1885, a period span during which the size of Atlanta had doubled and the size of the Sunday School had more than tripled. So obvious and great was the need now being met that, when the new building was completed and occupied in April 1906, celebration was the order of the day. The new 1906 structure has since been removed to provide space for the present Oglesby Building, but back at the time of its completion the joy of those who had worked and prayed for this accomplishment was almost ecstatic:

> The day of our dedication dawned out of a cloudless sky. The faces of the participants were as bright as the sunshine. What a sight it was when the children all assembled in our auditorium upstairs and filled it to overflowing. As one remarked, "There is hope for a Church which can look out on a scene like that." I wonder if any company of people were ever happier than we were as we gave our new building to God. (Dr. Rice writing in the *Weekly* of April 28, 1906.)

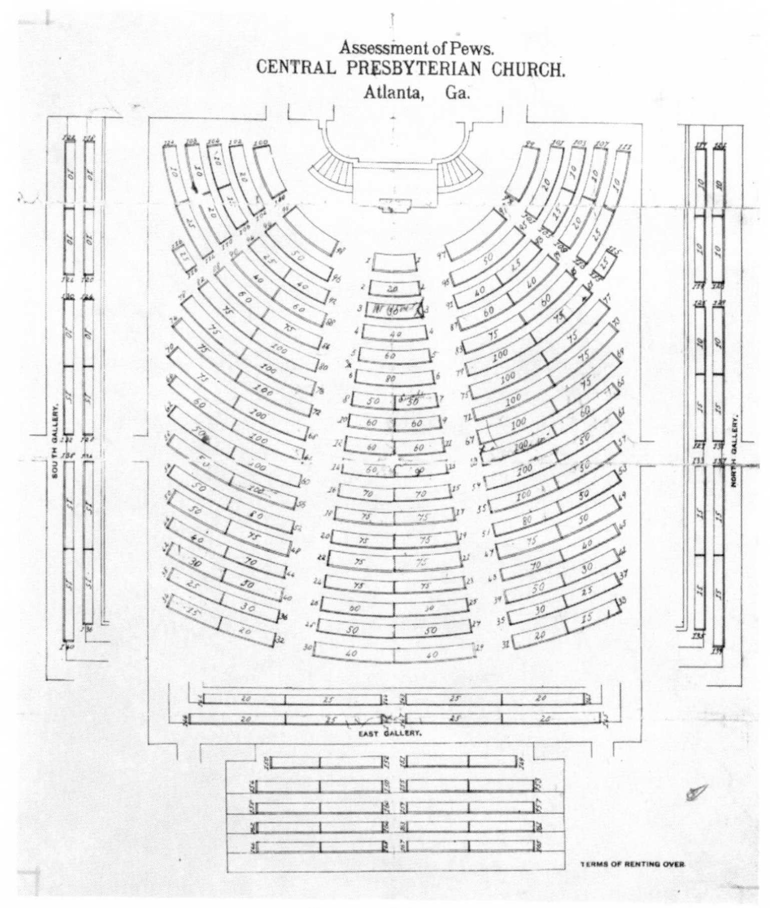

Terms of Rental

The pews in the Church will be rented on the FIRST MONDAY IN OCTOBER, *at 10 o'clock a.m., for one year, as follows:*

First quarter, cash in advance; notes payable in bank for the balance, at three, six and nine months. We have placed an assessment upon the pews of sufficient amount to enable us to meet the current expenses of the Church.

It is urged upon all persons wanting pews or seats in the Church to be present or represented on the day of renting to make their selection as the Pew Committee have no authority to reserve pews for any one before that day.

Very Respectfully,
PEW COMMITTEE

Until 1897, pew rentals provided the only systematic means of meeting current expense costs. This 1890 chart advised members of the annual rental value of each pew according to its size and location.

Equally ecstatic was an account of the dedication ceremonies for Central's new 1906 Sunday School Building which appeared in *The Earnest Worker,* a denomination-wide publication. The account was written by the denomination's Director of Sunday School Activities who had journeyed down from Richmond in order to be on hand for the occasion:

> The Sunday School of Central Church is the largest of our denomination. This church is easily one of the leading churches in the South in all that constitutes real spiritual eminence. For years it has been powerfully taught with rare skill. There has developed within its life a body of officers who for good sense, spiritual power and progressiveness are equal to the foremost. Its varied activities would make a long list, while its benevolent contributions in some sense adequately measure the devotion of its members to their Lord and His work. The Sabbath School is a development and has taken years to grow. It is splendidly organized in every detail, and its officers have not only rendered the progress made possible, but have by their harmony and progressiveness produced the progress.

No one could have been more pleased and thankful for the progress of the Sunday School than was its superintendent and prime mover. Exactly one year after the new building came into use, John Eagan was able to report that the added space had resulted in even greater progress and in even greater cause for thanksgiving:

> It has been a year of unity and a year of progress in Bible study and, we hope, in Christian character. With our enrollment (including Home Study and Cradle Roll) having reached 1,317, and with four times as many accessions to the Church from our Sunday School as the year before, and with a report from our House to House Visitation Committee showing between 300 and 400 visits made during the past week alone, it does seem as if God is filling our cup of blessing to overflowing.
>
> (*Weekly,* April, 1907)

While the Saints of Central were thus getting equipped for their educational future, they were also getting equipped for their musical future. From its beginning, Central had depended for the most part upon professional singers for its musical leadership. The choral renditions of its paid quartets were of the highest musical quality. Yet there was hardly a time during the almost half-century period that these paid quartets were in use that one or another discordant note was not threatening the peace of the Session's music committee. This committee was constantly beset by personality clashes among the

This 1903 panoramic view from the dome of the Capitol looks out over Atlanta's growing skyline. Central Church (1); Immaculate Conception (2); Fulton County Courthouse (3); Healy Building (4); Kimball House (5); Candler Building (6); Georgia Freight Depot (7); St. Phillips Cathedral (8).

musicians, salary squabbles, resignations, firings, reluctancies to perform at Sunday School and at prayer meeting assemblies, and propensities toward leaving the church worship service before it had ended. Such problems often caused the beleagured music committee to contemplate — but never actually resign itself to — the use of a precentor as an alternative.

The change-over, when it came, was to a full choir of volunteer singers, and was prompted less by disenchantment with the old paid quartet method of musical leadership than by the new evangelistic and missionary fervor seeking to find expression in all aspects of Central's life. Musically speaking, this was a people's movement fraught with all the spontaneity and growth the term implies:

> The choir was organized in the spring of 1904 for the purpose of leading the singing in the Sunday School. Most choir members were also teachers in the Sunday School and thus pressed for time. Nevertheless, the choir found time to rehearse regularly and faithfully and by doing so prepared itself for the larger work it was soon to take up.
>
> At year's end the professional quartet was released and on the first Sunday of 1905 the choir, now led and trained by a conductor engaged for that purpose, made its first appearance in the regular worship service of the Church.
>
> (*Weekly* August 31, 1907)

Despite their rugged schedule of rehearsing and singing and teaching Sunday School, the choir members found time for some good 1905-type fun together:

> Mr. and Mrs. H.G. Smyth entertained the members of the choir with a trolley ride last Saturday night. The moon was full and you can imagine what a delightful ride it was. We started out at eight o'clock in one of those large open cars and went on the delightful trip to Decatur and then out to Brookwood, returning two hours later. Everything imaginable was done for our pleasure by our host and hostess. (*Weekly*, June 10, 1905)

A tribute was also probably due Central's now decrepit old pipe organ that had somehow managed to hold together for so long a time. Built in New York City by Henry Erber, it barely made it through blockaded Savannah port, and was among the last shipments to clear over the Central of Georgia rails while they were still usable. It finally reached Atlanta and Central Church just ahead of General Sherman himself. Originally installed in the gallery in the rear of the old church, the organ was later relocated on the main floor of the same building in the northeast corner of the auditorium. There it remained until it was

The excellent Sunday School building, to the left of the sanctuary, was completed in 1906 as Central's first additional space since 1885. It enabled the school enrollment to become the denomination's largest.

re-installed in the new (1885) and present sanctuary where, with a specially built new front and with an additional set of pipes, it continued to serve until its honorable retirement in 1906 after a half-century of service. Central's new pipe organ (the one that served well into the 1930's) was much larger, much more modern, and much better suited to the new large and lively choir of the church. Elder W.D. Beatie as chairman of the music committee, after describing the new pipe organ in enthusiastic detail in the Feb. 23, 1907, *Weekly*, then announced with much satisfaction that, though Central now had a $5,150.00 instrument, its actual cost to the church was less than that "on account of using the wooden front from the old organ and some of the pipes from it whose tones were so sweet that we were unwilling to part with them." "The committee believes,"concluded Mr. Beatie, "that it has secured an instrument which for sweetness of tone, quickness of action, and durability of construction cannot be excelled, and only hope that this new instrument will give to Central as long, faithful and satisfying service as did the old."

That exciting new organ and the new "peoples" choir suited the new life and liveliness of Central to a tee. Satisfaction with this upturn in its musical fortunes reached high levels. The number of public organ recitals and choral concerts were now being reported in the *Weekly*, and the number of comments recorded in the sessional minutes of the period praising the excellence which had now been achieved in the area of choral music, all presage the even greater excellence waiting to be achieved under future leaders such as Lawrence G. Nilson and Hubert Vance Taylor and Don C. Robinson.

This era in the Church's history also presaged a much more meaningful stewardship program for the people of Central. Right up through 1897, the only systematic way they could express financial support for their church was by the regular payment of their pew rent. Each pew in the sanctuary, according to its size and location, had each year been assigned an annual rent value. Particular pews then were reserved to be occupied by the family units which had contracted and paid for them for that year.

Under the urging of Dr. Rice, the Board of Deacons devised a different and, they felt, more Christian way of raising church revenues. The officers then produced a special pamphlet which was printed and distributed to the people of Central, describing the new plan and explaining why they thought it superior to the old pew rent practice then so customary among the churches:

> With the beginning of the year 1898, Central Church begins a new plan of church support. By a vote of the officers of the church, it was determined to discontinue the system of renting pews, and to rest the financial support of the church upon the voluntary offerings of the people. This change was made after careful thought and earnest prayer for divine guidance. We were moved to it by a conviction that the pew-renting system is not in accordance with the teachings of the Scripture or the spirit of the Gospel.

In addition to areas such as Stewardship and Education, the Centralites of this period were becoming superbly equipped as a "spiritually" mature and sensitive people. It was this quality of spirit which greatly impressed Dr. Paul F. Brown, then a young man from Jacksonville, Florida, who was attending the school of dentistry in Atlanta:

> I came to your city just three years ago, a total stranger. Within a few days I was visited by two of the young men in the Young Men's Prayer Association of Central Church who invited me to their Church. I came, and so greatly has been the warmth of your welcome throughout my time in Atlanta that when it came time to

The funeral service for General John B. Gordon at Central Church early in 1904 was Georgia's top news event of the year.

> leave I felt I was leaving home to go home. God be praised that there is so much spirituality among you. (Letter printed in the *Weekly*, Oct. 20, 1906)

This spirituality, then so alive among the people of Central, was never allowed to become a thing apart from the other life and work of the church. For example, spirituality regularly found expression in Central's "Dorcas Day" collections of clothing for the needy, and in the ardent support given The Rescue Mission. It found expression in a continuing deep commitment to the establishment of local mission churches. The sessional records of the period refer to many additional mission points where Central now was leading out — locations and names such as Richmond Street, Randolph Street, Frazer Street,

Woodward Avenue, and, of course, Rice Memorial. The spirituality of Central Church expressed itself in the fervent support of the world mission program, especially through its Young Women's Foreign Mission Society. It also expressed itself in sensitive concern for people of all sorts and conditions, so that when there was a planned removal of a Red Light district from near Central, Dr. Rice cautioned that it "be done with care so as not to widen the gap between ourselves and fallen humanity."

G.B. Strickler returned for a visit to his old church late in the pastorate of Theron Rice, and, upon returning to his home in Richmond, wrote back recounting his highly favorable impressions of changes which had taken place at Central since his days there:

> I observe that many changes have taken place since I left the city twelve years ago. The Church membership has grown greatly. The Church building has been enlarged by the addition of commodious rooms for the accommodation of the Sabbath School and you now have one of the largest and best organized and most efficient schools in the denomination. But especially is it gratifying to see how harmonious and thoroughly united the Church is in its purposes and plans for the future, and how free from discouragement.

In 1908, Dr. Rice followed Dr. Strickler's example and accepted a professorship at the Union Theological Seminary in Virginia. But long before this, Theron Rice had done exceedingly well his part in equipping the saints of Central for the road ahead. That road, as soon would be known, held adventures aplenty.

It was in one of these open air street cars that the choir had its trolley outing in 1905.

Chapter 5
Discovering Its City (1909-1929)

There is a real sense in which Central had no need to "discover" its city, for the city and its people had always been an active concern of this congregation. Even back in 1878, when internal strife had its strongest hold upon them, the people of Central Church procured and gave to the Ladies of the Industrial School a large house and lot on Fair Street "to be used as a house for the indigent and old women of the city." The congregation then provided the funds needed for the ongoing operation of this charitable operation. Such acts of mercy were part of the essential character of this congregation from its very outset.

But Central was destined to respond to the needs of its city with involvements far more demanding and far-reaching than simple acts of mercy. As the Twentieth Century got underway, the congregation at the heart of Atlanta was already beginning to move out into concepts of ministry quite surprising for the South of that day. The seeds out of which these new concepts flowered were probably first planted in the year 1900. That was the year when Dr. Josiah Strong, then lecturing in Atlanta, spent a week as house guest of John J. Eagan, the up-and-coming young industrialist and leader of the Sabbath School at Central. Dr. Strong was the pioneering prophet in the America of his day in proclaiming the social and economic demands of the Christian gospel. His book, *Our Country*, was a fresh challenge to the church and a trumpet call of hope for America's poor and disadvantaged. The seeds he sowed during the many day's-end conversations he had with his young Atlanta host fell on exceedingly fertile ground. Dr. Sherwood Eddy, a kindred spirit and friend of both men has written describing the consequence of the 1900 encounter:

> Young Eagan's eyes were opened. For the first time he saw a world in deep distress, needing to be redeemed in its social relationships as well as man-to-man. As he thought and read along these lines there grew up within him a deepening sense of social obligation.

Thus began a new and growing dimension to John Eagan's Christian faith. Long before encountering Josiah Strong, he was possessed by a burning zeal for the learning and teaching and spreading of the gospel. This evangelical zeal continued ever as his first love. But now, equally evident and marching step by step with that first love was John Eagan's new and companion passion for social and economic justice for all people. It is not surprising, therefore, to discover Martha Tovell Nesbit in her 1975 doctorate dissertation at Georgia State University on *The Social Gospel in Atlanta, 1900-1920,* declaring that this layman from Central Presbyterian Church stands out pre-eminently as Atlanta's "most active leader pursuing social gospel activities during the years from 1911 until his death in 1924."

Though he died a comparatively young man, Eagan's achievements for Atlanta and the South and the nation in the area of social and economic justice were enormous. Within American Cast Iron Pipe Company, over which he presided, he established profit-sharing and board membership for workers. In the area of race relations, he inspired such authentic progress that the overflow from it was to serve Atlanta and the nation for years to come. As chairman of the Georgia Prison Reform Association and as the one appointed to lead certain areas of national welfare during World War I, he inspired progressive and wise reforms in crucial areas of human need throughout our country. And in order that more cohesive church strength among all denominations might be mounted for the achievement of social and economic justice, John Eagan became an initiating force for ecumenism not only in Atlanta but also nationally. A sampling of 1924 editorial comments written from a variety of perspectives will suggest both the breadth and depth of this quiet man's impact:

> John Eagan is a man of infinite courage, very gentle, very considerate, very kind — but very firm. His great love of God makes him one who loves his fellow man — a fine character, a fine citizen, a gentleman unafraid. *(Atlanta Georgian)*
>
> His life as a Christian and as a Churchman stands out as an example of what a man can become when his talents and material possessions are fully consecrated to God and to the service of his fellows.
> (Board of Directors of the American Cast Iron Pipe Company)
>
> He set himself to the task of Christianizing his possessions. No worthy cause appealed to him in vain. He was rated among the rich but walked with the poor. He was reckoned among the high but chose to be with the low. *(Journal of Labor)*
>
> He incarnated that spirit of service and esteem which broke down misunderstandings between class and class, race and race.
> *(Colliers Weekly)*

Ruling Elder John J. Eagan

His was not a religion which complacently cries "Lord, Lord," but which does justly and loves mercy and walks humbly with his God. *(Atlanta Journal)*

As superintendent of our Sabbath School his loss is irreparable. He poured the best of his manhood into its whole warp and woof. Eternity alone can reveal all the good that has been wrought through this man. His love for God and his faith in His word gave him a clear vision of his duty to his fellow man, filling his life with deeds of justice and charity and love toward all, it mattered not what their race or condition might be.
(Minutes of Session of Central Church)

The exceptional quality and impact of the life of this Central member must be explained at least in part by the great depth and realness of his prayer life. Trained as a youth and young man under the deeply devout Dr. Strickler ("He was the major spiritual force in my life.") and gaining much rich experience in prayer in the company of his peers in Central's Young Men's Prayer Association, John Eagan has left many of his written prayers among his papers. How well they suggest the simple and deep and almost saint-like quality of his Christian faith can be sensed from this typical prayer which he penned for his own personal guidance on November 13, 1907:

> Father, I submit my whole life to Thee. I would not withhold even the smallest or the largest thing. All I ask is to have no aim that Thou hast not inspired, and no object but to glorify Thee.

Few can doubt that that prayer was most beautifully answered. Even a casual reading of Robert E. Speer's biography of this fellow layman *(John J. Eagan — A Memoir)* makes this abundantly clear. It also makes clear that Eagan and Central Church were indeed products of each other:

> As Sunday School superintendent, Deacon, and then Ruling Elder, John Eagan always put his Church duties before all others, inasmuch as these were the earliest, deepest and most abiding claims he had upon him. Though an avid reader in many fields he read his Bible more than all other books combined, always seeking out its principles and applying them to life.

Such then was Central's strong and abiding stamp upon Mr. Eagan. In turn, his stamp upon Central lay primarily in a deepening sense of social justice and a growing awareness that the Christian gospel can and must be proclaimed in deed as well as in word. For as John Eagan grew in these respects, so also did Central and his fellow members there grow with him. Under the strong and encouraging pastoral leadership of Dr. Dunbar Ogden (1908-1918) and Dr. Ben R. Lacy (1919-1926) the people of Central carved out ever more responsibile roles for themselves at the heart of their city in applying the principles of the Gospel to help human needs and to heal human hurts.

It was out of the Brotherhood of Central, for instance, that Atlanta's now famous Union Mission had its beginnings. The Brotherhood (a 1906 reincarnation of the old Young Men's Prayer Association) represented the essential manpower of Central Church. The members earnestly believed that the learnings from their twice weekly meetings for prayer and Bible study were to be applied in Christian service. This search for their area of service came to a focus gradually but convincingly upon the plight of that sizable body of down-and-out men, usually alcoholics, who seemingly had no other home than the streets of downtown Atlanta. Under the prodding of deeply concerned Centralites like W. Woods White and John A. Whitner and president Marion Jackson, the Brotherhood was quick to take the bold steps necessary to get help and new hope to these defeated nomads. It leased a Decatur Street building in 1907, and went into the business of providing bed, board and baths as well as spiritual resources for men who could no longer help themselves. But soon, because the task was discovered to be too huge for any single congregation, the Brotherhood

The Rev. Dunbar H. Ogden
Central Pastor 1909-1918

called a meeting at Central of men representing all the Presbyterian Churches of Atlanta and organized them into the Christian Helpers League. With Central men still providing the leadership, the enterprise now had a broader and more sufficient base of support. One of the League's early reports to Central Church concerning its Rescue Mission provides impressive evidence as to the extent of their emerging urban ministry. The figures for the one year period ending March 21, 1910:

Meals served	11,352
Beds used	6,108
Baths given	4,834
Clothes furnished men	64
Physicians furnished men	102
Positions secured for men	100
Ex-prisoners served	59
Attendance upon religious services	5,442

(*The Weekly*, May 28, 1910)

The solid and sensitive response that Central mounted for the needy men of its city was matched by the congregation's response on behalf of Atlanta's needy women. These women, usually young, had moved to Atlanta seeking jobs in the rapidly growing city. They usually got jobs all right, but a woman's average weekly pay of eight dollars proved far too little for the bare needs of existing. It was sheer necessity, therefore, that drove a distressingly large number of these young workers to seek additional income in Atlanta's red light district. Central's leadership through the Men's Forward Movement took strong and immediate aim on the problem that this represented. A long-range goal was to improve the salaries of women workers, but along with that were two bold short-ranged goals.

The first goal was to get the red light district utterly abolished, because it was the heart of Atlanta's crime problem, and because it was exploitive of women. By 1912, to the great surprise of everyone except the crusading men of Central Church, that mission was accomplished.

The second short-range goal was to provide good inexpensive room and board for Atlanta's working women. With their improved salaries still years in the future, and with the added income from the district now cut off, the plight of these working women was still very acute. It was in response to this situation that the Young Women's Bible Class of Central went into action and established their boarding clubs for the women who had come to Atlanta seeking work. The sheer logic as well as compassion of what the Y.W.B.C. was trying to do, especially through its Annie Caruso Home, quickly gained additional support for their undertaking. By late 1912, these early boarding clubs had attracted leadership and funds, largely from Central, to become expanded into what soon became the interdenominationally-based Church's Homes For Girls.

Atlanta's success story on behalf of its working women excited national attention. *The Literary Digest,* in its May 3, 1913 issue, summarized that success all the way from red light district to Church's Homes in terms of the remarkable leadership of Central members Marion Jackson and John Eagan:

> They are David and Jonathan in their friendship, young men of the same age and in the same church, drawn together by the great tie of Christian fellowship. They had a New Testament passion for people. What these two laymen have done, with the full and efficient cooperation of the churchmen of their city, is a revelation and a fore-gleam of the new era (which can) bring to pass the reign of the Kingdom in this present world.

More remarkable still was Central's impact during that period upon the whole Trade Unions movement in Atlanta. The open support of organized labor by the congregation during those early years of the century is remarkable for its courage. Elsewhere in the South, stern opposition to labor was then all but universal. Atlanta's leading newspapers, rarely intimidated from taking stands on any other issue, shied off this one completely. They did not even make full information

Atlantans especially loved this parade because it celebrated the end of World War I. Dr. Ben Lacy was still clothed in his army chaplain uniform when he preached his first sermon as Central's new pastor in 1919. Central Church offices are at right, Werner Apartments at center, Second Baptist at left.

available. It was in order to fill this information and editorial vacuum that Central Ruling Elder Marion Jackson, a lawyer, began publication of a small newspaper called *The Way*. He sought in it to create a forum for applying moral leadership and Christian principles to Atlanta's more pressing social and economic issues. In the forefront of these issues was, inevitably, that of the trade unions. *The Way* was in a very real sense the public voice of Central Church, its pastors, and its people. Central, indeed, in those early days of the movement, may have provided for organized labor the most open support it had anywhere in the whole South.

When, for instance, there was a worker's strike at the Fulton Bag and Cotton Mill in 1914, it was Central, standing almost alone, that took up the cause of the strikers. When other centrally located meeting places became closed to the strikers, it was Central which acted "to tender to them the use of the Sunday School building to have such meetings as they desire." (Session minutes of May 31, 1914) When on June 28, there was a mass meeting at the Opera House in support of striking workers, it was Central member Marion Jackson who presented irrefutable evidence that many Atlanta children were having to work full-time instead of going to school since their mill-employed fathers earned so little money. And it was Central member John J. Eagan, as the other platform speaker for the occasion, who pointedly reminded that "no manufacturer has a right to discharge employees for seeking better wages or let them go hungry so long as he has bread for himself." Indeed it was Central's strong leadership which in the end tilted public support to the side of these woefully underpaid textile workers.

Less than two years later, Atlanta was in the throes of another big strike. This time, it was the street car workers and operators who were trying to improve their lot, and in the process much bitterness and some violence had been generated. Public and press support for the workers eroded to the point where their case was no longer being heard. The atmosphere became such that any outside group trying to get a fair hearing for the strikers would find itself in an unpopular position. But Central Church, still standing all but alone, refused to be intimidated by that danger. The same church officers who had brought Christian principles to bear in attaining just settlement in the earlier strike were again now in the vanguard of this effort. And the congregation stood with them. Thus its voice was strongly and effectively heard at the huge mass rally held on behalf of the workers on October 13, 1916, in downtown Atlanta. Dr. Dunbar Ogden and Mr. Marion Jackson, Central's pastor and one of its ruling elders, delivered the two major speeches of the day. In fact, they were the only persons on the speaker's platform who were not there by virtue of offices they held locally or nationally in the labor movement. Their only purpose was for justice and fairplay to become factors in any settlement of the dispute, and in this they were eminently successful.

It can probably be affirmed that the people of Central Presbyterian Church, by strongly insisting as a matter of Christian principle that all facts get full and fair airing, became a stablizing force in the early and subsequent development of labor relations in the city of Atlanta.

Such civic leadership was yet another confirmation that Central's good fortune in the quality of its ministerial leadership continued when Dr. Dunbar Ogden came to lead the congregation throughout the crucial 1908-1918 years. Believing profoundly in the social implications of the Christian gospel, he was able to inspire the men and women of his congregation in ministering to the needs of all Atlanta's people. By the time Dunbar Ogden left to serve a church in New Orleans, as had R.Q. Mallard more than fifty years earlier, Central Church had become permanently tilted toward responsible corporate action on behalf of its city.

During Dr. Ogden's pastorate, Central's practice of applying Christian principles to public issues was being tested in yet another arena of civic righteousness. Back in 1912, when Messrs. Eagan and Jackson led the Men and Religion Forward Movement in its successful campaign to shame Atlanta's red light district out of existence, their ringing declarations of Christian principles as they applied to life in the city were so convincing that Police Chief James L. Beavers himself became a permanent and enthusiastic convert. He became determined to fight for civic righteousness, wherever that fight needed to be waged, without fear or exception. Such convictions soon brought the police chief into open conflict with some powerful and prestigious social clubs of Atlanta when he ordered them to cease selling alcoholic beverages within their clubs and to conform to the prohibition law just as other citizens.

This tampering with their special privileges resulted in inconveniences which the power structures within these most prestigious of Atlanta's organizations were in no mood to tolerate. Forthwith, they applied appropriate pressure and Chief Beavers was promptly relieved of his duties. But just as promptly, the men leading the Forward Movement accepted the challenge and mounted their counterattack to get Chief Beavers reinstated. The real facts in the case got into the Atlanta newspapers almost daily in data written by Marion Jackson and paid for by John Eagan. Under such constant bombardment, and with public indignation against them increasingly all the time, the clubs finally acknowledged defeat, and asked that Beavers be returned to his post as Chief of Police. Central had once again made a difference in the affairs of the city simply by standing firm upon what was seen to be its Christian responsibility in the city.

It was about this same time that the congregation began making its contribution in the area of race relations. Long before now, Central had been performing outstandingly in its mission work among the Negro citizens of Atlanta. Less outstanding though had been its performance in reference to Atlanta's deep-rooted racial strife. Mission activities must certainly have been an ameliorating force in the midst of that strife, but until the 1910 period, there is scant evidence that Central had yet understood its role in terms of the deep socio-economic causes of racial strife.

Swift changes now began to take place. A more responsible stance toward the racial needs of its city became part of the corporate character of the congregation. It was a stance which took shape in the lives of hundreds of members of Central Church. It was a stance whose development grew out of the exceptionally strong pastoral leadership of Dr. Ogden and Dr. Lacy, both of whom saw the city as their second parish. It grew also out of the remarkable commitment of the Rev. R.G. Buford, an assistant pastor who was murdered in line of duty being performed in the city and who died in what the *Atlanta Constitution* described as a "hero's death." (He had been shot to death protecting a battered wife from her drunken husband.)

But once again, it is by means of the well-documented life of John J. Eagan that Central's growing stance in race relations can best be traced. The deepening sense of responsibility of the congregation toward the racial needs in its city and area are in fact personified in Mr. Eagan and in his special contributions. It was he, for instance, who in 1915, brought Booker T. Washington to Atlanta as part of an effort to enlist the power structure of the city to help achieve better education and increased income for Negroes. It was he who was tapped by the War Department to go to Washington during World War I, and there, assisted in his efforts by Central's Marion Jackson, to become national advisor on matters related to the welfare of all sailors, soldiers and communities involved in training camp activities. It was he, as Chairman of the Commission on Interracial Cooperation who formulated and helped carry forward national goals ("Equal administration of justice, better living conditions, cleaner and more courteous traveling accommodations, and improved educational opportunities") which, at least for that point in time, were remarkably on beam as regards the then basic Negro needs. It was he who established among his Negro counter-parts in Atlanta relationships so trustworthy that *The Worlds Work* in its 1923 article gave that relationship credit for Atlanta's remarkable racial progress:

> Racial crises may recur in Atlanta, but if they do we can be sure that John Eagan and Robert Morton (one of Atlanta's notable Negro leaders of that period) will be found fighting on the same side.

But a short year later Mr. Eagan, who had always had to battle frail health, was dead. There can be no doubt that his brief life had profoundly influenced the course of race relations. The life and activities of this officer and Sunday School superintendent in Central Presbyterian Church made an impact for racial justice reaching far beyond his own city and state. When he died, Fisk University, the famed Negro institution in Nashville, Tennessee, acknowledged its great feeling of loss and esteem by bringing out a special issue of its *News* devoted to honoring this quiet-spoken churchman who personified much that his home church was to stand for:

> John Joseph Eagan was the South's unquestioned leader in matters of righteousness in the adjustment of problems of race. His philosophy of race adjustment was so high above the halting principle of race expediency that his leadership was claimed and appropriated by the Federal Council of the Churches of Christ in

The Rev. Ben R. Lacy
Central Pastor 1919-1926
General Assembly Moderator
1950

America in its work toward better Christian relationships in race contracts.

John Eagan, who had been most fortunate in having had G.B. Strickler, Theron Rice and Dunbar Ogden as his earlier pastors and counselors, was similarly blessed during the last five years of his life in being under the invigorating leadership of young Ben R. Lacy. Central had gone all the way to France to get its first post-World War I minister, inasmuch as Dr. Lacy was then still overseas serving as a divisional chaplain in the American Expeditionary Forces when the congregation called in 1919. The kind of minister they got to lead them for the next seven years becomes revealed in a succinctly worded citation with which the University of North Carolina almost thirty years later awarded him its Doctor of Laws degree:

> Ben Rice Lacy:
> Student leader and football captain Davidson College,
> Rhodes Scholar at Oxford University,
> Hoge graduate fellow at Union Theological Seminary,
> Chaplain, captain, 13th Div. AEF, cited for bravery.
> In an age of confusion, a source of faith.
> His personality rises radiantly above the tumult of the times.
> His spirituality reaches robustly across the nation.

The sterling qualities which Chapel Hill discerned in 1948 were recognized far earlier by Central. In a move which must be considered radically uncharacteristic for such bodies, the Board of Deacons, only eighteen months after Dr. Lacy's arrival on the scene at Central, wrote begging the Session for permission to increase the salary of this exciting young minister. "Throughout our city," they declared, "the circle of his friends and the scope of his influence is constantly broadening. His consecrated life and capacity for leadership equip him for exceptional service in upbuilding and uplifting our community."

Unsurprisingly the Lacy years at Central did provide services notably "upbuilding" and "uplifting" for the Atlanta community.

One of these was Central's famed Baby Clinic. Dr. Lacy himself has written describing his recollection of its 1922 beginnings:

> It was at John J. Eagan's suggestion that the Baby Clinic was begun at Central. He informed me that he had talked with the Mother's class of Central about it and they like the idea, that the Mother's Class president and vice president had then conferred with the Red Cross which confirmed the timeliness of it. Eagan told me he was sure our congregation would support such a movement if a group of doctors would undertake the work, giving their services freely to charity patients. A conference with Dr. George McAliley resulted in an efficient staff of physicians which was matched on the part of Central with an admirable group of assistants headed by Mrs. Ralph Nolan.

In a subsequent chapter more must be said about the Baby Clinic and the remarkable urban ministry it has provided through the decades since 1922.

Also in the service of both Church and city since the Lacy period is the structure on Hunter Street known as the Campbell-Eagan Building. Again let Dr. Lacy's own memory describe its beginning:

> Mr. J. Bulow Campbell sent for me one day and asked if Central Presbyterian Church would receive a gift of a lot in memory of his mother, Virginia Orme Campbell, which would cost $25,000, and which he hoped to see erected a modern Sunday School building. It was not long after the purchase of this lot that Mr. Eagan died and his mother, Mrs. M.V. Eagan conceived the plan of erecting the John J. Eagan Memorial Building.

Mr. Bulow Campbell, the quiet and exceedingly effective churchman whose generous gift played a major part in bringing the Campbell-Eagan Building into being, was later to establish a signifi-

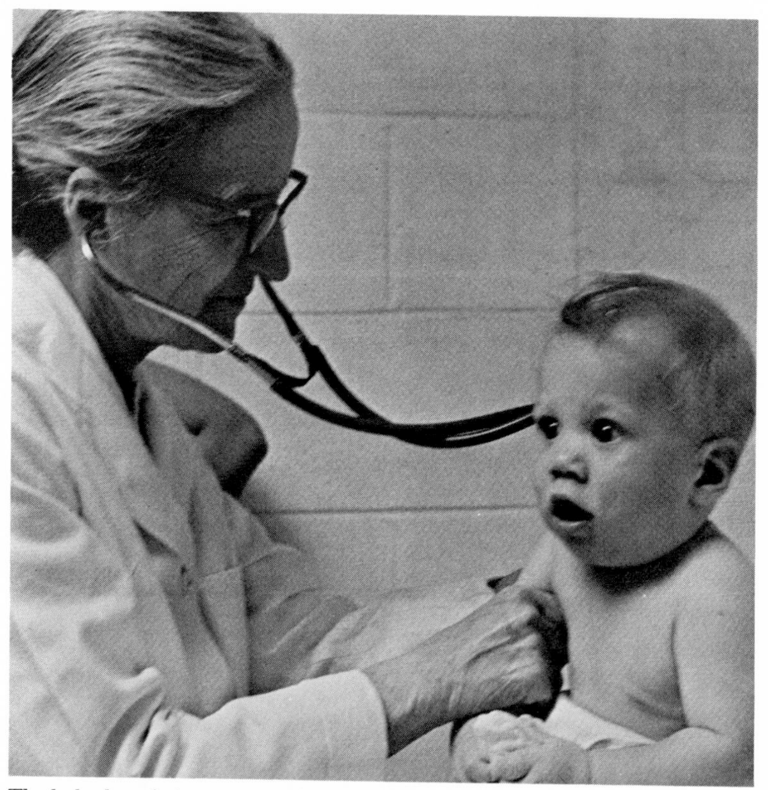

The baby here being examined by Dr. Leila Denmark at the Baby Clinic is but one among some 65,000 individual children who have received professional health treatments at this the oldest of all the clinics of Central Church.

cant trust fund on behalf of Central Church. The income from Mr. Campbell's legacy still continues to help support the vital work of this congregation just as it has been doing in most telling fashion for almost four decades. He was quite simply, as Dr. Oglesby once described him, "a noble Christian."

It is uniquely appropriate that the building erected in memory of John Eagan and which later served to memorialize J. Bulow Campbell as well should continue as part of the plant of the Church from which they gained spiritual strength in such large measure, and that it should continue to serve the two facets of the Christian faith and experience which were so wonderfully meaningful to them both. They and many another old Centralite would be pleased not only that the Campbell-Eagan Building continues as a place where the Christian gospel is taught and learned but that it has also through the years served as

Ruling Elder J. Bulow Campbell

home for dozens of welfare and public service organizations devoted to meeting the needs of the people of the city.

After the Campbell-Eagan unit stood completed and in full use, the already demanding program activities of Central Church became more time-requiring than ever. Dr. Lacy, like predecessor pastors before him, found the pressure of duties increasingly burdensome. The burden weighed so heavily upon him that on April 28, 1925 he wrote laying his quandry before the Session and asking its counsel and help in finding a solution:

> Many (of my friends) think that I should resign as pastor of Central and accept a field more compact and less exacting in its demands. Their advice is based upon no consideration of my physical health, which is unusually good at present, but because they feel that I will not attain my greatest usefulness without a better opportunity for study.
>
> You recall that Dr. Strickler had about twelve years in a quiet pastorate at Tinkling Springs before coming here. Dr. Rice had a much briefer pastorate at Alexandria. Dr. Ogden had been seasoned at Columbus and Knoxville. I have had no such seasoning, so no opportunity was offered me for study either during the three years as a home missionary or the two years as a Chaplain in the

> Army. The work of Central today is not less demanding than in the pastorates of my predecessors, yet they came to the field better equipped than I. My own experience tallies with the warning of my friends. It is with greater effort that I find time to read or study. Worse still it is with greater effort that I prepare a sermon. Some weeks I stay in a state of mental upheavel and uncertainty because the message will not be formulated in my mind. I doubt if any other than a pastor appreciates the difficulty of preparing two fresh sermons each week, besides prayer meeting and occasional addresses, and at the same time even partially leading the church in its larger enterprises. If I stay on at Central as at present, it will be with diminishing power in the pulpit. It is impossible for a man of my temperament to seclude himself enough to do more than the minimum amount of study. If it *were* possible, I doubt if Central would desire that kind of preacher as pastor.

Dr. Lacy, in his letter, then suggested several possible courses of action such as his resignation or his taking an extended sabbatical study leave. But the solution which seemed to him most feasible, and the one adopted by the Session, was that the pastor be allowed a two-month study leave annually.

Before his newly agreed upon policy was fairly underway, however, a familiar spectre arose to haunt the Session — Union Theological Seminary was once again after a Central Church pastor! Dr. Lacy was in Richmond when the seminary there extended him its call. Immediately then on July 6, 1925, he wrote informing the Session of this turn of events. Four days later the elders and deacons were in joint session pondering that unwelcome news. The task of persuading their pastor to continue at Central in face of the obviously strong appeal that the proffered seminary post held for him was hardly a new task. Officers of the Church had been at that arduous undertaking at repeated intervals reaching all the way back to 1883! Now they were at it again. Before the night was over the officers had adopted and telegraphed to Dr. Lacy their urgent resolution. It had a familiar ring to it:

> Resolved that in our judgment it is God's will that Dr. Lacy should remain at his post as pastor of Central Presbyterian Church, this being indicated by three things:
>
> First, by the way in which God has blessed the work of the Church under the leadership of Dr. Lacy and by the greater work and responsibilities which the Church and its members have recently been led to undertake by Dr. Lacy.
>
> Second, by the way in which our Father has blessed the leadership of Dr. Lacy not only in the Central Church and in the interdenominational work and civic life of the city of Atlanta

The Campbell-Eagan Building, which has served Central and the surrounding city since 1926, still bears its lively witness in the heart of Atlanta.

> where manifestly he has been called to a position of leadership and influence which the city cannot afford to lose at this time.
>
> Third, by the peculiar talent as a preacher of the Word which God has endowed Dr. Lacy with, a gift which enables him to appeal to the multitudes from the pulpit in a marvelous way, a gift which is peculiar to him as a man, enabling him to win others for the ministry and for the Christian life, but a gift which he cannot impart to others in a classroom, and which to use most effectively for the glory of God and the advancement of Christ's kingdom on earth, Dr. Lacy must remain in the preacher field, preaching the Word to a lost world.

The Session's inspired appeal at least partially persuaded Dr. Lacy, if not the seminary. For another full year he stayed on at Central's exciting and very demanding helm. But when in May, 1926, the seminary came urging upon him none less than its presidency itself, Dr. Lacy saw this as a call not to be refused and forthwith asked the congregation to concur with him in accepting it. On May 23, the congregation gave its concurrence, with profound expressions of esteem and with prayers "that the Holy Spirit, constantly strengthening and leading him, may make him to be an ever growing blessing to ever increasing numbers in his new field."

The Rev. W. E. Davis
Central Pastor 1927-1929

Any assessment of Dr. Lacy's long and notable service as President of the Union Theological Seminary in Virginia will leave no doubt that the congregation's prayer was abundantly answered, just as it was to be similarly answered regarding another Central Church pastor called to the same post forty years later.

After its peak years under Dr. Ben Lacy, the Church suffered some set-backs during its first few years without his leadership. Part of this can be laid to the onset of the Great Depression, with its adverse effect on every Atlanta institution. More significant though in the somewhat declining fortunes of Central Church was the lingering ill-health of the pastor called to succeed Dr. Lacy. The Rev. Dr. W.E. Davis was so beset by sickness after his arrival in Atlanta that he was barely able to finish out two years at the job before having to give it up and resign.

Because of this unfortunate circumstance, the years between 1926 and 1930 were lean ones. It was an era in Central's life distinguished primarily by such questionable achievements as beginning a Men of the Church organization and disposing of the church bell which had been a part of Central for almost seventy years. The bell, first hung in the tower of the 1860 building where it called hearers to worship until cracked and silenced at the time of General Sherman's invasion, was rehung in the tower of the new and present building erected in 1885.

By 1928, it was declared too heavy for its supports and was removed from the tower at a cost of $25.00. The last official word about it was that the bell was to be sold, presumably for scrap. No remaining record reveals that it actually was sold, nor for how much.

All in all, the Central Church which approached the year 1930 was at a low ebb and in dire need again of invigorating pastoral leadership.

The J. Bulow Campbell Class, 1926. (Mr. Campbell is 5th from left, front row.)

Chapter 6
Discovering Its Mission (1930-1958)

Central finally found the invigorating pastoral leadership it needed in the person of an Arkansan who had been theologically trained at the seemingly ubiquitous Union Theological Seminary in Virginia, and who, while there, had been a student under Central's ex-pastor, Dr. Theron Rice. Stuart Roscoe Oglesby was in the midst of his third pastorate when Central invited him to come and be its new leader. To be asked to serve one of the largest and most prestigious congregations in the whole denomination was both an honor and an opportunity for a rising young minister — and young Dr. Oglesby knew it. But he also knew the hazards that would lie ahead.

The invitation came to Stuart Oglesby just as 1929 was about to fade into 1930. The time was ripe for reversals in the fortunes of inner-city churches such as Central. In Atlanta, as in other big cities, the flight of fine residences from downtown areas, already a mass movement, was sure to become even more massive in the days ahead. Numbers of members who had moved residence from around downtown churches like Central were already transferring their memberships elsewhere, and the numbers were increasing. Parking, already a problem in downtown areas like Central's, would predictably grow into an even larger problem. And no crystal ball was needed to know that the economic depression, already hurting churches like Central, was going to hurt them a great deal more punishingly before it was over. All these hazards must have been known and weighed in the balance as Stuart Oglesby sat in his study at Hot Springs, Arkansas, and tried to decide whether he should stay there or go to Atlanta.

In addition to those hazards which Central shared with all other downtown churches of that period was another hazard which was then peculiarly Central's. Central Church had lost its momentum.

Of this there could be little doubt. The whole 1926-1929 period seemed to have drained away much of Central's past drive. The Church was simply not as sure now about its identity and its mission. After three trying years, attendance was off, membership was down, and confidence about the future was at low ebb. To reverse that trend and help Central regain some of its lost momentum was a monumental

The Rev. Stuart R. Oglesby

Central Pastor 1930-1958

Pastor Emeritus 1958-1977

task for any new pastor. Even to undertake to do so took a very special kind of courage.

Courage of that special kind was something Dr. Oglesby had. So, to Central he came. In fact, he came twice. First, by train, to look for a house in Atlanta and then, a week later, by car with Mrs. Oglesby and their four children. The second time it "took." Dr. Oglesby stayed to lead Central Church for the next twenty-eight years — the Church's longest pastorate of all.

If the young minister, traveling by Pullman from Arkansas, harbored any doubts about having made the right decision, they must have been more than dispelled once his train got to Atlanta's Terminal Station. The warm welcoming group was not only there to greet him but it had also plastered every passage and stairway the arriving pastor would traverse, as he moved from train to street, with placards announcing his advent and his sermon topic at Central on Sunday.

Dr. Oglesby was long to recall that first preaching service at Central. He remembered the wonderful congregation "that taxed the auditorium to its capacity." He remembered the text of his sermon that morning (Phil. 4:19) for he was to preach from the same text on each of the next twenty-eight anniversaries of that first sermon at Central Church.

It is remarkable how many new pastors throughout Central's history have felt enormously discouraged about the quality and productivity of the work they were able to do during their first several months on the job. Dr. Oglesby was no exception. Perhaps this early sense of inadequacy which plagued some of Central's most outstanding ministers grew out of sheer variety and magnitude of the work to be done there and the minister's realization that to perform all the duties of his office up to the high standards he had set for himself was simply an impossible task. At any rate young Oglesby approached the waning days of 1930 thoroughly dismayed that attendance, so reflective of a happy and effective pastoral relationship, had not been very good during the months past. As then he sat reflecting on it all at the end of his first Christmas day in Atlanta — a day which except for family had been a crushingly lonely one — he wondered in his diary whether the congregation itself found his performance disappointing.

But, Dr. Oglesby, like other ministers whose frustrations arise out of the commendably high standards they have set for their work, was dead wrong about how the congregation actually felt toward him and his performance:

> His pastorate will be one year old at Central Church on February First. When he first came our whole church was yearning for the leadership of a pastor. We were sincerely happy to see him, and the heart of the congregation waxed warm when we saw him in the pulpit. And that heart is still warm. Again, we firmly hoped and believed that Central Church could look forward to another fruitful ministry with the saving of many souls and a continuation of its services to the Master.
>
> After a year of Dr. Oglesby's ministry that belief has grown into Faith. Central under its great pastors in the past has made a noble history. We now have faith in its great future.
>
> (*Weekly*, Jan. 31, 1931)

That prediction was a correct one. Subsequent history has confirmed that Central did indeed have a great future. But the greatness was not to come easily in those unsettling early 1930's. Some mighty road blocks were squarely in the way.

For one thing, these were the Depression years. For a long decade of years surrounding the stock market crash of 1929, the whole nation languished in a sea of economic stagnation. Institutions of every sort had their progress halted or at least slowed down. Central was no exception. For lack of funds its cherished programs were shackled, and its goals delayed. Central's proud record of allocating more of its income for others rather than for self was spared only because the pastor insisted, instead, that the reductions be made in his own salary. By 1933, Dr. Oglesby had taken two sizeable salary cuts, and it was to be yet another decade before these reductions would be restored, if ever they were.

In fact, the only aspect of life at Central not reduced or slowed down by the Depression was the congregation's never-say-die spirit. It was a spirit which not even the euphemistically dubbed "Bank Holiday" days could dampen. At least not when those most devastating of Depression days happened to fall in the very midst of Central's celebration of its seventy-fifth anniversary:

> At the celebration of Central's 75th anniversary the hearts of our members were immeasurably cheered. There was evident in the faces of our people a lively hope which was quite unaccounted for from a mere external point of view. All that one could see from that standpoint were banks with doors locked closed, business brought to a standstill, and a mood of fear and uncertainty throughout most of the world.
>
> Yet the members of Central, gathered at our anniversary supper, looked with confidence on the future, sure that God was going to bless the ministry he had given us to do together at this place. (*Weekly*, March 18, 1933)

A sterner test for Central's confidence was the increasing pace with which its members were now leaving the downtown area. Central members were abandoning their big old mid-town dwellings in favor of those bright, new suburban settlements miles away from Capitol Square. Even as early as 1931, a chart printed in the *Weekly* gave graphic evidence of the outward movement of Central's membership.

By that year only eighteen percent of the membership still resided in the vicinity of the church building. All others had left. Most of them, fortunately, were still within five miles of the church. But as the years went on the outward trend was to continue, and the distance separating residences from the Church was to lengthen even more.

This, plus the fact that some of these members would transfer their membership to churches in their new neighborhoods, meant that Central now had to confront the most critical decision that mid-city churches have to make: To stay or not to stay.

Some inner-city churches have no where else to go. But Central in the 1930's clearly had an option. The area northward from the church was the one to which a preponderance of its members had moved. So also might Central itself. This possibility provided a thoroughly viable

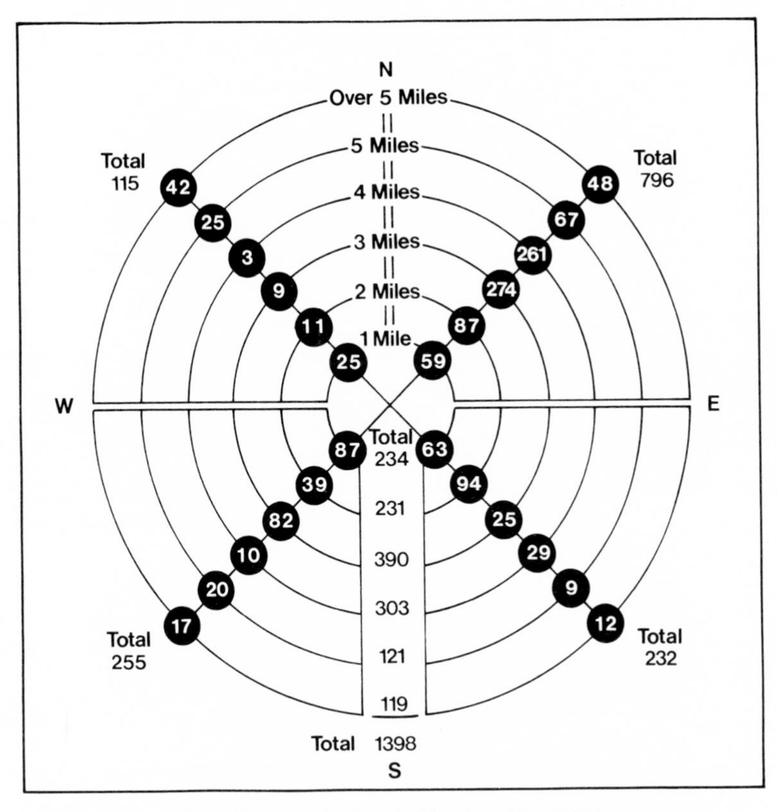

Distribution of Church Membership, 1931.

alternative to staying put. The more so since this northward section of Atlanta still had room aplenty for another major Presbyterian church to move into. And Central, by relocating in that growing, prospering area, would itself continue to grow and prosper. It would, in moving out, experience scant difficulty in maintaining its rank as the largest Presbyterian congregation in Atlanta and, perhaps, in the whole denomination.

For Central in the 1930's to have opted to make that outward move would not have been an unworthy decision. But the congregation had an even more worthy decision in its view. A majority of the people of Central, along with their new minister, held strongly to the conviction that for Central, at least, the only right decision was to stay right there in the heart of Atlanta. Dr. Oglesby's third anniversary message set the issue squarely before the whole membership:

> There are three classes of members in Central today. One class believes that the days of our Church (in the downtown area) are

> numbered, the problems insoluble, and the end of our usefulness — if not our existence — is almost in sight.
>
> Another class loves "dear old Central" and "wouldn't have it die for anything in the world," but yields to the urge of convenience in sending their children to nearer Sunday Schools as well as attending themselves most often in other churches.
>
> The third class believes there is a need of a great downtown Presbyterian church in Atlanta, that our problems, though great, are not insoluble, that our field of usefulness and service was never wider or more urgent than today, and that insofar as we give ourselves in unselfish and devoted service to our work, the Lord will cause the Church to prosper. The pastor is grateful that the third class is in the majority among our members and trusts that their tribe may increase. He takes his stand unequivocally with them. (*Weekly,* Feb. 4, 1933)

The pastor doggedly stuck it out on his unequivocal stand, and more and more of the people moved over to stand with him. The tribe of those determined to stay, already a majority, did increase by the month. By the beginning of 1937, Central's congregation was virtually of one mind. They were for staying. And, God helping them, they intended to do so. This was a decision which the city of Atlanta, then in the midst of its Centennial Year, found most praiseworthy:

> After seventy-five years of gracious history in its present location, the Central Presbyterian Church has decided to remain there. Instead of moving from downtown Atlanta as many other churches have done, it will continue its ministeries where they began.
>
> It will endeavor to make itself more than ever helpful to its old neighborhood by improving and beautifying its property.
>
> This is an admirable decision.
>
> Midtown churches in a growing and changing city face peculiar problems. As business claims more of the home areas around them and their membership is being scattered into new residential sections, they must make readjustments which are often difficult. But with their new problems come also new opportunities for well-doing, and the church that is prepared to meet them renders distinctive service. So has it been and will now continue to be with Central Presbyterian. For it is planned to spend some forty thousand dollars equipping itself for even more generous work exactly where it has always been.
>
> This church, which has numbered among its ministers some of the most distinguished in America, will continue carrying forward its noble traditions of service and the entire city will applaud its efforts. By acquiring adjoining land and making extensive improvements in its buildings, it is now saying to Atlanta: "Our life began here nearly eighty years ago in the center of this city. Our name has always been the Central Presbyterian Church, and that is what we intend to remain — Central."
>
> (*The Atlanta Journal,* May 9, 1937)

Early in the Oglesby years, Central shared its Hunter Street corner with Atlanta's Number Two (Mechanics) fire station, in the right foreground of this 1933 photograph. The 1905 Sunday School building can be seen to the left.

To remain "Central" was an uphill battle. The firm decision to stay downtown only made the staying sure; it never promised to make it easy. It was hardly an easy task anymore to sell the special merits of Central Church to the average member who now lived far away, had to fight traffic to get there, had to scrounge for parking when he arrived, and whose children constantly wondered why they were not going to the big neighborhood Sunday School like the rest of their gang.

Only because a majority of the people of Central believed greatly in their church and in what it was doing, were they willing to engage, as unceasingly as now they had to, in their battle to remain strong to serve downtown Atlanta.

During the entire 1930-1958 period, an enormously determined pastor and people fought endlessly: first, to prove to one and all that Central was decidely worth preserving as a strong congregation; and, second, to unite the people of Central in a loving and caring fellowship from which no member would lightly wish to transfer.

It was in connection with this latter goal that Dr. Oglesby initiated and carried forward till the day he retired what has to be one of the most remarkable pastoral ministries of all time. From the moment Stuart Oglesby arrived in Atlanta, he was on the move becoming what he believed every pastor should be — the friend and counsellor of every person remotely connected with his congregation. With him on his daily journeys was a little record book in which was listed every member of his congregation with careful notations as to when he had last had the privilege of visiting with each person. The care with which Dr. Oglesby kept tab of his work in this particular area of his responsibilities well indicates the importance he placed upon it. His records over many years reveal an average each month of more than 100 pastoral visits made in hospitals and homes and places of business and wherever his people happened to be. During his active ministry at Central Church, Dr. Oglesby logged an amazing 39,920 pastoral calls. He was busy at these and his other duties almost twelve hours a day and seven days a week as long as he served Central Church. He made few concessions to weather, or the painful headaches to which he was subject, or to the almost weekly breakdown of his not-too-faithful Chevrolet. So even on foot and on ice, by trolly and by telephone, Dr. Oglesby kept diligently at his pastoral responsibilities all the days of his ministry. Those who knew him well claim quite seriously that their pastor finally came to achieve a sort of sixth sense for perceiving, before anyone else, if there were special needs among his people where he might be of help. He developed a wonderful pastoral knack for being at the right place at the right time. And the people were grateful. Exemplary diligence to his pastoral calling may indeed have been Dr. Oglesby's greatest single gift to the congregation he served so lovingly for twenty-eight years. And if any one thing can be said to have saved and focused the strength of Central for the fulfilling of its mission, this was it.

An inevitable question seeks answer at this point. Is it possible to be *that* pastoral in a city the size of Atlanta and in a congregation the size of Central without a corresponding neglect of other responsibilities to which the minister is likewise called? That question, applied to the Oglesby years at Central, can be answered with an assured *Yes,* it is possible. Indeed the depth at which Stuart Oglesby carried forward pastoral responsibilities added even greater depth to the other duties he faithfully performed.

If there had been any dangerous over-balance toward the pastoral at Central, then Dr. Oglesby's preaching ministry would have been an obvious and serious casualty, and it wasn't. The more than 3,000 sermons he preached at Central were utterly winsome and powerful in their honesty. They were honest to the scriptures Dr. Oglesby knew so deeply, honest to his own personal knowledge of his people, and honest to his own clear-edged convictions as to God's will for Central's future. Excerpts from some of his sermons will suggest why the people heard him so gladly and why he was able to give such firm guidance to the church during a time of uncertainty.

The people who sat under his preaching through the years and who heard words like those which follow, could not remain unaware of the urgent needs about them in downtown Atlanta, nor of the need for

Central to remain there among those needs, nor of the vastly wider opportunities for service which the congregation enjoyed in that location:

> There are more people living in the community served by Central than ever before. However, with the movement of those who could afford it to the residential and suburban sections, the poorer people were left and those who have come in have a greater need for Christian ministry than ever before.
>
> The program of this church has been projected to meet the needs of this community. These needs cannot be met, and often are not even known or understood by prosperous churches located a great distance away.
>
> I believe in the downtown church because it offers to its members so many satisfying, Christlike opportunities for service. There are many Christians who seem not to be able to see human needs unless it is a great distance away. The downtown church does not neglect its ministry to those far away, as our benevolences show each year, but it concentrates on the need of its own neighbors.

Not only did the Oglesby sermons at Central honestly acknowledge the greater inconveniences members would experience by being part of a downtown congregation, but they were also bold to claim that the members would have more fulfilling experiences because they were serving in a downtown church:

> A downtown church does not have convenience of location to offer its members. Many churches are closer by, even many Presbyterian churches. Some of our members pass several of them on their way to Central. This is an inconvenience. But convenience is a small sacrifice we can make for the ministries of Central Church.
>
> The downtown church is a cross-section of the life of the city. The argument that children want to go to Sunday School with the same children with whom they go to public school is valid for children. But with long-range character development in mind, it is not valid. In a downtown church children come in contact with people from all classes and not just one class.
>
> This they are going to have to do when they grow up, and meeting children who have a different background is a real development of character.

Most of all in his preaching, Dr. Oglesby liked to remind his listeners of Central's unique and unequalled opportunity to be a constant influence for good there at the very heart of Atlanta:

> The influence of a church like Central, in front of the Capitol and near the City Hall and County Courthouse is great just for the fact of being here. The pastor of Central knows personally the officials of city, county, and state, and they know him. There are many ways in which we work together in a manner that could not be done if Central was not here at the center of the city. The pastor of a downtown church touches the life of the city through the newspaper, the social agencies, the character building agencies with which he is in intimate personal contact.

Dr. Ben Lacy once said that "...the pastor at Central Church is in a real sense, pastor to the whole city." Perhaps this explains how Dr. Oglesby somehow found and took the time to become a leading and ministering spirit not only among such notable civic enterprises as the Atlanta Union Mission, the Atlanta YMCA, and the Atlanta Council of Churches, but also among causes and persons utterly without name or fame. For example, his diary entries for a four year period beginning in December, 1939, recount the dogged compassion with which Stuart Oglesby fought for the salvation — the physical and mental and spiritual salvation — of a certain desperately needful and fameless young man who happened to cross his path. From the moment the lad was first found passed out on Washington Street in front of the church, his welfare was accepted by Dr. Oglesby as a God-given responsibility. Even though doubts as to the worthwhileness of the effort often assailed him, the crushingly busy downtown pastor never waivered in fulfilling his additional pastoral obligation he felt God had thrust upon him. As long as Paul (that was the young man's name) was in Atlanta, Stuart Oglesby was busy not only helping him get hospital care and clothing and work and a room at the "Y" but also patiently counseling him several times weekly.

When Paul, in spite of all this, persisted in his delinquencies and ended up in a Tennessee prison, Dr. Oglesby pursued him even there, doggedly continuing his seemingly futile efforts at rescuing the good that was in the boy. "...Am I casting pearls before swine? God forbid. I just can't break through to that center which controls him and touch him. But I must be patient with him as the Lord is patient with me."

The patience of which Dr. Oglesby was writing in his diary is the reason the story has a happy ending. It is a story best told by Paul himself. Now, almost forty years after his first contact with Dr. Oglesby, Paul is a respected citizen and family man and director of a museum in South Carolina. His story comes out in an inspiring letter he wrote to Mrs. Oglesby following the death of her husband, his benefactor, in 1977:

> "It is now many years since the day Dr. Oglesby found me sick on the street in front of the church. At that time my mind was so warped with hatred that even today I cannot understand how I

> was ever salvaged... I was without a doubt the most mentally twisted person alive.
>
> The few months that I lived in Atlanta were the most important of my life. Dr. Oglesby secured a job for me at the Atlanta Athletic Club and at the same time required that I attend church and Sunday School.
>
> One day I silently left Atlanta to go back to the life I had left, that of robbing and stealing and doing unto others before they could do me. This led to the Brushy Mountain Prison... Somehow Dr. Oglesby found where I was and constantly wrote to me there. I had never dreamed that one human being could actually care about another but here was a man who actually lived this way.
>
> After prison I went into the army. As an infantryman in Europe, I spent many a night pondering about the things that Dr. Oglesby had taught me. Things began to take shape and my mind began to see as it never had before. When I returned home from Europe I was a changed man.
>
> I shudder to think of what would have been my fate if I had not met Dr. Oglesby. Though I must have tried his faith to the breaking point, he never gave up. I doubt if he knew the meaning of the term. There is not another person alive who would not have given up on me. I am so glad he did not despair... He remains in my memory as the most considerate, kind, generous, and sinless person who has lived since Christ."

The feeling of gratitude which Paul felt toward Dr. Oglesby was probably also experienced by yet another prisoner whom we know of only because Celestine Sibley, popular columnist for *The Atlanta Constitution*, wrote reporting what must have been yet another typical Oglesby response to a needy person out there in "his city." It was in the late 1940's and Miss Sibley was eager to find an Atlanta pastor who could minister to a very special prisoner she had discovered and interviewed several times there in the old Fulton Tower jail:

> My first call was to a preacher whose name I had seen in the newspaper rather often. He was too busy. A few days later I happened to be passing Central Presbyterian Church and on an impulse I went in and introduced myself to the minister, Dr. Oglesby, and asked him if he would visit my friend — for he became my friend — in his jail cell. Without a word Dr. Oglesby picked up his hat and walked over to the tower. He went back many times, talking with the prisoner, praying with him, taking him books to read. And when time came to get a parole for him, Dr. Oglesby went with us before the parole board.
>
> He was pastor in what had been one of the town's stylish churches but it became, under his direction, one of the most active social forces in the city.
>
> (*The Atlanta Constitution*, Nov. 19, 1971)

The first meeting of the Board of Directors of Union Mission was held on May 28, 1942. Present were Dr. Stuart R. Oglesby, Dr. Paul F. Brown, Mr. James E. Jackson, Dr. William Huck (first Executive Director), Dr. C. P. Stauffer, Mr. O. J. Parker, Mr. William Hansell, all affiliated with Central except Dr. Stauffer from the First Christian Church.

Central's famed Baby Clinic in its ongoing existence since 1922 cannot be described as a social force in Atlanta. But in a unique way this clinic became the torch lighting the path along which Central itself became a social force in the city. One of Dr. Oglesby's earliest formed convictions after arriving on the Central scene was that the Baby Clinic, after only nine years of service to needy families, had already made itself far too indispensible to abandon by relocating Central somewhere else. Thus, when a few years later an Atlanta newspaper article about the clinic began by stating that in saving the lives of babies Central Church "also saved itself," the writer may have been stating a fact:

> The story of how this metropolitan church established a baby clinic and operated it for more than a score of years has become of such general interest that it has been told in magazines of nation-wide circulation.
>
> Now entering its winter season under the direction of Mrs.

Twenty years later (1961), five of the original seven directors were still serving (two were deceased). Dr. Oglesby (1), Dr. Huck (2), O. J. Parker (3), James E. Jackson (4), Dr. Paul F. Brown (absent).

John J. Eagan, chairman, the clinic is providing invaluable service for people of all denominations. And of the staff of some 60 persons providing this service, only one is receiving pay.

Besides giving medical treatment to children of parents of little or no income, the service has been broadened to provide for many other needs.

There is a professional staff of 15 doctors. There are 40 women members of the church who work one or more of the three clinic days of each week. Mrs. Ralph Nolan is the capable and hard working full-time director. But working with these doctors and nurses and medical dispensers are other groups. One of these is the baby clinic sewing circle which makes garments needed by the little patients who range in age from a few days to six years. Another group is the hospital committee which provides layettes for newborn babies. And there is another committee which is in charge of devotional services held at the beginning of each clinic.

In addition there is a visiting committee which carries a friendly, helpful Christian ministry into the homes of the clinic mothers. All these committees have made the clinic something that is contributing substantially to the welfare of needy people of this entire community.

While statistics are sometimes dry reading, here are a few that will give some conception of the scope of operations of the clinic as based on the 1941 report:

Total number of patients on file 11,692
New patients received 711
Treatments given during year 4,520

> Treatments given to date 75,934
> Prescriptions given 4,540
> Visits made by Mrs. Nolan 979
>
> The figure showing 979 visits paid by Mrs. Nolan in a year gives a hint of her scope of activities. She is at once the director of the clinic, clinic nurse and social worker. She has used up five automobiles in 20 years and all of them have been paid for through voluntary gifts of individual members of the church.
>
> (*The Atlanta Journal*, Sept. 20, 1942)

It is noteworthy, if not surprising, that two of the women connected with Central's Baby Clinic have won two of the highly cherished "Woman of the Year in Atlanta" awards. Because of her work in the clinic, Mrs. Nolan in 1945 was named Atlanta Woman of the Year in Social Services, while in 1954 Dr. Leila D. Denmark, an outstanding pediatrician who for many years had regularly given an unselfish portion of her time to professionally serving the Baby Clinic, became Atlanta Woman of the Year in Professional Fields.

Meanwhile, Dr. Oglesby himself was winning his share of awards in token of the leadership he was giving to a wide variety of organizations for helping needy people, while at the same time managing to author no less than nine published books and to read 1,750 additional books authored by others. These were incredible accomplishments in light of the priority Dr. Oglesby was giving to the pastoral needs of Central. More incredible still does it all become in light of the lengthy list of additional services rendered by Central's pastor and which the *Weekly* printed in 1934 as part of its campaign to prove the worth of downtown churches:

> The pastor of a large downtown church is usually called to render services to the community and to the church as a whole such as is not asked or expected of the pastor of suburban or neighborhood churches. The pastor of our Central Church, for instance, has the following responsibilities largely by virtue of the fact of being pastor of a large, working downtown church:
>
> 1. Member Assembly's Committee on Home Missions
> 2. Member Assembly's Committee on Stewardship and Finance
> 3. Member Trustees of Mountain Retreat Association
> 4. Member Presbyterian Ministers Association
> 5. President Evangelical Ministers Association of Atlanta
> 6. Member Executive Committee of Atlanta Christian Council
> 7. Chairman Committee on Columbia Seminary Extension School
> 8. Chairman Religious Education Committee of Atlanta Presbytery
> 9. Chairman Synod's Committee on Church and Society

10. Chairman Committee to Revise Synod's Work
11. Associate Editor *Presbyerian of the South*
12. Member Executive Committee of the Atlanta Community Chest
13. Member Speakers Bureau of the Atlanta PTA

The above stated duties are in addition to numerous demands of speaking engagements and other forms of service which daily come to the pastor's desk. All these things ought to be kept continually in mind in evaluating the work of a downtown city church. (*Weekly*, Oct. 20, 1934)

At no time during Dr. Oglesby's ministry was the congregation allowed ever to forget the real significance of Central as a downtown church. In sermon after sermon and in issue after issue of the *Weekly* was the congregation reminded of the very special role it was to fulfill there in its city setting. So persistently was this indoctrination carried forward that the congregation came to have a remarkably clear-cut image of itself and its mission. Few people in Central remained unaware of the distinctive nature of their church. They came rather to have a precise awareness of who they were as the congregation of Central Church, why they were staying where they were, what their mission there was to be, what was the urgency of that mission, and why it was important for Central to survive with strength in its inner-city location.

That Central indeed did survive downtown with strength during those years has to be one of its major achievements. For it happened in spite of the Depression, and in spite of World War II and the loss of its residential community, and, perhaps most important of all, in spite of what might have been a debilitating image crisis. In terms of its self-image, what Central achieved was a major victory and not just survival room. An enthusiastic Centralite probably spoke for most of his fellow-members in the December 27, 1947 issue of the *Weekly* when he said, "I like Central because it is a downtown Church, because it is a Democratic Institution where rich and poor may meet on one ground and join together in furthering the work of the Kingdom. I like the spiritual life one gets from such an institution and such people. I just like Central and its work."

This feeling was unanimous. Every member took immense pride in Central's image as a church at work. Indeed "*A Church at Work*" became the title of a major brochure with which Central celebrated its ninetieth anniversary in 1948. Through the dissemination of this excellently developed brochure, the whole denomination became aware, as the congregation already was, of the distinctive image the Central Church in Atlanta had achieved for itself. The image was of a downtown church performing a remarkably sensitive ministry in a remarkably first-class fashion. Praise and appreciation for what

Celebration marked Central's Centennial observances in 1958.

Central was doing in a situation known for its high degree of difficulty began pouring in from all sides. The Central image was not only well-established but also now well-known. This was a victory which belonged to every person of the congregation; but more than to anyone else, it belonged to Stuart Oglesby. He had worked ceaselessly to achieve it for Central Church.

The Central image became enhanced in a more visible way in 1951 when its new Rand Chapel building stood handsomely completed and ready to take its place among Central's earlier buildings, all serving the work of this Church at Work. Made possible through the unusually generous gift of Elder Fred L. Rand, this strikingly beautiful chapel was a visual announcement to the world that Central Church, far from engaging in mere holding actions, was boldly on the offensive in meeting the city's challenge.

Dr. Oglesby probably could have rested on his laurels a bit during the final decade of his ministry, but he didn't. Right up to the day of his retirement, he continued giving his best energy and effort to the congregation, so that by the time the Church reached its 100th birthday in February, 1958, the Central image had become known and honored in secular as well as church circles. Columnists and editorialists and feature writers of the Atlanta newspapers vied with each other, as excerpts will attest, in rendering homage to the occasion:

The reception line. *right to left:* Henry L. Hills (Chairman, Board of Deacons), Frances Oglesby Hills, Dr. Oglesby, W.B. Oglesby (Dr. Oglesby's twin brother), Mrs. S. R. Oglesby, J. M. Harvey (Church Visitor), Mrs. Harvey.

Everyone from the Mayor to the General Assembly of the State of Georgia is felicitating Central Presbyterian Church this month on the observance of its 100th birthday.

Other great churches may have left Capitol Square, but Central Presbyterian, wearing its dignified coat of gray granite, still thrusts its spires heavenward from the same downtown location where it has always stood.

It stands as a fountain in the arid heart of the city, not only of faith but of good works.

There are other churches, of course, who have broad and effective social service programs. But because it stands on a downtown curbstone, handy to the jail, handy to the slums, handy to the push and pressure of commerce, Central is just one of a kind.

To have merely existed for 100 years isn't much. But to have been the alive, going, giving concern that Central Presbyterian has been — that's truly a cause for celebration.

Central's celebration was sobered only by the knowledge that Dr. Oglesby, now 70, would soon be retiring. When the day finally came, later in 1958, Central made Dr. Oglesby its Pastor Emeritus — the only one of its pastors so honored. Then, when Central's magnificent new clinic-administration building stood completed a few years later, Dr. Oglesby became further honored when that new structure was named the Oglesby Building.

This is the cemetery monument which Mrs. Oglesby will share with her husband. This remarkable lady was most integral to her husband's great ministry at Central, as were other wives to their husbands at other times.

After Dr. Oglesby's death in 1977, following 28 years of active service to the people of Central and many additional years in their midst, the words then penned in love by Ruling Elder Douglas MacRae well express the esteem felt by all:

DR. STUART R. OGLESBY
1888-1977

Stuart R. Oglesby was born July 10, 1888 in the little Arkansas town of Hope. How fitting for his life is the name of his birthplace.

For Dr. Oglesby's life was an epitome of hope. For him hope was both destination and origin: hope rooted in the sure and certain knowledge of life's essential meaning and life's intended destiny.

Dr. Oglesby was, therefore, abundantly able through his long and distinguished ministry to enable thousands to understand, as he did, the meaning and the destiny of life.

His first pastorates were in Oxford, North Carolina, Monticello, Arkansas, and Hot Springs, Arkansas. From Hot Springs, Dr.

Oglesby was called to Central Church in Atlanta. On February 2, 1930, he stood in the historic pulpit at Central and proclaimed the solid assurance of the great Philippian text, "My God shall supply all your need according to his riches in glory by Christ Jesus."

One of the most remarkable and loving ways in which God has supplied the need of Central Church was to give her people the leadership of Stuart Oglesby for 28 years. Dr. Oglesby took Central's pastorate in trying times, and led the church to new strength. He converted the complex problems of community transition to exciting arenas of community service. He brought the impact of the church upon business and government, press and industry, city and state.

Stuart Oglesby was a pioneer in ecumenism in Atlanta, a chief architect of the Atlanta Christian Council. His compassion for the needy led to years of leadership at the Union Mission.

It was Dr. Oglesby who began the practice of church night suppers at Central. It was Dr. Oglesby who brought to the church a new concept of ministry of music which has spread to so many churches elsewhere.

Dr. Oglesby was one of the strongest and most courageous pulpit preachers in Central's history. And in the counsels of the General Assembly he was regarded as a church statesman. He served as Moderator of the Synod of Georgia. He wrote nine books.

But despite the pressures that always accompany prominence, Stuart Oglesby was personally available, on instant call, to those who needed him. The sick felt the healing of his visits (he always knew precisely what to say) and little children loved him and felt secure in his presence.

And so we shall thank God upon every remembrance of him. We share with his beloved family, just as genuinely if not so intimately, the solemn pride of loving him and being a part of his work.

One of Dr. Oglesby's amazing gifts was his tender, loving spiritual art of conducting a funeral. His hallmark here was simplicity, though the way he blended the solace and hope of the Scriptures with the sincerity and confidence of his prayers was a thing of elegaic loveliness.

At a funeral service, Dr. Oglesby always used the death of the departed one as a signal for others to assume the mantle of leadership and to go forward full-speed with the work of God's Kingdom.

He invariably included in his closing prayer that great exhortation from I Corinthians: "Therefore, my beloved brethren, be ye steadfast, unmovable, always abounding in the work of the Lord, forasmuch as ye know that your labour is not in vain in the Lord."

And this is what Dr. Oglesby is saying to us today.

The truly compassionate ministry eulogized that day by Dr. MacRae was one which Church and State alike could join in honoring, and they both did. As the Oglesby funeral service ended in old Central, the bells began sounding out from the neighboring towers of Immaculate Conception and Trinity, while the great flags at the State Capitol across the street flew at half mast.

A major heritage left the church out of the long, eventful pastorate of Stuart R. Oglesby was the emergence of a definitive Central image — an image which during that pastorate, became known to the congregation and to the denomination and to the city.

Later on it was to become known to a much wider world as well, and there also Central was to make its impact.

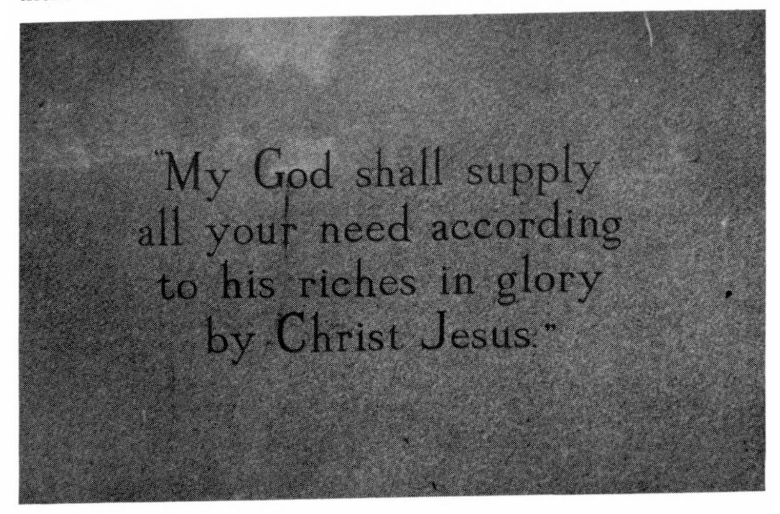

The reverse side of the Oglesby monument.

Chapter 7
Making Its Impact (1959-1978)

Even while Central's first century was drawing to an end, the people there were busy planning for the second century. They dreamed of an even stronger future. They dreamed of Central with facilities vastly improved, with services much enlarged, and with a capacity for ministry more equal than ever to its task.

Century Two and its hopes were thus very much in mind as the congregation probed for its just-right new minister. More than a year of careful search passed before the forward looking old church and a forward looking young minister found each other, and Fred Rogers Stair, Jr., became Central's minister for the Sixties — or, at least, for most of them.

He was, as a Davidson College citation declared in awarding him an honorary degree at about the time of his going to Central, "...a preacher of power and perspicuity, a skilled administrator, experienced alike in academics and in theology, with a mind incisive and creative and dynamic."

Like some of the best of his counterparts before him, and perhaps after him, Fred Stair was a bit awed at the thought of tackling the work at Central. The achievements-against-odds of that century old church and the reputation it had earned both within and without church circles added up to some enormously high expectations ready to challenge any new minister coming to serve. Fully to live up to all that was now expected was probably too tall an order even for the best of them.

As Dr. Stair pondered this uncertain prospect from among the relatively more modest demands which the church at Hickory, North Carolina, placed upon him, he felt an ambivalence too real to go unacknowledged:

> I am terrified, moving from a small town to a bustling metropolis, from a small congregation to a large one, facing the prospect of becoming acquainted with a congregation of almost 1,500, along with the families and occupations and homes, learning to fight traffic, and trying to get caught up with the enormously varied work of Central. I shall be frank to admit that I was terrified. But also very optimistic.
>
> (*Weekly*, Sept. 12, 1959)

The Rev. Fred R. Stair, Jr.
Central Pastor 1959-1966

There was much in Central at that time to inspire the confidence Dr. Stair felt. Interim leadership, led by Assistant Pastor Walter Cook and ably assisted by Dr. Tom McDill, who did the preaching, had brought Central through what could have been a treacherous between-pastors period in perfect shape. Stair was encouraged also by the high level of excellence evident in Central's music ministry, then under the leadership of Hubert Vance Taylor. Most of all, though, he was encouraged by the Church itself — one hundred years old, yet eager and bracing to take on its second century; its people scattered twenty-five miles in every direction, yet a remarkably close-knit and caring church family.

Eager to maintain the family feeling that permeated the membership of old Central, Stair and his staff undertook the process of making a pastoral visit in the home and business of every individual and family of his big, scattered congregation. This undertaking was in addition to the constant pastoral visiting needed by the sick and shut-in, and it took the first five years of Dr. Stair's ministry just to get around to everyone the first time. But it was done. Meanwhile, the Session was seeking additional, and perhaps more efficient ways of carrying forward Central's pastoral ministry among its people. Out of this search came Central's "Family Plan" and its new Counseling Center. The Family Plan was simply one of dividing and subdividing the whole metropolitan expanse into segments sufficiently small for every member of Central to become part of a reasonably compact neighborhood group which, in partnership with all other such groups, could serve as a constant communications network for the entire far-flung congregation.

The Counseling Center at Central came into being because there was then a dearth of professional services of that sort in Atlanta, and because Central had some especially knowledgeable leadership ready to guide the congregation in that direction. Dr. Tom McDill, professor of counseling at the Columbia Theological Seminary, did much to inspire interest during his months as interim preacher at Central. Dr. Stair, who himself had had extensive training in counseling ministries, not only maintained but also enlarged the congregation's interest. Elder Richard Oglesby, finally, as head of the responsible council, was an informed and effective advocate for getting Central's Counseling Center into operation. It continues to serve the counseling needs of Central's own people as well as those of the city at large.

If the ministers and officers of Central had to run just to keep up with the pastoral and counseling needs of the congregation during the Turbulent Sixties, even more did they have to run to keep pace with the congregation's Second Century eagerness. Dr. Stair and his family had hardly unpacked in Atlanta when, on a pivotal 1959 Sunday, the congregation met and took its first giant steps into Century Two. First, it launched itself into an enormous expansion dream which it named the Second Century Program. Then, as if to lend both faith and substance to that still indefinite Second Century Program, the congregation immediately authorized the purchase of the "Baptist property" located almost next-door on Washington Street. This was the church building and land in and on which Central's wonderfully good neighbor, the Second Baptist Church, had long served before moving out in the 1930's. The property continued in the hands of the Baptist denomination until put on the market in 1959, and that is when Central bought it — an act of sheer faith.

It was also a Rubicon-crossing act. In exchange for its $206,000.00 check, Central's bank now held deed to the Baptist property. In the context of the total Second Century Program this purchase was but a small first step, but there was now no turning back. The congregation was now committed to a dream.

This dream, however, as it developed, came to have some nightmarish elements. It aimed at erecting new buildings not yet on the drawing boards with funds not yet in sight. It aimed at purchasing two additional land areas not yet on the market, and again, with money nowhere in sight. It meant coming up with the purchase price, whether ready or not, whenever either one of the still needed land areas should become available, with no assurance that the State and County and City governments would later pick up their part of what was to be a four-way negotiation looking toward an eventual and hoped-for development of Georgia Plaza. This hoped-for development was considerably sidetracked in 1960 and the program further compli-

Central's bold Second Century Program was soon to create a scene radically changed from that offered in this 1959 aerial view. The Baptist property (1) was to be bought and cleared of buildings, as was the Werner Apartments property (2) next to it. Central's 1906 Sunday School Building (3) was to be removed to make way for the new Oglesby Building, and the Smith property (4) was to be purchased for use. Except for the church plants of Central and Immaculate Conception (5), the whole remaining block was to become magnificantly developed as Georgia Plaza.

cated when a proposed City bond issue, which would have given an early green light to Georgia Plaza, was voted down.

Through it all, Central stuck as resolutely as it could to its Second Century goals. By mid-1962, not only had Central finished removing buildings from its newly-purchased property so that the cleared area could serve the interim parking needs of the congregation, but had also completed its purchase of the adjacent Werner property. This property consisted of some old apartments occupying the only remaining Washington Street frontage in the whole block not yet in Central's possession. Its procurement meant that the Second Century Program was almost back on schedule.

It was about at this stage of things that the strains of so many major transactions upon Central's decision-making apparatus began to show up. The Joint Officers group, the body through which all important matters were required to clear, was an unwieldy 100 member body divided into more than thirty large and small committees. As it became

Goodbye to a beloved neighbor. The demolition of the Second Baptist Church.

more and more evident that a streamlining was now urgently needed, the officers early in 1963 acted to scrap their whole committee set-up, including the big one responsible for the Second Century Program and replaced it with five new church councils, each served by one of the ministers and together covering every aspect of the life and work of Central Church.

Once its administrative logjam had been broken, Central became ready to tackle the crux of its whole development package: a very major structure to replace the old 1906 addition south of the sanctuary. More expensive and more strategic than all the rest of the Second Century Program together, the proposed multi-purpose building, later to be named honoring Dr. Oglesby, was to be a sort of omni-structure to serve as the Church's administrative headquarters, for educational activities, and especially, for Central's service programs and clinics. The cost of this much needed building was very large, but so also was the incentive with which the people of Central sought to meet this challenge. By mid-1964, the congregation by pledge and grant had $700,000 in hand — enough, at least, to start the bulldozers moving.

The fact that another giant step had been taken was cause enough for celebration. And celebrate is exactly what Central did on September 27, 1964 with a big, happy church-wide service of thanksgiving. Then, just two months later, there was further cause for thanksgiving.

Not only had the old Simpson home site, now the "Smith property," become available, but Central, once again, had been able to come up with the money required to buy it. This was the last of the land areas required for meeting Second Century challenges. Its purchase was yet another bit to add to the already floodtide of evidence that Central not only meant business about staying downtown, but it also meant business about providing for the needs of people there with ministries as excellent as could possibly be provided.

Meanwhile, Atlanta's huge and very powerful downtown sector was in the midst of a development program of its own. In a comeback effort involving enormous amounts of money and planning, Downtown Atlanta was going all-out to achieve some of those downtown victories which have since been so notably won. In those early stages, though, the Downtown Association needed every ally it could find. And Central Presbyterian Church, for all its relative smallness, was perceived to be such an ally. It was not only staying downtown, but was also improving and stablizing its surrounding area. At a time when there were fewer and fewer churches trying to improve the lot of downtown people, Central was doing more and more for them. Far from being remote from the downtown's recovery efforts, Central's Dr. Stair had a leading role in the Plaza Park feasibility studies and was active in the powerful Downtown Association itself.

By reason of all this, Central gained many high-level friends and admirers who not only applauded what the church was striving toward in its Second Century development, but who also became staunch supporters of that effort. This support probably had some bearing on what happened next: that finally after six long years of negotiations, it all came together. Plaza Park became approved by all parties concerned. The State now had funds to proceed with its proposed land purchase and development. This meant that Central, which had gone deeply into debt to buy the land in the first place, finally would have the means to pay off that particular obligation.

Relieved of this huge part of its debt burdens, Central was now in a position to borrow sizeable additional funds. These, together with other sizeable sums already raised or granted, brought Central's Second Century dream near to splendid reality. Means were now in sight to finish paying off all remaining costs of constructing the new building and refurbishing the old ones, including a most excellent new Tull Fellowship Hall given by the foundation of Joseph M. Tull, one of the South's leading industrialists.

The quietly effective Mr. Tull, who came into Central during the Lacy years, clearly personified qualities characteristic of the congregation of which he was a part. As a business executive he was concerned enough about his employees to institute retirement and stock purchase plans for them long before most industrialists had

Parking Available! The Sunday School building borders expanse created when Central bought and removed Werner Apartments and the buildings once used by Second Baptist Church. Central soon also bought the Smith property (left foreground).

embraced such progressive practices. And as a judge of persons, he was perceptive enough to have tapped young Robert W. Woodruff as his business assistant long before most people could have recognized in him the makings of the future "Mr. Coca Cola." But undergirding J.M. Tull's obvious executive talents, according to one Central pastor, was his "...solid character, personal charm and warm heart." The words well describe also the nature of the fellowship hall which honors this one-time deacon of Central Church.

Central Church by late 1964 had each one of its huge Second Century goals ripe for achievement. Added to all these victories was the pleasure of anticipating a soon-to-be completed Georgia Plaza which, together with Central Church and Immaculate Conception Church, would constitute one of the handsomest and most useful blocks in the entire city.

The block would have been even more useful to Central if it could have included ample underground parking alongside the Oglesby Building and with direct access to it. But when the builders encountered unexpectedly extensive sub-surface water table problems under the old Werner property, that greatly cherished hope had to be relinquished.

Completed in 1967, The Oglesby Building along with the neighboring Georgia Plaza stand today as worthy and people-centered Second Century accomplishments for Central Church and Downtown Atlanta.

This one big disappointment was far out-weighed, however, by the truly remarkable successes crowning every other aspect of Central's Second Century effort.

Meanwhile, up in Virginia, the Union Theological Seminary was beginning its search for a new president and, since Dr. Ben Lacy, who forty years earlier had gone to that post from his pastorate at Central, had performed so outstandingly as the seminary's President, it came as a surprise to no one that the seminary once again looked to Atlanta's Central Church for the very special new leadership it now needed. The notable service provided the seminary by Professors Strickler and Rice as well as that of President Lacy himself, all three having been called to Union directly from the pulpit in Atlanta, was probably all the assurance the seminary board needed that they were once again on the right track. The seminary board was specifically aware of the very surefooted way Dr. Stair had guided his Central Church congregation which, among a plethora of administrative and fiscal and relational pitfalls along its way, had achieved a truly remarkable Second Century victory.

A brief but most interesting period was to transpire between Fred Stair's departure and arrival on the scene of John Randolph Taylor. Those months were alive with activity. The sights and sounds of

The Rev. J. Randolph Taylor
Central Pastor 1967-1975

construction were everywhere evident as Central's new building took shape and its old ones became renewed. Protestors and demonstrators, never in short supply during the turbulent Sixties, continued to personify the urban-racial crisis of the period, and Central continued to welcome and include such groups rather than to oppose and deplore them. And through it all, Central itself continued on its lively way under the lively leadership of Ed Grider and Zee Holler, its first Associate Pastors.

Such was the scene at the end of 1967 when the Taylor family, bright as the Christmas season about them, first arrived at Central.

Dr. Taylor in his wildest dreams could hardly have imagined even half of the crucial events waiting to be loosed upon him, his church, his city, as well as the nation during his first twelve months at Central. Month One saw the Viet Cong launch its Tet Offensive, thereby ending all dreams of a quick victory for us and the allies. Month Two saw President Johnson, tarnished by the now winless war, remove himself from any re-election purpose. Month Three saw Governor Wallace of Alabama announce his bid for the Presidency as a Third Party candidate. Month Four saw civil rights leader Dr. Martin Luther King, Jr., unbelievably slain in Memphis, and that slaying followed by violence sweeping the nation in shocked reaction. Month Six saw Presidential Candidate Robert Kennedy, again unbelievably, meet his death at the hands of another assassin. In Month Eight, Richard Nixon and Spiro Agnew were nominated by a riotous Republican Presidential Convention in Miami, and Hubert Humphrey and Edward Muskie were tapped by an even more riotous Democratic Presidential Convention in Chicago. Finally, the Month Eleven national election results put Mr. Nixon in line for the the White House. All this was part of Central's world during Randy Taylor's first year at its helm.

The one crucial event of 1968 that shaped Central's future development more significantly than all the rest was the tragic slaying of Dr. King, and then, a few days later, his moving and emotion-wrenching funeral service in Atlanta. Notables and unknowns poured into Atlanta not by the thousands but by the scores of thousands, an army of wounded persons, unpredictable both as to number or mood. All public facilities and services of the city would be strained to the breaking point. Countless numbers of visitors would find themselves utterly without hope of food or shelter or toilet facilities during their days in Atlanta. Human needs would reach critical proportions. That, and the explosive possibilities of the event itself were matters of grave concern to all, especially to the top leadership of the city.

Chief among these deeply concerned leaders was Mayor Ivan Allen, Jr., then Atlanta's nationally-admired City Hall occupant. In his book, *Mayor: Notes on the Sixties*, Mr. Allen has described his feelings at that particular crucial moment in Atlanta's history when success or crashing failure teetered in the balance depending upon the as yet unpredictable responses of two hundred thousand visitors and a million Atlantans. The Mayor, responsible for the city and its visitors, was pacing the floor and pondering all this when his private line telephone rang:

> I don't know how he got the number, but it was the young minister named Randy Taylor from Central Presbyterian Church — a huge church across the street from City Hall, one that had managed to survive despite the fact most of its congregation had moved away to the suburbs. Randy Taylor had called on me recently when he had first come to Atlanta, and I vaguely recalled our meeting. Now he was calling me to say he had a problem, and I felt like snapping back at him that I could match any of his problems ten times over.
>
> "Mayor," he said, "it was unanimous. Our Board of Deacons voted on it and we are housing 300 Negro citizens already tonight. We'll provide meals for several thousand and living quarters for as many as we can take. We're going to need 600 blankets."
>
> So this was how Atlanta was going to react. In the back of my mind all along there had been great fears that the major factor in whether Atlanta was going to have serious trouble was not with

> the black people but with the white racists. I had received telegrams and phone calls from a surprisingly large number of those people, and from some people I had respected in the past suggesting that the city ignore the funeral. But here was a young Presbyterian minister saying his church was opening its doors to Negro visitors. Later in the day other white churches, following Central's lead, made similar announcements. Randy Taylor has shown me the attitude Atlanta was going to take, and it took only a minute to call Third Army headquarters and get 600 blankets.

With its Army blankets, Central also got its army of visitors. There were the strangers which the Church, obedient to its faith, took in. In need of food and shelter and friendship, they came in steady stream. For three days and nights, every facility and resource of Central Church strained to respond to the vast tide of human need which had suddenly become its neighbor. Only after the event was over and the visitors had departed was there time for the people of Central to stop and take stock of those crucial days:

> Amid feelings of sorrow and perplexity over the assassination of Dr. Martin Luther King, Jr., we at Central were called upon to minister to the thousands who arrived in Atlanta Monday and Tuesday to attend his funeral. Dr. King's organization, the S.C.L.C., requested that this church be a communication and service center in their efforts to provide food and lodging in this flood of visitors. Our own members, supported by the generous voluntary efforts of other congregations throughout the city were able, working around the clock, to provide hospitality and assistance to literally thousands. Though the reassurance and hope which this ministry expressed cannot be measured, those of us who were privileged to be part of it will long remember the spirit of good will that united us with one another and with those who were served. (*The Weekly*, April 13, 1968)

Central was far from alone in noting that good will and unity which its ministries during the King funeral had helped generate. The nameless hundreds whose needs had been served by those ministries noted and reflected the same spirit. A typical thank-you note was one which Central received from a black couple from Chicago:

> I was a bit reluctant to go to the funeral in Atlanta, knowing that this city is in the South and feeling there would be unpleasantness for us there. But being a dedicated civil rights worker and one who has marched with Dr. King on many marches, my husband and I felt it our duty to be there on this last march.
>
> When we arrived at S.C.L.C. headquarters in Atlanta we were shocked to find this beautifully integrated group working together in love and harmony. The next surprise was when we were given

> living quarters with a white family. We almost turned this offer down, but decided we would take it and were treated warmly. This young white man was nice enough to suggest that we go over to Central Presbyterian Church for our downtown meals, and we followed the suggestion and here was another beautiful surprise for us. The people in charge at Central met us with so much love and warmth and made us feel so welcome that we returned again and again during our stay in Atlanta. This was our first trip to Atlanta. From what we experienced there we feel that the South is going to be the first to become FREE. Please accept our grateful thanks. /S/Mr. and Mrs. Samuel A. Blowe
> (quoted in *Weekly*, May 4, 1968)

So it was that Central, due as much to circumstances to be met as to a premeditated plan to be followed, found itself immersed in a ministry of bridge-building, helping to span some of the spaces between Blacks and Whites in Atlanta. And having begun a bridging of that space, it suddenly became unthinkable that the Church could now leave unbuilt any still needed span within its power to build. Such a span took shape soon after Dr. King's death when Central put up a permanent plaque in the Stair Courtyard of Central Church signifying that this very old and very southern and predominantly white congregation wished to honor the memory and principles of Martin Luther King, Jr. The King family along with other leaders of the black community and leaders of Atlanta's white community were on hand for the unveiling ceremony, and heard Dr. Taylor recount his Church's purpose in erecting the plaque:

> The decision to erect this plaque in this place was made by the Elders and Deacons of the Central Presbyterian Church meeting jointly on Saturday, April 6th within forty hours after the tragic assassination of Martin Luther King, Jr. It reflects the desire of our officers to communicate their concern to Dr. King's family and congregation and to make permanent record of our commitment to the principles which were embodied by his life. This plaque in this place means that by the grace of God in the critical year of 1968, men and women in a predominantly white church in the heart of this Southern city sensed and saw and said that the dreamer shall not have died in vain.
> (quoted in *Weekly*, August 31, 1968)

Central was destined to construct yet one more span in the bridge it had been building when the S.C.L.C., exactly one year after its leader's death, planned a Holy Week vigil to be held on the State Capitol grounds. This meant that from afternoon on Friday through afternoon on Sunday, a cross-section of America's angered or concerned or committed or disenchanted people would be gathered in vigil but a

Dr. and Mrs. Oglesby at the dedication of the Oglesby Building.

street breadth away. It also meant that Central had to choose between two different courses of action. It could follow the course that Governor Lester Maddox had taken, and secure itself away from the people who would be gathering there at the Capitol, or it could open itself to them. Central decided that for a bridge-building congregation, there could be but one choice. It opened its building and its hearts to care for the needs of the hundreds of vigil participants:

> The church was open for them to be able to rest and talk and get something to eat and go to the bathrooms. Members of the church took four-hour shifts, morning and afternoon and through the night, and provided a ministry of presence from mopping the floors to midnight conversations. The crowd included black and white, dropout and dignitary, hippie and policeman, the very old and the very young, clergyman and agnostic, the dirty and the clean, heads that were bald and those far from bald, the bearded and the unbearded, the hungry and the wet. Many vigil participants could not believe that Central was open for them and seemed to care about them. One soggy young man who had come in out of the heavy rain on Saturday to get dry and rested said, "I thought the church had given up on us, and I sure had given up on the church." Many others asked our volunteers, "Will you get in

> trouble with the church authorities for doing this?" They found it surprising and stimulating that our Session had, after discussion, made the decision that we be open, and that we felt it our Christian mission to answer human need wherever we are confronted by it. (*Weekly*, April 12, 1969)

Central's by-now-predictable responses to human need wherever it is confronted, along with its well demonstrated skills at bridge-building were among the factors prompting Atlanta's Community Relations Commission, for the first time in its history, to give its Annual Award for the year 1969 to a whole congregation of church people. The scroll which Rabbi Jacob Rothschild presented at Central's morning worship on May 11, 1969, read as follows:

> The Atlanta Human Relations Commission presents its 1969 Annual Award to the Central Presbyterian Church of Atlanta:
>
> For its spirit in rendering to the citizens of Atlanta and the citizens of the world tangible assistance during the tragic death and funeral of Dr. Martin Luther King, Jr., Nobel Peace winner and citizen of Atlanta,
>
> For providing a center for the continuation of a dialogue for all citizens of Atlanta,
>
> For maintaining a children's clinic for all the children of Atlanta,
>
> For its creative approach to solving the problems of the Atlanta community,
>
> For courage in moving into areas where problems are compounded,
>
> For exercising its influence in the creation of a climate which embraces the true meaning of the church, and
>
> For providing a new kind of leadership for the entire city and its citizens. (quoted in *Weekly*, May 17, 1969)

Growing out of all this came additional honors to the church and its pastor, as when Dr. Taylor was made co-chairman of the General Assembly's Committee to plan for an eventual reunion of the two major Presbyterian denominations of the nation; when he was chosen to chair Atlanta's strategic Community Relations Commission; and when The Georgia Region of the National Conference of Christians and Jews named him Clergyman of the Year for "...both the individual ministry of the man and the corporate ministry of the Church he serves."

A few of Central's own members, however, were less than enthusiastic about some of these corporate ministries. They were unhappy about the social activism which, they felt, had become paramount in their Church's agenda. One by one, over a period of years, they quietly departed. They had been members of the sort that no congregation

Dr. Taylor, Dr. Stair, Dr. Oglesby at the dedication of the Stair Courtyard in front of the Oglesby building.

could lose without a profound sense of loss. But in a congregation as diverse in all respects as was Central's, and given the basic decisions that Central had to make, the only surprise is that the attrition was not of larger proportions.

This smaller-than-expected loss of members during those years of urban-racial crisis was due perhaps to the fact that the same ministries which were viewed by a few members as "new social activism" were accepted by the overwhelming majority of members as being entirely in character with what Central had long stood for. In opening doors to serve all who came to the King funeral or the striking Georgia Power Company workers, or to the S.C.L.C. vigil, the officers of the Church were simply responding as had their counterparts sixty years earlier in opening Central's doors to the striking street car workers of Atlanta. In providing leadership on behalf of Presbyterian reunion, Central was but echoing a stance which reaches back at least to 1896 when Elder John C. Whitner's stirring advocacy of re-union gained national attention. In providing leadership for Atlanta's civic and human needs Central was but continuing to do what it had begun back at the turn-of-the-century through leaders like Dunbar Ogden and John Eagan.

The big difference now, though, was that Central's actions of the Sixties and early Seventies all took place in a national atmosphere charged with deep emotions ignited by highly polarized differences between races, generations, sexes and communities. An Age of Protest had engulfed the country. Individuals and groups no longer hoped for or politely requested changes in their status; they were demanding and even seizing advantages. Where once the sit-in demonstrations against racial segregation in 1961 were the burning issue of the day, the Civil Rights movement was now joined in quick succession by other causes: the Free Speech Movement on college campuses, the emergence of Students for a Democratic Society, protests against the war in Vietnam, the appearance of a "hippie" counter-culture, a strong feminist drive, Gay Liberation and other movements. It was not a time in which one could easily retire from the confrontations to the sidelines, because everyone's life was being touched by them in one way or another.

As already indicated, Central's pastors and other leaders did take positions. Predictably, because of the very diversity that has characterized Central's congregation in this century, some members found themselves unable to support the church's positions and actions, and left. Yet, these very actions were precisely the ones that induced other members to join — and in almost like numbers to those who departed. The newcomers were, though, on the average, much younger, considerably less conservative and decidedly less weathly. On the whole, they were not so well schooled in Reformed faith and practice and had less experience in church leadership.

However, what the new members who appeared during this crisis period did bring with them was fresh energy, a great variety of talent, a deep commitment to what they believed and the conscious knowledge of why they were casting their lot with Central Church. They enjoyed the spirit of fellowship in the congregation and the energetic leadership of the ministers. They valued the challenge posed by Randy Taylor's prophetic sermons and appreciated Central's excellent ministry of music under the direction of Don Robinson. They were attracted by the involvement of the church in the community and in the events of the times. Especially were they attracted to Central's ministries of service, and to the enormous variety of ways they themselves could serve and be served. Some of the newcomers — many of them raised in other denominational and doctrinal settings — were frank to confess that they had sought out Central as their last hope for continuing to remain affiliated with the organized church.

It was late in 1975, after eight eventful years at Central's helm, that Randy Taylor decided to accept a call which had come to him from the

The Rev. P. C. Enniss
Central Pastor 1976-

Myers Park Presbyterian Church in Charlotte, North Carolina. Dr. Taylor is the sort of person whose departure is never a gentle happening. Like his predecessors, he had stamped his mark so indelibly upon this church that, according to one wag, Central had come to be known as "Lord and Taylor's." Although a quip, the comment gave fair warning that the interval between Dr. Taylor's departure and the arrival of his successor could be a difficult one indeed.

Once again, however, Central proved exceedingly fortunate in the leadership qualities of its remaining ministers. Throughout the long interval after Randy Taylor's departure, Associate Pastor Steve Bacon, demonstrating effective administrative abilities, kept the entire work of the church on even keel. In this, Mr. Bacon had the able help of Central's skilled and committed staff. Especially helpful during the interim was the continuity personified by Miss Dorothy Woods who for more than three decades has served as special secretary for every minister of Central Church from the time of Dr. Oglesby to the present.

After almost a full year of careful work, Central's search committee found exactly the minister it was looking for. As far as the Rev. P. C. Enniss, Jr., was concerned, this admiration was mutual and he promptly agreed to come to Central.

The First Presbyterian Church in Tallahassee, Florida, where Mr. Enniss had been serving, was not unlike Central and his ministerial skills were well proven. His reputation in the denomination was that of a strong preacher, an outspoken advocate for creative social change, and a leader committed to an urban ministry from a downtown base.

Interestingly enough, Mr. Enniss was also the first one of Central's senior ministers who had received his theological education at the nearby Columbia Theological Seminary. The relationship between Central Church and this excellent institution has been a particularly close and mutually helpful one from the time, earlier in this century, when the seminary first moved to the Atlanta area with Central's Dr. Lacy and Elder J. Bulow Campbell sparking the effort. Teachers and administrators as well as students of Columbia Seminary have long been a valued part of the Central Church family. It is particularly appropriate that the church's newest minister now contribute to that ongoing relation just as prior ministers have done in respect to relating Central to the Union Theological Seminary in Virginia. The close and invigorating connections of Central with these two theological institutions is a notable fact of its history.

With the arrival of Buddy Enniss late in 1976, several things became quickly evident. First, Central's long and unbroken succession of excellent preachers would continue unbroken. Second, Central's habitual good fortune in gaining a delightful pastor's family along with the pastor would continue to hold true. Finally the hope of the people of Central that their new pastor would share some of their own enthusiasm about their old downtown mission-minded church was a hope well-fulfilled.

A church-wide opinion survey among Central members early in 1975 etched out a profile of what the people saw as the most important aspect of their church life and as their hopes for it. Central's service ministries along with its strong pulpit and excellent choir got top applause while an improved pastoral ministry peaked as the top hope of all.

If a similar opinion survey were conducted in 1978, it would probably indicate that Central's pulpit and service ministries and choir were still earning the top applause of the members. The Chancel Choir continues, not only musically superb, but also as a major source of new members and new leadership for Central Church. The service ministries — a variety of clinics to meet a variety of human needs, as well as the Child Development Center, which is considered a model for day care services — now keep Central's big and functional church plant in almost constant use seven days a week. The space facilities of the church also provide a "home" for such diverse non-profit groups as Literacy Action, The Georgia Hunger Coalition, Alcoholics Ano-

Central's highly acclaimed Child Development Center is but one of several ministries within which members daily respond to the needs of their surrounding city in vital and sensitive ways.

Instructing tutors at Literacy Action.

nymous, and the like. Central furnished the famous Protestant Radio and Television Center space for its first home. On April 3, 1978, the Urban Design Commission of Atlanta placed Central Church on the city's official Roster of Historic Sites and Structures. Historical certainly, but most definitely not gathering dust. Central's buildings are now being used more constantly and more fulfillingly perhaps than ever before in all their long history.

Today, 120 years deep into its lively history, Atlanta's Central Presbyterian Church is much more than just holding its own. Although some of the members have to assemble on Sunday mornings from as far away as forty miles, the congregation, as it always has done, still comes to involve itself in corporate worship and study; to hear sermons that maintain the great tradition of both prophetic and pastoral concern; and to be uplifted by superb music. The rest of the week, the members come to involve themselves in ministry to the community and to each other. It is a rare moment in any seven-day period when Central's rooms and halls are not filled with the sounds of people coming and going and engaging in the work of the church: helping, healing, sharing, reconciling, or receiving these services and ministries. To try to depict the lively present-day activities of this church at work would challenge even the considerable talents of Central's newly resurgent Drama Troupe.

But the real drama of Central Church, the one being written in its own day-by-day history, continues on its forward-looking way. Old Central's sense of fellowship continues to grow; its commitment to a

Central at worship.

life of mission continues secure; and the very idea of resting on past laurels continues as foreign as ever to the way Centralites think and feel about themselves and their church.

If any one aspect of life at Central could now rest on its laurels, the Baby Clinic would be it. The grandmother of all the service ministries of the church, it is the liveliest 55 year-old around. But laurel resting is not its line. Baby Clinic files now contain case records of 65,230 separate individuals who have received medical care there, most of them many times. Workers at the clinic, however, are not nearly so interested in yesterday's statistics, as in tomorrow's sickcall which will bring another batch of ill youngsters to be helped. In March of 1978, both the Senate and House of the State of Georgia adopted impressive resolutions honoring Dr. Leila Denmark, who during her years of volunteer service in the Baby Clinic developed the medical world's Whooping Cough vaccine, and commending this remarkable lady for her "high professional skill and love and understanding." But Dr. Denmark savored this signal honor not half so much as the opportunity to continue the work she has been doing for half a century — her ministry of health and hope on behalf of the sick children at Central's Baby Clinic. With a past stretching back to 1922, the Baby Clinic is still looking forward.

Forward, in fact, may be the only direction this old downtown church now knows how to look. Centralites were so busy looking forward, that the 1978 church budget was subscribed beyond best expectations. So busily were they looking forward, that their additional special subscriptions enabled the hope of a much-needed new organ in the beautifully refurbished Rand Chapel to become a 1978 reality. So busily were they looking forward that, when at midyear, their 95-year old sanctuary suddenly developed major repair needs expensive enough to make a shambles of their 1978 operating budget, Centralites automatically tightened their belts, borrowed some money, made temporary repairs to their budget, and continued on still looking forward.

But Central was not so busy looking forward as to forget for one moment its old-time compassion. One bitter cold week-end, about a year after Buddy Enniss' arrival, Capitol Square was once again a mass of humanity, again without the amenities to meet their needs. This time they were Georgia farmers who had converged by the thousands to protest their plight. Concrete-bound old Central Church doesn't know much about farming, but it does know about simple, ordinary human need and how to go about meeting it. It had been at that business for a long, long time. So, with warm buildings and warm hearts and gallons upon gallons of hot coffee, Central welcomed the crusading farmers of Georgia, just as they had welcomed the strikers and the mourners and the vigil keepers before them.

There could no longer be any doubt: Central was still Central. It was still the Church at Work. It was still the Church that Cared. It was still the Church that Stayed.

Chapter 8
The People Who Stayed (1858-1978)

The Church, in essence, is People. This concluding chapter seeks to name all the people who, under God, fashioned the history of Central Church from its beginning in 1858 through the year 1978.

What follows is the product of diligent research on the part of many people. Among these, very special credit must go to Roy Greene, Margaret Carlisle, Maud Nardin, Iris and Jack Yarbrough, Dorothy Woods and Patsy Wiggins.

THE PROCESS

Insofar, as possible, all names are listed alphabetically within the year of joining. Every existing record — every sessional record, every *Weekly*, every Central church register and every published roll of members — was carefully researched in the process. Wherever determinations were to be made as to spellings or as to the manner in which married couples are listed, the actual minutes of the Session meeting at which the members were received were considered to be the final arbiter.

THE PROBLEM

The major difficulty encountered in the process is the absence now of all official records of Central Church covering periods totaling sixteen years of its history. The records from Feb. 14, 1858 until April 4, 1870 were burned and lost. No explanation has been discovered as to why the Session minutes from March 30, 1901 till April 1, 1905 are likewise missing. The latter group of minutes, we must hope, may yet someday be discovered. Missing records are the reason why the researchers for this chapter had to prepare one large list of known members separately and without the year of joining being specified.

THE FOUNDING MEMBERS

The newly rediscovered list reproduced on page 116 will serve to satisfy finally Central's long-felt need for an official naming of its first members.

In far greater numbers than most congregations, has Central been blessed with the services of ordained ministers who have made it their church home. These ministers, usually administrators for denominational organizations or institutions, have membership in presbyteries rather than in local churches such as Central. Their names have been appropriately listed in this chapter, however, for they too are a real part of the history and work of Central Church.

Proudly listed on the pages which follow, are all the People Who Stayed.

Central Presbyterian Weekly

PUBLISHED WEEKLY BY THE
Central Presbyterian Church and Sabbath School
WASHINGTON STREET.
Printed by the Foote & Davies Co., Atlanta, Ga

All notices for publication must be sent to CENTRAL PRESBYTERIAN WEEKLY, 75 Washington Street before Wednesday.

Entered at Post office at Atlanta, Ga., as second-class mail matter, April 18, 1900.

HISTORY.

Examining some old church papers, we found what seems to be the long lost list of the charter members of the Church. We think it will be haled with delight, as there has always been some doubt as to the lists that have been published being exact. We give the exact copy of the paper:

"GRIFFIN, GA., Dec. 28, 1858.

"Mr. M. Cole.

"Dear Sir: In compliance with request I herewith send a list of the names of persons that signed the memorial to F. R. Presbytery, requesting a division of the Atlanta church. My absence from home must explain the delay of this letter.

"Yours, &c.,

"(Signed) JAMES C. PATTERSON.

"Jos. P. Logan, Ann E. Logan, A. W. Stone, Mrs. C. A. B. Stone, John R. Rhea. 2nd, M. Cole, Jo. L. Lockhart, I. Newton Beach, Julia B. Beach, Mary C. Hull, Emily A. Rogers, Fannie G. Wallace, Joseph Thompson, Nancy P. Farrar, Robt. M. Farrar, Richard P. Farrar, W. P. Robinson, J. L. Crew, Mary J. Calhoun, Laura D. Ripley, S. D. Gilbert, James Craig, Martha A. Boyd, Mary R. Boyd, Sallie H. ColemanMary E. Calhoun, Mrs. Joshua Whitney, M. Frank Whitney, Julia U. L. Fraser, Mrs. M. T. High, Mrs. A. E. Hamlieter, S. D. Parr, M. A. Parr, Calderwood Shaw, Elizabeth Clark (for'y McLin), Mrs. C. R. Du Bose, Mrs. Amanda S. Corley, Mrs. Jane Gill, Mrs. L. R. Rice."

Exactly as it appeared in the July 15, 1905 issue of the *Central Presbyterian Weekly* is this story of the 1858 letter from the Stated Clerk of Presbytery officially naming the founding members of Central Church.

CENTRAL PRESBYTERIAN CHURCH MEMBERS 1858-1978

1858

Adams, Mrs. Mary R.
Beach, I. Newton
Beach, Julia B.
Calhoun, Mary E.
Calhoun, Mary J.
Clark, Elizabeth
Cole, Marie
Cole, Moses
Coleman, Mrs. Sallie H.
Combs, Mary A.
Corley, Amanda L.
Craig, James
Craig, Mrs. Julia A.
Crew, Mrs. J.L.
Dubose, Mrs. C.R.
Farrar, Nancy P.
Farrar, Richard P.
Farrar, Robert M.
Foy, Mr. & Mrs. James M.
Fraser, Julia U.L.
Gilbert, S.D.
Gill, Mrs. Jane
Grant, Jane L.
Grant, Mrs. L.L.
Hamlieter, Mrs. A.E.
High, Mrs. M.T.
Hull, Mary C.
Lockhart, Joseph D.
Logan, Mrs. Ann E.
Logan, Dr. Joseph P.
Parr, M.A.
Parr, S.D.
Rhea, John
Rhodes, Sallie
Rice, Mrs. L.R.
Ripley, Mr.
Ripley, Laura D.
Robinson, Mr. & Mrs. W.P.
Rogers, Emily C.
Shaw, Miss Calderwood
Stone, Amherst W.
Stone, Miss C.H.B.
Thompson, Dr. Joseph
Toy, Mrs. John M.
Wallace, Alexander M.
Wallace, Fannie G.
Whitney, Mr. & Mrs. Joshua
Whitney, Miss M. Frank

1859

Gilbert, Henerritta
Gilbert, Theodore
Grant, Col. Lemuel P.
Harden, Sarah J.
Harden, Dr. W.P.
Kilby, Mr. & Mrs. William J.
Luckie, Mary Rushton
McNaught, William M.
Orme, Dr. Henry S.
Rushton, Martha
Rushton, Mary A.
Rushton, William
Thomas, Mr. & Mrs. George S.

1860

Barth, Carl F.
Clarke, Mr. & Mrs. John M.
Craig, Julia A.
Forsyth, Ann
Forsyth, William
Grant, Anna
McDowell, Elizabeth
McDowell, Thomas M.
Willis, Mr. & Mrs. James
Wyly, Sarah H.

1861

Clarke, Mr. & Mrs. Edward Y.
Dabney, Martha
Dabney, William A.
Logan, Miss Anne
Patton, Julius M.
Wiley, Nancy H.
Williams, Mrs. Corrie

1862

Boyd, Martha C.
Boyd, Nancy E.
Calhoun, Florida
Calhoun, Georgia
Calhoun, Lucy
Clayton, Caro
Dabney, Wiliam A.
Patton, Mary D.
Rushton, Eva
Steele, Mary

1863

Pease, Emma
Pease, P.P.
Rushton, Eva

Whitehead, Charles
Whitehead, Julia C.

1864

Clarke, Mr. & Mrs. Thomas M.
O'Keefe, Mrs. S.H.

1865

Alexander, Harriet E.
Jeffries, Dr. Francis M.
Kirkpatrick, Miss C.E.
Kirkpatrick, Mr. & Mrs. H.A.
Phillips, H.T.
Ward, Addie C.
Ward, Dr. Robert C.
Whitner, John C.
Whitner, Sarah Martha

1866

Alexander, Mrs. Georgia J.
Bard, Martha
Barrick, James R.
Barrick, Mrs. L.B.
Campbell, Virginia C.
Crook, Amanda M.
Crook, Joseph W.
Crook, Mary W.
DuBose, Mrs. Anna
DuBose, Dr. Wilder
Edwards, Virginia M.
Elliott, Isabella
Ellis, John
Farrow, Cornelia S.
Farrow, Col. Henry P.
Fox, Mrs. Lizzie S.
Knight, George W.
McGuire, Anna M.
Mullen, Mary Alice
Newton, Charles S.
Towns, George W.

1867

Anderson, Jane E.
Anderson, Robert A.
Bradfield, Josiah
Brumby, Mrs. A.E.
Brumby, Col. A.V.
Campbell, Mrs. F.E.
Campbell, Mrs. Isabella
Cannon, Mrs. M.E.
Cole, Mrs. Maria D.
Few, Mary B.
Force, Benjamin W.
Force, Julia A.
Grant, W.W.
Harris, L.L.
Holliday, Mrs. M.L.
Jackson, Sallie Cobb
Jones, Charlotte G.
Jones, Cornelia
Jones, Darwin G.
Jones, E.L.
Jones, Ed H.
Jones, Hattie H.
Jones, Sarah S.
Jones, W.R.
Knight, Clara Corinne
Moore, Mrs. N.S.
Moore, Thomas
McNaught, John
Porter, Mrs. Jane
Van Epps, Julia C.
Van Epps, A. Carroll
Winn, Dr. E.E.
Winn, Mary A.

1868

Austin, Mrs. E.
Baker, Mary
Barry, John A.
Beatie, David A.
Beatie, Mary L.
Beattie, Mr. & Mrs. D.
Boyd, J.C.
Brumby, Dr. A.B.
Camp, Laura
Campbell, V.M.
Chapman, Mrs. C.M.
Dallas, Martha
Emery, H.F.
Floyd, Jane
Floyd, Miss L.C.
Fox, Louisa S.
Fuller, Caroline
Fuller, Henry A.
Garrett, Caroline M.
Garrett, Dr. William M.
Glover, Mrs. A.B.
Harrison, Miss S.N.
Ketcham, Mrs. G.A.
Knapp, Mrs. Effie
Mallard, Mr. & Mrs. William J.
Marks, Maj. M.R.
Mynatt, Mrs. Alice L.
McNaught, Effie
Nesbitt, Ruth Lowndes
Parkhurst, Mr. & Mrs. Wm. Francis
Patton, Emily E.
Porter, Lillah D.
Simms, Edward
Stacy, Dr. & Mrs. R.Q.
Symmes, Edward
Whitner, Eliza A. Spann
Wight, Clara S.
Wight, Ella B.
Wight, S.A.G.
Wight, S.B.
Woodruff, John W.

1869

Anderson, Mrs. R.A.
Brumby, Leigh R.
Brumby, Sue
Clayton, Katy W.
Grace, Juliet T.
McNaught, Mary
Patton, Mrs. J.M.
Patton, Josephine D.
Pease, Orpha H.
Stokes, William

1870

Bacon, Mrs. E.J.
Barry, Mary E.
Campbell, L.M.
Cannon, L.M.
Clarke, Mr. & Mrs. S.E.
Cooper, Mrs. W.L.
Crosby, Gertrude B.
Dabney, Mrs. T.G.
Eckford, Belle Gates
Eckford, Charles Gates
Eckford, William H.
Fain, John A.
Fain, Mattie C.
Grant, John A.
Grant, Lettie H.
Grant, Septine F.
Harris, Elizabeth A.
Hull, Mary C.
Ketner, Julia
Leftwich, Adelia
Mynat, Pryor L.
Phillips, Bettie W.
Spencer, Mary E.
Spencer, S.B.
Whitner, John A.

1871

Alexander, Sallie A.
Alexander, Thomas G.
Block, Frank E.
Block, Maggie D.
Bodega, Charles A.
Boroughs, Mary Eliz
Bowie, Mrs. John A.
Bowie, Lucy J.
Boyd, Mary A.
Burges, Jesse N.
Charles, O.D.
Clayton, T.A.
Coleman, Carrie
Coleman, Julia
Dodson, Julia A.
Dodson, Mary
Dodson, W. Carey
Dunwody, Mrs. E.W.
Dunwody, Mary E.
Force, Irene H.
Fox, Anna H.
Fraser, Mrs. Lucretia
Hale, Prof. A.I.
Hancock, Carrie
Hunter, Benjamin T.
Hunter, India
Jones, Caroline
Jones, Jane A.
Jones, John C.
Ketcham, Sarah E.
Kingsbury, Joseph
Kirkpatrick, John C.
Kirkpatrick, Mary A.
Link, Fannie
Link, J.A.
Link, Flossie
Morrison, Mrs. John
Murphy, Mrs. E.C.
Murphy, Dr. I.B.
Montgomery, Ellen M.

McKinly, Mrs. M.
McKinnon, Ellen
Nolan, Emma
Orr, Eliza C.
Orr, Mary E.
Patton, Sallie
Rainey, Mr. & Mrs. Charles V.
Rainey, Della
Rainey, L.B.
Rainey, William W.
Rainwater, Jessee F.
Rigdon, Mrs. L.M.
Rushton, Ellen M.
Rushton, Julia
Shackleford, Mrs. V.A.
Simpson, Dr. Carolus A.
Simpson, W. Wallace
Sleymaker, Helen Christie
Spencer, Mrs. George C.
Spencer, W.A.
Stokes, Frances A.
Thompson, Evert M.
Turner, James A.
Valentine, Mr. & Mrs. Louis T.
Vance, D.F.
Walker, Mrs. A.E.
Walker, Alice
Walker, Mr. & Mrs. W.G.

1872

Anderson, Fannie E.
Brooke, Lilla E.
Brumby, Mamie
Clarke, William H.
Cotton, Eliza
Cowles, Miss C.I.
Crane, Benjamin S.
Cromwell, Addie
Field, Lyda A.
Frasier, Mary A.
Gee, Mr. & Mrs. A.
Gowdy, Katie E.
Green, Susan
Heath, Eliza A.
Jones, Mrs. S.A.
Jones, Sheppard A.
Ketchum, Annie M.
Kirkpatrick, Annie
Kraft, H.F.
Lee, Dr. Henry B.
Mitchell, Mrs. C.E.
Murphey, Marion G.
McConnell, Ann
McConnell, Ella
McConnell, Mrs. M.E.
McConnell, S.D.
McConnell, Miss T.E.
McCulloch, Eliza W.
McKoy, Ada I.I.
McKoy, Catherine E.
McKoy, Judge Henry K.
McKoy, John L.
McKoy, Laura S.
McMahon, Mrs. California V.
McMahon, Matthew B.
McPherson, Mary
Newman, Mrs. F.A.
Phillips, Mattie
Pollard, Sarah A.
Rice, George
Robinson, Ann K.
Robinson, W.G.
Rocheubeau, Ida
Rokenbaugh, Lydia W.
Sharp, Ann Francis
Smith, Henrietta H.
Spencer, Macon B.
Wallace, Maj. Campbell
Wallace, Campbell, Jr.
Wallace, Fannie E.
Wallace, Susan E.
Whitehead, Maria
Williams, Laura L.

1873

Abbott, Mrs. M.J.
Allen, Florence S.
Ansley, Ann E.
Ansley, I.A.
Ansley, J.R.
Ansley, Louisa S.
Barry, Charles M.
Barry, Jane E.
Beach, Mrs. C. Isabella
Beach, D. Payton
Beattie, John L.
Bowie, John A.
Boyd, Thomas J.
Camp, Ann E.
Camp, H.
Campbell, William B.
Clarke, Mary H.
Clarke, Robert C.
Clayton, Mrs. Wm. H.
Cofer, Lizzie
Cofer, Mattie E.
Dryer, Susan
Eagan, Mary
Eckford, Joseph I.
Eckford, Marshall T.
Ellis, Hallie F.
Field, James P.
Fife, Aolia
Fraser, Colin M.
Fry, Mary A.A.
Hall, Lucia C.
Harris, Lucy P.
Hill, Thomas
Hopkins, J.G.
Howard, Sallie A.
Howard, Sallie R.
Hoyt, Miss L.M.
Hoyt, S.B.
Hulsey, Alice E.
Jamison, T.W.
Jarrett, Simpson Y.
Jones, Henry H.
Kennedy, Jennie
Kilby, Fannie
Kilby, Florence
Kilby, Kate
Lacy, Jasper N.
Lanneau, Eliza G.
Launeau, Julia L.
Leake, George G.
Logan, Eliza C.
Logan, Emma D.
Logan, F.R.
Logan, Jennie M.
Logan, Prof. John
Logan, William W.
Mallard, Florida
Mallard, Josiah
Mallard, Sarah
Merriam, A.B.
Merriam, Hannah M.
Milner, Mary Ann
McClintock, Mrs. C.A.
McConnell, Laura E.
McCormick, Ann
McDearmid, Angus
McDouough, Etta
McDowell, Lizzie C.
McDowell, Marion C.
McDowell, Mary B.
McMahon, John M.
Rhodes, Willie W.
Richards, Mrs. M.J.
Rigdon, Rebe D.
Robinson, Richard V.
Rockenbaugh, M.K.
Rushton, Robert E.
Russell, Miss Georgia B.
Russell, Jane
Russell, Jessie
Shannon, John
Shannon, William
Simpson, Isabella
Simpson, Ossein F.
Sloan, Cooie
Smith, Benjamin Hall
Smith, Capt. H.I.
Smith, Henry L.
Smith, Hugh S.
Smith, Sarah
Thompson, Mrs. Joseph
Torrence, I.E.
Torrence, Mrs. M.R.
Torrence, Miss V.A.
Toy, Emma D.
Wallace, Campbell, Jr.
Wallace, Elizabeth
Wallace, John R.
Way Corine C.
Werner, Florence C.
Whaling, Julia M.
Whaling, William J.
Whitner, Mary Ann
Whitner, Sallie Roots

1874

Aiken, Mary E.
Akers, Lilly
Ansley, Harry C.
Barry, Mary E.
Bee, Emma P.
Born, Eliza H.
Bowie, Isabella
Bowie, Lillie
Brier, H.D.
Cassels, Mr. & Mrs. Walter O.
Castleman, Humphrey
Doggett, Rose
Fechner, Virginia L.
Fuller, Mr. & Mrs. William
Green, Susan
Hulsey, Augustus I.

Johnson, Cynthia
Knight, Minnie S.
Lacy, Thomas
Launeau, Hannah
Leftwich, Thomas
Montgomery, Charles D.
McCormick, Dora B.
McCormick, Jeanie
McGee, Catherine
McMasters, Julia
Pease, Clara E.
Pease, Julia A.
Pinson, Cornelia A.
Pinson, John L.
Porter, Mrs. Fannie T.
Pugh, Josephine
Russell, J.G.
Shepperson, Clement C.
Slaughter, Georgia
Thomas, Maria
Thompson, Sallie
Ward, Susan T.

1875

Beall, Samuel O.
Bowdoin, Florence E.
Bowdoin, Miss I.B.
Boyd, John L.
Boyd, Mrs. M.A.
Bradfield, Louis H.
Bridwell, Ella
Brown, Hugh
Cone, Annie E.
Cotton, John W.
Crawford, Mary
Force, Florence C.
Gilbert, R.J.
Howard, W.J.
Kendrick, Dr. Wm. S.
Kingsberry, Edwin
Kingsberry, Rosea
Little, Carrie
Little, Dr. George
Livingston, Ida B.
Livingston, Wm. S.
Loughridge, H.
Mell, Anna
Palmer, Josephine
Platt, George A.
Platt, Miss S.A.
Platt, Miss S.C.
Riach, Mr. & Mrs. W.A.
Richards, Mrs. James E.
Smith, J.Bruce
Smyth, J.M.
Turner, Juliet
Turner, W.S.
Walker, Lizzie
Wallace, Fannie A.
Wallace, Joseph S.
Wallace, Minnie C.
Werner, Florida
Wrenn, Florida

1876

Akers, Mary E.
Alexander, Jennie Orme
Bankston, Lydia A.
Bell, Maria J.
Bell, William
Berry, Hettie
Blalock, Alford
Bowie, Ema A.
Bowie, Rosa
Bradfield, Howard W.
Buck, Mrs. E.B.
Clarke, Annie B.
Clarke, Edward Y. Jr.
Cunningham, Addie Jones
Dabney, Martha B.
Dagett, Col. H.S.
Evans, Minnie
Farrow, Janie J.
Floyd, Lelia B.
Floyd, Rosa
Frierson, Charles F.
Frierson, Sarah A.
Gilbert, Eugenia H.
Gobay, Emma L.
Grant, L.L.
Hamilton, L.E.
Hancock, Robert A.
Howarth, Mr. & Mrs. James L.
Hoyt, William R.
Hudson, William James
Humphreys, John T.
Humphreys, Mildred M.
Jeffries, Maria
Johnson, Martha
Jones, Ida T.
Jones, Mrs. M. Addie
Kelly, Florence
Ketcham, Clara A.
Ketcham, Julia P.
Logan, Charlotte A.
Logan, Minnie M.
Maclean, Edwin
Mitchell, Henry C.
McKinley, Jennie
McKinley, Miss S.M.
Owen, Minnie
Patton, Mary D.
Platt, Annie
Porter, Alice L.
Rankin, Jesse W.
Rigdon, Kattie
Robinson, Annie
Robinson, W.P.
Rokenbough, Lydia W.
Rokenbough, Miss M.K.
Scott, Laura
Smith, Georgia M.
Spencer, Mary
Stevens, Jennie Orme
Torrence, John E.
Van Epps, Minnie
Ward, Susan T.
Warner, John
Willis, Nellie

1877

Bell, Mrs. A.E.
Bowen, Miss E.A.
Brooks, Caroline
Clarke, Andrew
Clarke, Emma P.
Hesterly, Mary
Hesterly, Indiana
Jones, Cornelia A.
Killen, Elizabeth
Lanfasty, James
Meador, Mary E.
Moffatt, James G.
Morgan, David
Morgan, Elizabeth J.
McDowell, Ada J.F.
McLeod, Mrs. Ada
Patton, Leila A.
Quick, Mary
Roberts, Nancy
Robinson, Annie M.
Robinson, William P.
Smith, Mrs. C.B.
Walker, Sarah
Wallace, Mattie
Weeks, Margaret
Wight, Mrs. C.B.
Williamson, Elizabeth
Williamson, Martha L.
Wilson, Benjamin J.
Wilson, Carrie

1878

Blackman, J.B.
Brown, Elizabeth J.
Brown, Julia
Brown, Nancy
Calhoun, Dr. Abner W.
Calhoun, Lula P.
Clarke, Nora V.
Curry, Jane
Dozier, Miss Willie
Eldridge, Lizzie
Fain, Virginia A.
Franklin, Joseph
Gaines, Idella
Gay, Lucy M.
Grant, Miss Callie
Harper, Elizabeth
Harper, Julia
Harper, P.O., Jr.
Higgins, Martha
Robinson, Callie L.
Rogers, Hattie L.
Ross, Leonard G.
Shaw, Mrs. Kindness
Sheftall, E. Tatnall
Smith, Mrs. Willie
Sneed, Fannie
Snow, Mrs. Kindness
Sysle, George
Sysle, John W.
Sysle, Mammie B.
Sysle, Mary
Valentine, Sarah
Voss, Susan

1879

Bankston, Creed T.
Bowie, John A.
Bowie, Lilly
Bowie, Lucy J.
Braden, Margaret
Dunwody, E.M.
Dunwody, Mary E.

Young Men's Class taught by Mr. W.J. O'Callaghan (last row, 4th from left). The day, February 2, 1930 was Dr. Oglesby's first day at Central (first row, 5th from right).

Emmons, Mary
Gillam, Miss J.B.
Gillam, Dr. L.M.
Gillam, Mrs. M.E.
Hawkins, Lizzie
Jones, Cornelia A.
Langston, Eliz
Logan, Mrs. Lettie H.
Maxey, Mrs. P.T.
Merriam, Alfred B.
McMaster, Ida T.
Pass, Martha Jane
Pass, Sarah Jan
Patton, Mary D.
Pugh, John
Pugh, Maggie
Quick, George D.
Ray, Mary M.
Ray, Nannie E.
Spencer, Mrs. M.E.
Spencer, Col. S.B.
Spencer, Samuel B.
Stephens, John S.
Stephens, M.L.
Torrence, Catherine
Wells, Julia
Whitner, Tom Cobb

1880

Anderson, Mrs. H.W.
Anspach, Frederick
Bain, Donald
Bain, Rebecca
Barnet, Mary Jane
Bass, Mrs. Jessie Orr
Boggs, Marian A.
Brooks, Harriet E.
Bynam, Mark B.
Byrum, Caroline
Clayton, F.H.
Clayton, Mollie C.
Crist, Mrs. Mattie Flora
Crist, Mattie Thelma
Crosby, Gertrude B.
Dabney, Mrs. M.B.
Dunwody, Mary Jane
Emery, Abbie
Emery, Alice R.
Emery, Anne
Emery, Sarah
Fain, Mamie A.
Fain, Mary A.
Fain, Mattie Flora
Ferriday, Emily A.
Greensbough, S.P.
Gunsborough, A.P.
Gunsborough, Bertha
Henderson, Mrs. E.J.
Henderson, I.J.
Hill, Mary Y.
Hunter, Mary E.
Hutchison, Jennie A.
Johnson, Mary J.
Jones, Jane A.
Jones, Martha G.
Jones, Mary Anna
Jones, R.M.
Kingsbury, Emma
Kingsbury, Louisa J.
Logan, George W.
Morgan, B.E.
Myatt, William
Orr, Jessie O.
Powell, Elizabeth
Rankin, Fannie G.
Rawson, Miss M.P.
Rice, Elizabeth S.
Robinson, Allie M.
Rogers, Charles
Schoad, Lizzie
Skelton, Mr. & Mrs. William L.
Speer, Jane
Torrence, John E.
Tuttle, Mrs. A.J.
Wallace, Emma McComb
Wyatt, William
Wylly, Sarah A.
Wyly, William

1881

Barry, Maggie A.
Barry, Nancy
Barry, Robert E.
Carlisle, James C.
Carlisle, Mary J.
Cole, Clarke P.
Collier, John T.
Collier, Dr. Thomas E.
Conrad, E.F.
Cosby, Martha A.
Fraser, Susie
Hansen, Julia
Heath, George P.
Heath, Mary J.
King, Barrington J.
King, Estelle
King, Frances P.
King, Ida P.
King, James R.
King, Oliver W.
Milner, Mattie M.
Moore, Mrs. Idora
Morgan, Annie E.
Morgan, Jennie I.
McMaster, Maggie
McMaster, Martha G.
Orr, Robert C.
Patterson, George C.
Planghman, Idora
Prathen, Jane Y.
Pratt, Julia E.
Puckett, S.E.
Richards, Sallie J.
Ripley, Sallie M.
Ripley, T.R.
Robinson, Elizabeth
Robinson, Rosalie
Skelton, Eliza J.
Skelton, Martha
Smith, Mrs. Annie E.
Smith, Minnie E.
Speights, Miss Clyde
Speights, Mary W.
Speights, W.T.
Spencer, Macon B.
Thomas, Charles S.
Thompson, Janie
Thompson, John S.
Tuttle, Nannie E.
Whitner, Mattie M.
Woolf, Mary Ida
Woolf, Winfield
Woolf, Winfred P.
Wrenn, Albert B.
Wrenn, Sallie

1882

Beatie, William D.
Bell, Mary P.
Berry, Charles M.
Bleckley, Logan M.
Brown, Carrie
Clarke, Annie Lee
Dowda, Mr. & Mrs. C.A.
Eagan, John J.
Edmondson, L.E.
Edwards, Ella
Edwards, Mickleberry E.
Findley, Jessie
Forbes, Brice
Forbes, George B.
Forbes, Mary M.
Forbes, Mattie
Fuller, Henry W.
Goodman, Mary C.
Hesterly, Miss Julian
Hoyt, Corrie
Hunter, Katie C.
Isham, John
Madge, Annie
Madge, Charles H.
Mann, Isabella R.
Mann, Matilda Louisa
Maude, Annie Bell
Maude, Ellen J.
Morgan, Ella M.
McCombs, James M.
McGhee, Nancy J.
McPherson, Mary W.
McPherson, Mattie E.
McPherson, Susan W.
Palmer, Ida
Peacock, John T.
Rankin, Jesse W., Jr.
Rankin, Mamie M.
Richards, Emma
Spencer, Frank S.
Wallace, Emma B.
Wallace, Margaret Jessie
Wallace, Marion C.
Whitner, Charles Frank

1883

Ansley, Catherine Urguhart
Ansley, Ida
Ansley, John M.
Baker, Sarah M.
Barili, Alfredo
Bibb, Rebecca L.
Camp, Rosa Leigh
Cassels, Lula Clifford
Cassels, Thomas M.
Cox, Mrs. Lon
Fain, John W.
Fry, Mrs. George T.
Hardwicke, Mrs. R.W.

Harper, Mrs. E.E.
Hillyer, Mrs. Eleanor H.
Lumpkin, Mr. & Mrs. W.W.
Mallard, Jennie Law
McClellan, Mr. & Mrs. John W.
Newton, Florence
Van Epps, Howard
Wilson, Robert Edward
Wingfield, James P.

1884

Ammons, Saddie M.
Ammons, William A.
Anderson, William A.
Barford, Annie
Bell, Mr. & Mrs. Frank
Bellingrath, Albert F.
Boyd, Mattie B.
Boyd, Roger D.
Calhoun, Andrew E.
Cameron, Benjamin H.
Cameron, Irene C.
Camp, Mrs. Maria C.
Campbell, Percy
Campbell, Percy D.
Clayton, Mrs. F.H.
Coursen, Lucy L.
Crosby, Warren B.
Dallas, George J.
Dunwody, Matilda E.
Emery, Lizzie B.
Fry, Elizabeth C.
Gholstein, Nancy R.B.
Hackett, Ida M.
Hackney, Edward
Haines, Fannie D.
Haines, Mary A.
Harris, James O.
Henderson, Mrs. J.M.
Henry, F.D.
Herbert, Mr. & Mrs. George S.
Hill, Gussie Parkhurst
Irvin, Annie F.
Irvin, Elizabeth J.
Irvin, Julia
Irvin, S.D.
Jackson, Henry
Jones, Nannie
Lake, Mrs. Frank
Leas, William
Link, Alliene
Link, Bessie
Link, William P.
Martin, Mrs. Isabel
Martin, John Bowie
Martin, Samuel
McCay, Catherine
McDermaid, Anna
McNair, Julia
McNair, Henry S.
Owen, Mary L.
Parkhurst, Daniel McD.
Parkhurst, Gussie H.
Pelham, Mattie
Pelham, Mrs. T.H.
Pope, William H.
Quarterman, T. Elliott
Smith, Marie Candfield
Sperry, Emma Mary
Stokes, Frances A.
Stokes, William F.
Strickler, Mrs. Mary F.
Strickler, Nettie M.
Strickler, Miss V.M.
Taylor, Isabella V.
Waller, Mary L.
Way, Alice
Way, Samuel Y.
Way, W. Findley
Way, Wallen A.
Wilson, J. Ben
Wilson, Mary E.

1885

Alexander, Annie T.
Alexander, Mrs. E.Y.
Alexander, Mary Eloise
Baker, Miss L.M.
Barry, Charles Wm.
Barry, Eugene Taylor
Beath, Lucy B.
Bender, Barbara
Bender, Charles H.
Berkley, Edward
Berkley, Julia
Brumby, Campbell Wallace
Buford, Mr. & Mrs. J.M.
Buford, Rosa Therese
Byram, Caroline
Byram, Mark B.
Carllton, Bell M.
Clarke, Cora B.
Clarke, Samuel E.
Clayton, Caroline M.
Clayton, Robert M.
Clayton, William H.
Cofer, Mattie E.
Cole, Florence M.
Cole, Minnie E.
Cooper, Dora
Corlett, E.H.
Corlett, Eda E.
Cotton, Annie Kate
Floyd, Charles Lewis
Handy, Mr. & Mrs. Charles
Hil, Annie Lee
Hunter, Addie J.
Hunter, W. Hugh
Joyner, Clio Bell
Kennedy, Belle
Knight, Lucien L.
Knight, Marie Bertha
Kosborough, Mrs. E.P.
Link, James Allen
Mallard, William J., Jr.
Markham, Laura
Martin, Mr. & Mrs. Charles J.
Mashburn, Mr. & Mrs. A.W.
Mashburn, George W.
Mashburn, Miss M.C.
Meakin, S.
Milner, B.C.
Mitchell, Guy
Morgan, Benjamin D.
Mynatt, Joseph L.
McGregor, Mr. & Mrs. D.W.
Nagle, Charles Mark
Niles, Mrs. C.C.
Owen, Charles J.
Phillips, Sallie P.
Pinson, Chester Dewitt
Powell, June P.
Quarterman, W. Palmer
Rankin, Gussie
Richards, Katie
Roseborough, Mrs. Edward Palmer
Rushton, Charles Emmett
Rushton, Clara Belle
Rushton, Ella B.
Rushton, Robert E.
Rushton, Robert Elwood
Rushton, William Wight
Saunders, J.L.
Saunders, Virginia D.
Smith, John A.
Sparks, Ida
Spencer, Mary
Spencer, W.A.
Strickler, Cyrus W.
Wallace, William Lyon
White, Agnes D.
White, Annie A.
Williams, Noble C.
Woodruff, Julia Beasley

1886

Akins, Mr. & Mrs. William M.
Arnall, Charles S.
Arnall, Mattie D.
Avery, Cora L.
Bennett, M. A.
Block, Nellie D.
Boykin, Laura N.
Boykin, Lauretta N.
Callaway, Joshua T.
Cole, Mrs. C. P.
Coursen, Bertha L.
Craig, Bessie
Craig, James Newton, Jr.
Craig, Lydia H.
Craig, Maude
Cumming, Carrie E.
Earnest, Laura Virginia
Edmondson, John A.
Fain, Eppie M.
Force, Philip H.
Grace, Juliet A.
Hamilton, L. E.
Helmer, Elizabeth
Helmer, F. D. S.
Helmer, Harriet S.
Hull, Joseph A. B.
Hunter, Florence F.
Hurtell, Gordon N.
Kennedy, Cora L.
King, Marion P.
Logan, Alice R.
Mallard, Sallie B.
Maltry, Julia
Maltry, Philip
Martin, Florida C.
Meador, Sallie B.
Meyrowitz, Paul A.
Morrison, Angus
Maynatt, Pryon L., Jr.
McConnell, H. H.
McPhail, Pattie G.

THE PEOPLE WHO STAYED (1858-1978)

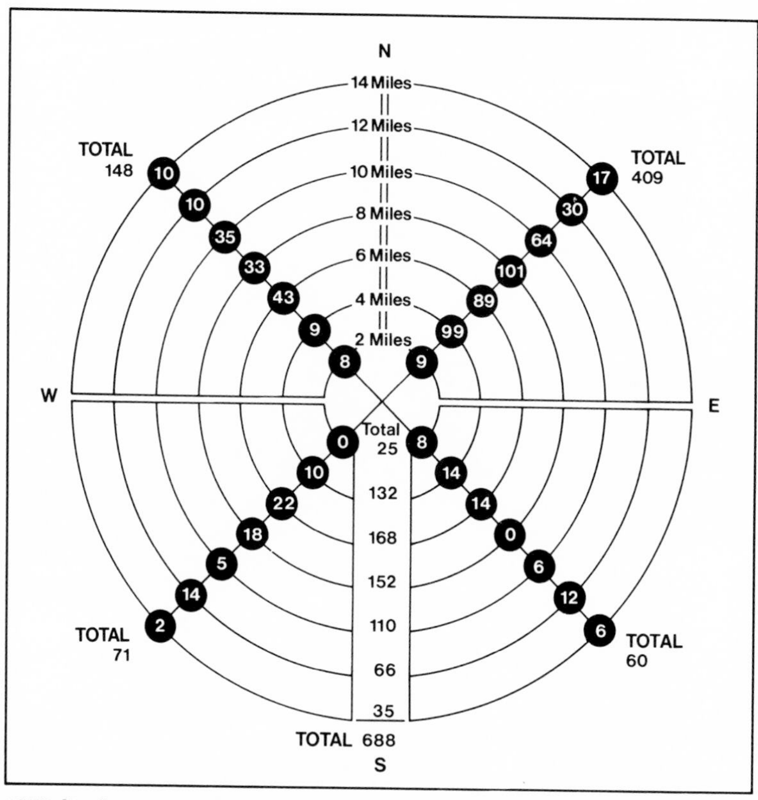

1978 distribution of Central's 688 members living within 14 miles of the church. 176 members live farther than 14 miles, some out of the state. See 1931 chart page 77.

McPhail, T. H.
Nagle, Mary
Pattie, Barton D.
Payne, Margaret B.
Powell, Jane P.
Rawls, Sarah
Redus, Anna
Redus, William R. K.
Reid, Gertrude
Reid, Judge Harry M.
Rhea, Maggie F.
Shaw, L. W.
Shaw, Mary
Simpson, Belle
Wallace, Annie N.
Warner, Felicia H.
Way, Nannie R.
Whitesides, Fannie S.
Woolf, Mary L.

1887

Alexander, Carrie F.
Alexander, J. Harvey
Anderson, Robert H., Jr.
Barna, Annie
Barna, T. M.
Barna, Thomas A.
Barnard, Jennie
Barry, John Leftwich
Beall, J. O.
Beardsley, Joseph R.
Beatie, Edward B.
Beatie, Nora L.
Bible, John F.
Bowie, Jennie
Boyd, Edward W.
Boykin, Eugenia Nisbet
Brown, Alice
Brown, Jessie
Brown, John N.
Brown, S. C.
Buzbee, Minnie
Cohen, Sallie I.
Cole, Arthur E.
Cole, Fred W.
Conley, Thomas J.
Cooper, Dr. Hunter Pope
Douglas, Corinne
Douglas, Hamilton
Edwards, John F.
Fife, Mary E.
Fuller, Annie R.
Grady, Jennie
Haines, Bertha D.
Hamilton, Mary Lee
Hammond, Harry
Hammond, S. G.
Hammond, M. E.
Helmer, Ethel G.
Helmer, Ora G.
Hood, Robert J.
Jackson, Callie Cobb
Jackson, Marion M.
Johnson, Emma
Jones, Johm Ashley
Jones, Rosa Belle
King, Clara Belle
Kirkpatrick, Walter W.
Larkin, Mary P.
Luckie, Mary R.
Maud, Attie C.
Meador, James J., Jr.
Mitchel, Walter G.
Morgan, Thomas
Mynatt, Alice W.
McCay, Benjamin F.
Nagle, Lucy
Newton, Edward T.
Nisbet, Miss C. D.
Nisbet, Charles R.
Nisbet, Marie S.
Nisbet, Mary S.
Orchard, Angus E.
Orr, Angus E.
Overby, Mary Fife
Reid, Mrs. B.

Richards, Charles H.
Richards, Fannie H.
Robinson, Thomas A.
Rushton, Clara Belle
Simpson, Miss Azile
Stevens, Lula E.
Stevens, Dean P.
Stevens, Nora F.
Stewart, Mr. & Mrs. A. J.
Stokes, Charles A.
Stokes, John W.
Stokes, William T., Jr.
Strickler, Mary R.
Thompson, Margaret C.
Thompson, Thomas Perrin
Toffe, Bertha D.
Wade, Mr. & Mrs. J. C.
Wade, Mrs. M. E.
Wallace, Jessie O.
Webb, William B.
Woolf, Winfield P.
Word, Matilda

1888

Alexander, Annie T.
Alexander, Mrs. E. F.
Alexander, J. H.
Alexander, Mary Eloise
Baker, Miss L. M.
Bell, Mrs. O. R.
Benson, Mrs. Louisa P.
Benson, Perrin
Bowen, Ida T.
Brewster, Dr. T. F.
Brewster, Mrs. M. R.
Brown, Mrs. L. M.
Evans, Mrs. Annie C.
Evans, Annie S.
Forbes, Mattie
Hale, Lillie
Hale, William C.
Hall, Mrs. M. F.
Harrison, Mrs. Eliza W.
Hawkins, Lillie
Hayden, Luke F.
Hayden, Mrs. M. Camilla
Hayden, Mattie A.
Haynes, Lillian M.
Hoyt, Bettie E.
Inghram, W. H.
Joice, Jennie J.
Jones, Ruby
Jones, Sarah S.
Kendrick, Mrs. R. L.
Kendrick, Dr. William S.
Kennedy, Charlotte
Langley, Thomas J.
Luckey, Ellen
Luckey, May
Miller, Bessie J.
Miller, Miss Frank
Milner, Willis J.
Morgan, Eglon T.
Murrey, Ira
McLellan, Grace L.
McLellan, Mrs. H: A.
Nesbitt, James T.
Orchard, Eugenia
Orchard, Miss Helen E.
Orchard, Mrs. Helen E.
Orchard, J. Edward
Orr, Cornelia Agnes
Orr, Jennie Joice
Page, Mrs. E. L.
Parkhurst, Mrs. Emma S.
Patterson, Emma D.
Pickard, Fannie L.
Pickard, Katie Helen
Pickard, Lillie B.
Pinson, Lizzie
Quarles, A. H.
Scott, Harriet K.
Stillman, Ellen King
Stillman, King
Stillman, Leona
Stillman, Lowe
Stillman, Mrs. M. E.
Thompson, James R.
Thompson, Mr. & Mrs. L. C.
Thompson, Mrs. Maggie C.
Thompson, Mamie P.
Thornton, Mrs. E. C.
Thornton, James A.
Thornton, Dr. James R.
Thornton, Mollie H.
Wade, Hattie King
Weatherneux, Mrs. D.
Werner, Julius
Willsen, G. B.
Willsen, Hattie

1889

Ackerman, A. K.
Ackerman, Lillie K.
Bell, George K.
Bryan, Mary Jane
Campbell, J. Bulow
Coursen, Virginia Calhoun
Cunningham, Julia
Cunningham, Kate B.
Ebbert, Allen P.
Ebbert, Anna R.
Ebbert, Belle B.
Ebbert, Joshua
Ebbert, Margaret R.
Ebbert, Mrs. Margaret
Evans, Mary
Eve, Robert C.
Finkell, Mr. & Mrs. A. E.
Fisher, Mr. & Mrs. James
Fletcher, Maggie
Foster, Mrs. Marvin
Foster, Samuel L.
Huff, Gertrude T.
Irvin, Mrs. Sallie
Joyner, Kittie
Joyner, Mildred
Joyner, Mrs. Sue
Joyner, Mr. & Mrs. W. H.
Keith, Addie M.
Keith, Charles M. L.
Keith, Elizabeth
Kelly, Maxwell M.
Kennedy, Dr. Luther P.
King, A. S.
King, Laura
Lawrence, Birdie C.
Lawrence, Mrs. L.
Link, J. Allen
Longley, Thomas J.
Lovejoy, Mary
Mallard, Thomas
Miller, F. W.
Moffett, Louis G.
McBride, Mrs. Bell
McBryde, Mrs. Bell
McCarthy, Mrs. E. M.
McCarthy, Lila W.
Peat, Jacob F.
Philpot, Annie
Powell, Mrs. N. Bessie
Rankin, Julia Toombs
Reid, Gertrude C.
Reid, H. M.
Robertson, George
Robinson, Will J.
Russell, Mary Jane
Simmons, Mr. & Mrs. J. C.
Sims, Isaac
Sims, Rebeckah Logan
Smith, Mary Ellen
Smith, Carrie S.
Stall, George
Stephenson, J. T.
Stephenson, Mary G.
Thompson, Mary E.

1890

Ackerman, Belle
Bastrum, Earnest A.
Bastrum, Ella S.
Bell, Margie K.
Bullard, Tallulah Whitner
Calloway, Joseph
Chamberlain, Mrs. Lida W.
Close, Rebecca J.
Cotton, Marvin L.
Dantzlar, Maggie
Davis, Benjamin C.
Davis, Emma J.
Davis, J. Walter
Denman, Mattie P.
Duman, Mattie P.
Emmerson, Lillie
Eve, Martha
Franklin, William T.
Green, Miss Charles Della
Groves, Mrs. R. J.
Hale, Harrison
Hale, Moses A.
Hale, Sue
Hall, W. Stovall
Hamilton, L. E.
Hamilton, Mary
Heard, Isaac T.
Howard, Mattie Cobb
Hoyt, Belle
Hunter, James
Hunter, W. B.
Hyman, W. B.
Inghram, Laura S.
Jefferson, Mollie
Jefferson, Mrs. S. C.
King, Josie
Logan, George W.
Lucus, C. E.
Lumsden, John O.
Lumsden, Maggie
Lumsden, Mary
Lumsden, Mattie
Lunsden, Margarette
Mallard, Clara Jones
Mallard, Thomas
Massey, Mary Calhoun
Milner, Ella V.
Milner, T. C.
McAllister, Mr. & Mrs. W. E.

McCarthy, Maurice, Jr.
Niebuhr, Lewis C.
Ottley, Mr. & Mrs. John K.
Parkhurst, Wm. Francis, Jr.
Pickett, Mattie
Pinkerton, Jane R.
Rushton, Robert E., Jr.
Small, Alexander Felfair
Small, Eliza
Smith, Isaac B.
Thompson, Charlotte
Thompson, Virginia
Tolbot, Mrs. L. B.
Wells, Janie
Wells, Julia R.
Whitlock, Lelia L.
Whitlock, Martin Thomas
Wolf. Lena

1891

Adamson, Margaret H.
Allen, Mrs. E. E.
Allen, Joseph B.
Askew, Bessie
Askew, Laura E.
Askew, Maggie E.
Askew, Mary R.
Askew, Pauline
Askew, Sadie
Askew, Samuel H., Jr.
Askew, Thyrsa S.
Askew, Warren T. I.
Barfield, Anna
Beatie, David Leftwich
Bellingrath, Mary A.
Bradwell, Elizabeth
Bradwell, Pauline E.
Brantly, Brainard
Brantly, Mr. & Mrs. John R.
Brantly, John W.
Brantly, Kate
Brown, Mrs. C. Brownie
Brown, Jacob W.
Calhoun, Indiana
Claiborn, J. H.
Cooney, Martha Stuart
Cooper, Janie F.
Davis, Mr. & Mrs. Edwin D.
Doyle, Ella W.
Doyle, Florence A.
Doyle, John H.
Doyle, Mrs. Nancy W.
Foster, F. O.
Foster, Mary A.
Fowler, W. A.
Grant, Laura Lee
Griffith, Mary B.
Grigsby, Hugh S.
Hale, Anna M.
Haynes, Laura Lee
Hunter, Alice
Hunter, Hugh
Irwin, Julia
Irwin, Col. S. D.
Lake, Frank G.
Leftwich, David
Mabray, Mr. & Mrs. J. S.
Miller, T. C.
Morris, George A.
Morris, Sadie V.
McClelland, Nannie
McDonald, Flora A.
Nesbit, James T.
Nolan, Lucile
Powers, William Horace
Rainey, Mrs. C. V.
Rainey, Charles V.
Rainey, Della
Rainey, Lila
Rainey, T. B.
Rainey, Willis W.
Robinson, Almira Treat
Sawtell, Myrtis
Shannon, Willis
Simpson, Jannie
Smith, Miss Georgia B.
Taylor, Alex S.
Tolbert, Emma D.
Waits, W. A.
Walker, Floyd
Wilson, Mrs. T. G.

1892

Allen, Lola
Atwood, Eliese B.
Badgar, Margaret Fitzzibbon
Beatie, Nellie May
Berkele, Hattie Ann
Berkle, Mary
Block, Lucretia Parker
Boozer, Eleaner D.
Boozer, Dr. J. H.
Calhoun, Ferdinan Phinzee
Carlisle, Annie May
Carlisle, I. Reid
Carlisle, William H.
Clarke, Arthur
Clarke, Burton
Cole, Lucy N.
Cotton, William U.
Culp, Julia E.
Davis, Edwin Raymond
Davis, Rosa Standish
Dayton, Emma F.
Dayton, John C.
Dennis, Maud
Ebbert, Elizabeth
Fraser, Fred C.
Fraser, Irene Virginia
Fraser, Mary
Fraser, Ruth
Garfield, Walter S.
Goodman, Agnes
Gowdy, Musette
Greenlee, Mary
Gunby, Hattie
Hackett, Cora Estelle
Hackett, John Robinson
Hale, Harrison
Hale, Moses A.
Hale, Mrs. Sue
Hall, Mrs. W. Stovall
Hancock, Mary P.
Haynes, W. G.
Helmar, L. Belle
Hulis, John
Hunter, Mr. & Mrs. Benjamin F.
Hunter, India
Hussey, E. M.
Kingsbury, Lulu
Kirk, Henry M.
Knapp, Wilford
Lawrence, Leila S.
Lawrence, Miranda E.
Mabry, Mrs. S. B.
Mallard, Logan L.
Miller, Harriet H.
Morgan, W. A.
Morrow, Imogene H.
McCants, Mary C.
O'Callaghan, John Hollis
Oliphant, James T.
Payne, Annie E.
Payne, Elizabeth A.
Payne, Howard Lansing
Payne, Mary Amelia
Payne, Porter
Poole, Lena
Rawls, Early H.
Richmond, Mrs. J. S.
Ripley, Laura D.
Ripley, Sallie
Rogers, Jennie May
Rushton, Alice Mary
Rushton, Charles E.
Rushton, Willie W.
Ryan, Mrs. Frank T.
Saunders, William Edward
Sawtell, Minnie H.
Sawtell, Thomas R.
Selby, Eliza A.
Selby, J. W.
Shackelford, John
Shackelford, Minnie
Stewart, Addie Ray
Stewart, John Patrick
Stewart, Willie
Stoddart, Ina May
Stokes, Minnie
Strickler, Effie Virginia
Strickler, Janie
Thompson, Lewis
Thompson, Lewis Collin
Van Epps, Amos C.
Van Epps, Lillie
Waddell, Adell S.
Warren, Whittier
Werner, Annie Marie
Werner, Lynn
Whitner, Lida F.
Whittington, Wm. Walter
Wolf, James Jay

1893

Awtry, Ella King
Beaumont, Sarah
Bellingrath, Herman
Blake, Edna P.
Brock, Mrs. H. L.
Bunting, George H.
Bunting, Harry S.
Bunting, R. F.
Burnette, Charles
Burnette, Edner Kerr
Burnette, Jennie S.
Calhoun, Willie J.
Chears, Mary A.

Clarke, Edward John, Jr.
Clarke, Francis West
Clarke, J. Caleb
Denman, George
Derman, Mrs. George
Fain, Marie E.
Fitts, Barton O.
Freeman, Else Lee
Fuller, Laura
Hancock, T. A.
Hawpe, Clarence D.
Hay, B. B.
Helmer, Janie
Hooks, India
Howard, Whitner
Jackson, Cornelia A.
Johnson, Allie
Kinkle, James E.
Kirk, James Edwin
Kirk, John Charles
Kirk, Margaret N.
Kirk, Mary C.
Kirkpatrick, John C., Jr.
Kirkpatrick, Leila Edith
Kirkpatrick, Wallace M.
Martin, Daisy
Mathews, James T.
Miller, John C.
Moore, Mrs. Cornelia A.
Moore, Cornelia J.
McIntire, Mr. & Mrs. James G.
McIntire, Mr. & Mrs. James Warren
McIntire, Mrs. Lon
McIntire, Minnie May
Rankin, Alberta
Rankin, Dalene
Rankin, Eli S.
Rankin, Fannie Lamar
Rankin, Lamar
Rankin, Valeria
Rogers, Mr. & Mrs. James
Runnette, Charles
Runnette, Edner Kerr
Runnette, Mrs. Jennie S.
Runnette, Jessie S.
Shields, D. H.
Shields, Mrs. E. A.
Smith, Daisey Turner
Smith, J. Stovall
Smith, James H.
Smith, Tommie Rubie
Spencer, Frank Burnett
Spencer, Mary P.
Thornton, Jessie
Thornton, Laura
Thornton, Mollie
Trowbridge, Jennie B.
Trowbridge, Henry Treat
Waddell, James D.
West, Ernest E.
Wiselogle, Clara Lucella
Young, Anna I.
Young, Bessie E.
Young, Mrs. Elija C.
Young, Mrs. Samuel
Young, William C.

1894

Adgate, Corra L.
Barth, Frederick Carl, Jr.
Barth, Raimond H.
Bears, Mrs. J. O.
Brown, Mrs. W. W.
Bryan, William L.
Bussey, Salonel McKinley
Chears, William Oliver
Clarke, Julia Beard
Coffin, Isaac G.
Cole, Joseph W.
Corrie, Alma
Corrie, Jennie Louise
Davis, Mary E.
Dennis, Mrs. W. C.
Dillon, Mr. & Mrs. John R.
Everett, Mary C.
Everett, Willis M.
Hale, Annie D.
Halkett, Robert
Hayden, Mrs. M. C.
Hunter, Benjamin T., Jr.
Irwin, Cora Clayton
Johnson, Susan E.
Laird, Alice L.
Laird, Emma A.
Laramore, Birdie B.
Laramore, Mrs. L.
Lind, E. G.
Logan, Margaret Grace
Martin, Isabella
Martin, Samuel
Morgan, David Bruce
Nisbet, James T., Jr.
O'Callaghan, Mary Lyly
Ottley, Charles W.
Pickard, James Donald
Reid, Mr. & Mrs. L. H.
Ryan, Anne Louise
Taylor, Mrs. M. E.
Thornton, Annie Susie
Underwood, Mrs. H. C.
Waddell, Laurie
Wallace, Jennie O.
Weddell, Louise
Wilson, Mrs. B. G.
Woodruff, Mary Louise

1895

Alby, Elizabeth A.
Alexander, Alice Lucile
Alexander, Carrie F.
Alexander, E. F.
Alexander, James H.
Alexander, Mary E.
Alexander, Virginia Ethel
Baker, Miss L. Matilda
Barfield, Frances Eola
Barfield, Fannie
Barfield, Roma Lee
Barfield, Mr. & Mrs. Thomas J.
Barry, Robert Moore
Berry, Maxwell Rufus
Berry, Rigdon
Brooks, John B.
Brooks, Lillie D.
Brownlee, Annie Otelia
Burruss, Frederick W.
Burruss, John Campbell
Burruss, Mary Catherine
Burruss, Mary Ross
Butler, Richard L.
Calaway, Carrie Coleman
Case, Isabella
Clarke, Fannie R.
Clarke, George A.
Cummings, Lula Edwards
Dalrymple, Mary Isabel
Dalrymple, William H.
Ebbert, Frank B.
Ebbert, John M.
Ebbert, Virginia Wright
Field, Minnie A.
Fields, Fannie
Fraser, Wallace J.
Godell, Homer Roscoe
Grant, Ellen Mary
Grant, George W.
Hale, Charles H.
Hale, Mr. & Mrs. Dayton
Hale, John S.
Hale, Lizzie S.
Jackson, Cornelia
Jones, Mrs. W. J.
Keister, W. S.
Kirkman, Thomas Watts
Kirkpatrick, Hugh Wallace
Lamar, Ella G.
Leake, Alphea Beatrice
Leake, Genevine A.
Leake, Mr. & Mrs. George G.
Leake, Paul Edward
Lenmont, John F.
Lenmont, Mrs. M. S.
Marien, Robert T.
Marsh, Mrs. R. B.
Marvin, Robert F.
Mashburn, Mrs. L. E.
Miller, Rachel C.
Moore, Carrie Isabella
Morgan, Emma Estelle
Motes, Eliza S.
Motes, William F.
Orr, R. H.
Payne, Howard Lansing
Richmond, Janie S.
Rushton, Ella B.
Smith, Victor Lamar
Stillman, Mrs.
Stokes, Florence Newton
Tennent, John F.
Tennent, Mrs. M. S.
Torrence, William Clayton
Wallender, Cornelia Milpass
Wilson, Mrs. E. T.
Zanzeroff, Ben Zen

1896

Arnall, Brooke Bunkley
Arwood, Odah
Barry, Andrew Barron
Bell, Amanda E.
Berkelle, Eugene
Blake, Thomas R.
Bosher, Virginia H.
Brownlee, Annie Ottelia
Brownlee, John Marion
Butt, Ella Rose
Butt, James William

Butt, Serena
Calhoun, Lowndes
Calhoun, Susan W.
Clarke, Carrie
Cummings, Lola Edmonds
Cummings, Tabitha E.
Daniel, Joseph P.
Delay, Annie
Dorn, John S.
Fisk, Miss Alice
Frierson, Carroll Reid
Frierson, Mary Lenora
Fry, Fredrick William
Gonzales, Emma W.
Graham, Zeb
Grant, Mr. & Mrs. George W.
Hall, Charlotte
Harry, Otis R.
Hiett, Mrs. G.B.
Hunter, Hattie
Hunter, Vance
Jackson, Florence King
Jones, Janie D.
Jones, Mary Dunwoody
Knapp, Mary Margaret
Lake, Mary Irene
Lamar, Ella G.
Letford, Mrs. William
Letford, Sarah Stewart
Meador, Mary Bell
Milner, Charles Whitner
Mobley, Nancy
Montgomery, Charles D.
Mounce, Whitman L.
Neville, Charlotte E.
Neville, J.E.
Neville, Margaret A.
Nice, A.W.
Pickard, Fannie Durant
Ransom, M.S.
Ransom, Maggie
Reid, Prentice B.
Roberts, Ida Hays
Ryan, Paul
Steffner, John P.
Stillman, Lowe
Stokes, Margarett Grace
Stone, Mrs. Emma
Stone, Frank
Stone, T.T.
Stone, William K.
Thompson, Mary
Troy, Frederick William
Van Epps, Minnie
Werner, Edward A.
Werner, Edward Alfonso
Werner, Florence
Williams, Hettie
Williams, Virginia Coursen
Wood, Nettie

1897

Adams, Miss Covisse
Askew, Warren S.
Boatfield, Sidney S.
Bostwick, Mrs. M.E.
Brooks, Mrs. Baxter
Butler, Miss Abby C.
Butler, Mary S.
Cameron, Mrs. Benjamin H.
Cameron, Mrs. Irene
Causey, Blache M.
Causey, Edward Lewis
Chisholm, Nellie R.
Clayton, Miss Aline
Clayton, Miss Lotta
Delay, Arthur H.
Delay, Hettie Deloach
Dickert, Annie Fuller
Dickert, Jefferson S.
Hardin, Minnie
Hines, Rosemary
Hooker, Fannie Isabell
Hooker, Mary Lizzie
Jones, Edward G.
King, Clyde L.
Kirkpatrick, Miss Myrtis
Knight, Mrs. Edith Nelson
Lake, Mary Irene
Lyhne, Marine
Mabery, Sarah B.
Massey, William C.
Meyers, Miss Annie
Morrow, John S.
Murphy, Miss Augusta H.
Murphy, Mr. & Mrs. George E.
Mynatt, Mrs. Annie R.
McCabe, Mrs. Ellen G.
Nelson, Mrs. Edith
Nunemacher, Mrs. Sallie C.
Nunemacher, Walter C.
Owen, Mary L.
Pierce, Emma May
Reid, Jessie Cecilia
Reid, Miss Willie Kate
Rice, Lucy B.
Scattergood, Mrs. Eliz H.
Scattergood, Miss Nellie H.
Scattergood, Wm. Ballie
Schroeter, Bertha
Schroeter, John Fritz
Schwitzerlet, Ann Marie
Schwitzerlet, E.C.
Steele, James A.
Stone, M.I.
Stone, T.J.
Stout, Rane McWilliam
Stout, Mr. & Mrs. T.E.
Switzerlet, Mrs. Ann Marie
Tickner, Irving L.
Tickner, Mrs. Mary E.
Thompson, Mary
Thompson, Walter C.
Tracy, Mr. & Mrs. W.L.
Tyler, John Bass
Tyler, Mrs. Mattie Elizabeth
Wilby, Eva
Wilby, Guy
Wilby, Mr. & Mrs. R.G.
Williams, Miss Adah
Williams, Mr. & Mrs. G.O.
Williams, Hettie
Williams, Miss Lula E.
Wiselogle, Harry R.
Wood, Mr. & Mrs. W.S.
Wright, Elizabeth
Wynatt, Mrs. Annie R.

1898

Anderson, Louis W.
Arwood, Odah
Bell, Earnest Clark
Bellingrath, Julia Martin
Bellingrath, Henry Leonard
Blount, Marshall Howell
Boatfield, Ellen T.
Boatfield, Jacob S.
Boathwell, George E.
Brown, C.V.
Calhoun, Mary
Calhoun, Nettie Aline
Carlisle, Lallah Rhodes
Coffin, Ida Bowen
Coffin, Walter G.
Cole, William H.
Cummings, T.A.
Dargan, James Thornwell
Dargan, Therese
Deckner, Pauline Emma
Dennis, John H.
Ebahart, Emma A.
Edwards, J.F.
Endicott, Jessie
Force, Anna Lumpkin
Hooker, W.D.
Hunter, R.E.
Jackson, Nattie T.
Johnson, Fannie B.
Johnson, Helen
Johnson, Rockwell W.
Kingsbery, Carrie
Kingsbery, Cleveland
Kingsbery, Edwin
Kolb, Annie P.
Kolb, P. Valentine
Kolb, Roberta
Mallard, Miss Leonora L.
Mann, Jamie Inez
Martin, Mrs. J.A.
Matheson, Gertrude
Melson, Ida
Melson, Marianna
Moore, Stonewall
Paden, Millie Melida
Patterson, Ada H.
Payne, Emma
Reed, Henry N.
Reynolds, Eva May
Robinson, Esther B.
Robinson, John B.
Robinson, Mary Platt
Rogers, Lucia L.
Sinclair, Edward McQueen
Sinclair, Mrs. J.W.
Stewart, Dollie
Stewart, Libbie Martin
Stewart, Zula Zelena
Stone, Charles Fredrick
Tidwell, Cleo S.
Tidwell, William D.
Tillander, Boyd
Tillander, Lewis
Tillander, Stonewall Moore
Watts, Millie M.
Webb, Anna Lula
Werner, Ray Coles
West, Mr. & Mrs. John A.
Woolf, Henry Ashby
Wright, George P.
Wright, Mrs. Stephen H.

A winning team in 1934

1899

Allen, Hubert L.
Allen, Mamie Baker Marcia
Boinest, Inez Lucile
Bothwell, Annie Belle
Brazwell, Millie
Butler, Aron G.
Butler, Edna I.
Butler, Lillie D.
Butler, Margaret D.
Calhoun, William Lowndes
Campbell, Mary K.
Cassen, Georgia Agnes
Chappelle, George
Chappelle, Nellie
Chunn, Rebecca O.
Dunlap, Arthur John
Dunlap, Edith
Dunlap, Mrs. M.E.
Dunlap, Minnie Margaret
Dunlap, William H.
Erwin, Mrs. Allie M.
Farrie, Laura Cordelia
Forbes, Evan Howell
Gayle, Margaret
Harris, Mrs. Sarah
Haselkus, Addie
Hawley, Ema C.
Hawley, John L.
Hay, Rose E.
Hay, Sarah Amelia
Helmer, Lillian
Herren, Alice N.
Herren, Katie Lee E.
Herren, Mollie May
Herren, Sara Amatha
House, Mary Ella
House, Thomas Frank
Hudson, Mrs. E.G.
Irvise, Allie M.
Kendrick, George F.
King, Mary Etheleen
Latimer, Alice
Latimer, Thomas
Lauren, Edness C.
Lauren, Mrs. Elizabeth
Lauren, Hester L.
Lauren, Minnie E.
Lauren, Thomas M.
Mann, Mrs. Robert
Mann, Robert C.
Mason, Mr. & Mrs. C.B.
Miller, Thornton Parker
Milner, Mary Etheleen
McLendon, Katie
McMasters, Anna
McMillan, Garnett
Neal, Mrs. E.G.
Parker, Mrs. Joseph H.
Pickard, John F.
Pittman, Mary
Porter, Fannie T.
Redding, Jessie
Saunders, Harry Graham
Sharp, Augustus N.
Sharp, Mr. & Mrs. B.S.
Sharp, Mary E.
Shelton, Polly
Shelton, Winniefred M.
Smith, Fred B.
Smith, Mrs. G.V.
Smith, J. Bruce
Stillman, Birdie
Stout, Martha A.
Thompson, Augustus
Thompson, Katie
Tilander, C.G.
Tilander, C.M.
Trobridge, Kenneth Miller
Tucker, William S.
Wells, Malvern Hill
Wells, Stella Bledsoe
West, Clifford
West, Lillie
Wetmere, Annie L.
Winn, Cornelia V.
Winn, J.P.
Wolf, Bernard P.
Wolff, Mrs. W.B.
Wooding, Jennie
Wright, Wade Hampton

1900

Barth, Alfred L.
Baxter, Bessie W.
Baxter, Mr. & Mrs. Thomas W.
Beasley, Alice May
Beasley, William L.
Blanton, Maggie
Broome, Lillian Z.
Brown, Annie
Brown, John
Bryam, Roundtace

THE PEOPLE WHO STAYED (1858-1978)

Burruss, Mrs. B.H.
Caldwell, Lucy
Caldwell, Rebecca
Cooney, Anna G.
Corrie, Eugene
Corrie, Jennie
Corrie, Marion
Cotton, Evelyn
Cotton, Mamie
Cumming, Miss Derrell McK.
Davidson, Lavancia
Dean, Mrs. S.M.
Deckner, James J.
Deckner, Josephine I.
Erwin, Annie
Erwin, James L.M.
Farmer, Essie May
Farmer, William T.
Farris, Mrs. Edwin D.
Ferris, Ethel Rebecca
Gramling, Stella Lois
Grigsby, Mr. & Mrs. Hugh S.
Hill, Katie Mustin
Hill, Sallie Mustin
Hodnett, Amrose W.
Hodnett, Alma Lois
Hodnett, Ella
Hodnett, Ethel
Hook, Annie
Hook, Catherine
Hook, Clarence L.
Hudson, Marion A.
Jacks, Carrie Lou
Jeffreys, Mrs. E.L.
Johnson, Frank Gilbert
Kendrick, Mary
King, Ophelia G.
Kirby, Alton Raymond
Kirk, Rose Lovell
Laird, Anna E.
Lawhon, Mrs. J.L.
Logan, Margarett Grace
Mangun, S.
Miller, John
Miller, Lillie N.
Milner, B. Charles
Murrell, Mr. & Mrs. J.W.
Mustin, Katie
Mynatt, Joseph L.
McGaw, Mrs. D.E.
O'Neal, Claudia
Peel, Miss Edie
Pellew, Marion Carter
Pittman, Nellie Florence
Roberts, Gertrude
Roberts, Jettie G.
Roberts, Mr. & Mrs. T.H.
Robinson, Blanche B.
Sattergood, Nellie
Sattergood, Mrs. W.B.
Selby, Gerald
Sharpe, Elizabeth
Stewart, Addie
Stewart, Willie
Stone, Annie Lucile
Stout, Margarett O.
Stuart, Agnes M.
Stuart, Mrs. J.H.
Swase, Mrs. John
Thomas, Fannie
Trader, Charles F.
Tucker, William John
Williams, Isaac
Wilmar, B. Charles
Wilson, Green
Wright, Lucey

1901

Abernathy, Eva Rubie
Ashe, Rufus R.
Bobo, Mrs. Roberta H.
Brice, Helen
Carmichael, Mr. & Mrs. L.R.
Cartledge, Dr. E.C.
Cartledge, Hattie
Cartledge, May
Chappelle, Clara Barton
Clayton, Edwin M.
Clayton, Lillie P.
Cole, Mrs. Dottie
Cotton, Mrs. Lucy Whisenant
Crenshaw, Mrs. R.L.
Crow, Nettie Lee
Davis, Eva Osgood
Denson, Ettie
Denson, Joseph A.
Dickert, Etoile
Dickert, Miss Ray
Ebbert, Nellie Q.E.
Evans, Martha J.
Everett, Mary C.
Everett, Willis M.
Farrar, Abraham
Finley, Ada
Freeman, Annie
Greenlee, Ethel
Greenlee, Henry C.
Gunter, Gippie Beatrice
Harper, R.T.
Jackson, Eunice Almentine
Jackson, Sue Thompson
Jackson, Wallace McPherson
Jeffreys, Katie
Jenkins, Annette
Johnson, Laura H.
Kadel, Dottie Cole
Kemp, Mary E.
Knapp, John Crosby
Knox, Mr. & Mrs. Samuel M.
Langford, Ralph
Leake, George Gunnnels
Leas, Mr. & Mrs. J.E.
Lee, Elizabeth G.
Lee, Mr. & Mrs. John W.
Lindorme, Annie Maude
Marsh, Katie Gowdy
Marsh, R.B.
Melvin, Florence P.
Melvin, James A.
Miller, Eva
Miller, James Trimble
Milner, Willis Justus
Morris, Ella M.
Morris, Hattie
Morris, Margie
Morris, Marion
Morris, S.L., Jr.
McKinley, John E.
O'Neal, J.W.
Overby, T.H.
Reid, John C.
Rutledge, Anna L.
Rutledge, O.P.
Seabrook, Nannie L.
Smith, Bertha Irene
Smoak, Eugenia S.
Smoak, Rudolph
Thompson, Belle Simpson
Tygart, Algia
Wallace, Tom Lyan
Watson, Mrs. Rob Ray
Whisenant, Lucy
Whitner, Mr. & Mrs. Thomas Cobb
Wood, Marion Morris
Wright, Miss M.G.
Young, Susan B.

1902

Dickson, Mrs. Juliette Clayton
Leake, George G.
Smith, Hattie Lee
Tygart, Algia

1903

Cloud, Elizabeth
Cloud, Joel
Cloud, Mr. & Mrs. O.L.
Dallas, Mrs. G.J.
Edmondson, Mrs. Charles J.
Foster, Mrs. J.H.
Fuller, Robbie P.
Hanifan, David L.
Mallard, John L.
Mallard, Virginia Ebbert
McIntyre, Mrs. Ferdinande R.
Reed, J.C.
Seymour, Mrs. H.A.
Van Fischt, Mrs. Kate C.
Whitner, Miss Lidie

1904

Anderson, Jennie
Barry, Mrs. John L.
Calhoun, Harriett Hays
Campbell, Mrs. J. Bulow
Elder, Mrs. Leila J.
Fraser, S. Alex
Hearn, Mary Charlotte
Hearn, Orena Bell
Hodnett, Mrs. A.W.
Kemp, Pearl Marinda
McDowell, Edwin K.
Rodgers, Mrs. M.E.
Rodgers, Woods White
Scully, Mrs. Lula Wright
Smith, Mr. & Mrs. Lucius E.
Wingo, Alice Logan
Wingo, Mrs. Ida

1905

Asenath, Miss Willie
Brice, Mabel C.
Brice, Walter
Carson, Marietta M.
Carson, Samuel M.
Chase, Effie Lorena
Chase, Lela Beusell
Claiborne, J.H.

Crouch, Mrs. Blanch
Fain, Miss Maria E.
Farris, Edwin D.
Farris, Ida May
Farris, Laura C.
Farrow, Col. H.P.
Frierson, T.A.
Frierson, Thomas Raymond
Hale, Lilly W.
Jenkins, Jim C.
Jenkins, Mrs. M.C.
Kemp, Fannie E.
Kennedy, Mr. & Mrs. W.H.
Mangun, Mr. & Mrs. S.
Meoos, Terry M.
Mizzell, William C., Jr.
Moncrieft, Charles
Morris, Miss Willie A.
McMillan, Mrs. Garnett
Nottingham, Stonewall J.
Pike, Harry Hale
Plummer, Bertha Estelle
Rainey, Mr. & Mrs. C.V.
Redus, Catherine A.
Scott, Robert B.
Shann, Miss M.E.
Spencer, W.A.
Stevenson, Shelton J.
Stokes, Mr. & Mrs. C.A.
Stokes, Florence
Stokes, Julia
Stokes, Margrethe
Stokes, Minnie
Stokes, W.F.
Sutton, Bessie Smith
Thompson, Jeff
Webb, Lucy
Wilson, Alexander E.
Woodruff, Frank L.
Worther, Mrs. I.E.
Worther, Mable
Worther, Jennie

1906

Allen, A.A.
Badger, Allison Louise
Baird, Henry Stewart
Baird, Mary Louise
Baldwin,Mary E.
Barnett, Albert N.
Brice, Mable
Brice, Walter
Brown, Mr. & Mrs. Frank S.
Buchanan, Kathleen
Burrus, Anna E.
Butt, Cecil Gasson
Calhoun, Wm. Dabney
Candler, Mattie Claude
Clayton, George Wharton
Cone, W.D.
Cook, Jesse Burns
Cook, Kate Jeffrey
Courtney, Faith Russell
Croft, George N., Jr.
Croll, Witt
Crusoe, Mr. & Mrs. R.D.
Dickson, Mrs. J.M.
Dickson, Thomas C.
Eckford, Burges West
Eckford, Mrs. William
Eckford, Mrs. William H.
Elder, Thomas G.
Evans, Minnie Owen
Fiel, Josephine
Fraser, Addie Matilda
Fraser, Gussie Louise
Fraser, James Martin
Fraser, William Farrow
Frazier, Mrs. V.K.
Fuller, Mrs. Cami
Green, Alice Coffin
Green, Hattie
Green, Mr. & Mrs. J.E.
Greene, Frank Harrison
Hardin, Lucile
Harper, Corinne Louise
Hart, Mildred May
Jackson, Evelene Bozeman
Jackson, Mrs. Marion
Jones, William Percy
Kilpatrick, Harry Thomas
Kilpatrick, Hollis William
Kirkpatrick, H.W.
Knott, Mrs. E.L.
Knott, Edward Lee
Lynch, Laura Geraldine
Lynch, Nora Aline
Mable, Robert
Martin, James
Mathews, Carolyn C.
Mathews, Catherine M.
Mathews, Clara W.
Mathews, James T.
Mitchell, Mrs. Guy
Mock, Emma Gertrude
Moore, Miller Nesbit
Morgan, Miss Claude LeRoy
Morgan, Myrtis Beatie
McIntire, Minnie M.
Neely, Claude B.
Neely, George
Neely, Mrs. N.O.
Overby, Mammie F.
Palmer, Effie
Perkins, William Dearing
Price Mamie
Rawson, Julia
Rigutte, Emily
Ringer, Marvin G.
Ryan, Frank T.
Scully, Ruth Elizabeth
Sharpstein, Hannah M.
Shear, J.O., Jr.
Skillman, Mr. & Mrs. C.M.
Smith, George Thomas
Smith, Harry M.
Smith, Sarah Falconer
Smith, Mr. & Mrs. W.F.
Stanford, Earnest
Stone, Mrs. Fred
Straus, Lena Bell
Strauss, Nellie
Thompson, Charles
Thompson, Charlotte M.
Thompson, Ira
Thompson, Jeff
Thompson, Mr. & Mrs. R. Charles
Thompson, William Wardlaw
Tomlinson, Stella
Vawter, Bessie Louise
Wallace, Emma R.
Wallace, Charles B.
Watson, Kenneth
Wells, Frances Colzy
Wilt, Mr. & Mrs. R.W.
Whitehead, Fred
Whitner, John A.
Whitner, Lidie F.
Williamson, Mrs. Georgia M.
Wiselogle, Charles Roy

1907

Anderson, Benjamin A.
Anderson, Mr. & Mrs. R.G.
Anderson, Robert Bruce
Armistead, Annie
Armistead, Ethel
Armstrong, Adron
Armstrong, L.A.
Bachman, Ida May
Berkele, John
Califf, Mr. & Mrs. J.G.
Campbell, Sarah
Cole, Laura Haygood
Cooper, Kate Scales
Crossing, Elizabeth
Dunwoody, Kessie
Easterwood, Alice
Fowler, Bessie
Fowler, Clara May
Fowler, Lula
Fowler, Mrs. R.C.
Fowler, Mr. & Mrs. W.C.
Goodrich, Mr. & Mrs. D.S.
Harvey, Orville R.
Hodges, John L.
Jansen, Pearl
Jones, Mrs. Edward G.
Knox, Maud
Knox, Roscoe C.
Lynch, Martha Eliz
Milner, Bessie G.
Milner, Clifford Glen
Milner, James F.
Milner, Jessie A.
Milner, Lula A.
Milner, Nellie J.
Munger, Charles H.
Muse, Bell
Muse, Joseph K.
Muse, Keith Bassett
McAllister, Mr. & Mrs. D.B.
McCulloch, R.W.
Parker, Mrs.Augusta
Parker, Edward Cabell
Patrick, Mr. & Mrs. P.H.
Pratt, Miss Willie S.
Reid, Dr. & Mrs. Louis H.
Ripley, Laura Katherine
Ripley, Mattie Bell
Sharp, Mr. & Mrs. Henry M.
Skillman, Dorothy Witham
Stewart, Mrs. Dollie
Stewart, Dovie M.
Stewart, Levie M.
Stewart, Nina C.
Stewart, Zula Z.
Telford, John Alexander
Thompson, C.P.
Thompson, Mr. & Mrs. E.H.
Thompson, W.C.

Ward, John L.
Waters, Willie Kate
Weddell, Laurie
Weddell, Reid
Wenner, Mollie A.
Whitner, James Ticheanor

1908

Barfield, Alonzo A.
Beem, Carlton Elmer
Beem, Jessie Ureta
Beem, Stanley
Boyd, Jennie Louise
Brown, Dr. Paul F., Jr.
Brown, Roberta
Bruce, Etoile Deckert
Califf, Carrie Bell
Campbell, Mrs. C.H.
Campbell, Eudora L.
Cleckler, Benjamin Davis
Coffin, Grace Bowen
Coleman, Eleanor Preston
Davis, William B.
Dean, Lucius
Dickert, Majorie Dolores
Duncan, William
Dupree, Julius Worcester
Esterlin, John W.
Farris, Ida Mae
Fife, Herschel A.
Finch, Daisy
Hart, Joseph M.
Harville, Mamie B.
Hayney, Mrs. Eudora Campbell
Holland, Mr. & Mrs. W.W.
Jackson, Floyd Brewer
Jones, Ray Rogers
Kendrick, George F.
Kendrick, Miss M. Agnes
Kendrick, Mary E.
Kendrick, Miss P. Lucile
King, Irene Tift
Lambdin, Barbara
Lambdin, Mary
Marsh, Mrs. Elizabeth
Marsh, John
Milner, Carl
Milner, Spann Whitner
Moore, Walter T.
Morgan, Mrs. David Bruce
Murrell, Mr. & Mrs. John M.
McCallie, Samuel W.M.
McConaughy, Hazel Bruce
McCord, Isabelle
McGaughy, Georgia Eulalia
McIlwain, W.F.
McManus, Lucy May
Norris, Mr. & Mrs.W.E.
Orr, Alma Elizabeth
Owen, Mrs. C.M.
Patton, W.H.
Pavitt, George T.
Rhodes, John E.
Rice, Jimmie
Rice, Mary P.
Rice, Meta
Robinson, Louis D.
Savage, Anna R.
Sawtell, Annie E.
Sawtell, Mrs. E.N.
Sawtell, Mary F.
Saxe, George Henry
Seary, Charles D.
Spurlock, Exonia
Stillman, Sara Lois
Strickland, Daisy Allen
Strickland, Mrs. T.L.
Taggart, Mr. & Mrs. A.D.
Warner, Lewis Stanley
Waters, Ella Agnes
Waters, George Maro
Williams, Emory Colquitt
Williamson, Steven Douglas
Womack, Lewis M.
Wood, Mrs. Beulah
Woodruff, Jennie Towns

1909

Aiken, Ellison
Aiken, Janet
Allen, George Earle
Austin, Mrs. D.H.
Axon, Randolph K.
Baker, Ida C.
Baker, William O.
Barmettler, Caroline
Barmettler, Marie
Beam, Mrs. M.E.
Beam, Maud B.
Bird, J.H.
Boer, Annie E.
Brazell, Hettie
Brazell, Jennie Smith
Brock, Annie E.
Campbell, Harry Crumb
Carson, Mrs. Sam M.
Cassels, Clare Scott
Cook, Rosemary M.
Corley, Samantha Thomas
Craig, Arthur Alexander
Craig, Mary Jordan
Craig, Milton Scott
Darst, John
Davis, Herbert Charles
Dickerson, J.E.
Duff, Martha A.
Eckford, George Adair
Elliott, Annie Kennedy
Elliott, Olivia
England, James Richie
England, Mattie
Ervin, Ruth Elizabeth
Feebeck, Mary
Finley, Thomas R.
Floding, Elizabeth
Floding, Mary
Floding, W.E.
Franks, Joseph
Freeman, Mary Ella
Frieson, Dr. Karl
Fuller, Claudine J.
Gillispey, Alice A.
Gillispey, Fannie B.
Gillispey, James
Gillispey, Laura K.
Godhe, Max A.
Haiston, William
Herren. Miss Neal
Humphries, Mrs. W.F.
Jansen, Walter R.
Jones, William Robert
Knight, Lucien L.
Kyle, F.T.
Kyler, Mr. & Mrs. T.T.
Land, Eva Elizabeth
Lane, Mary Bun
Lord, Claude
Lyle, Ophelia
Mann, David M.
Mann, Emma Rea
Martin, Annie Laurie
Meacham, Ethel Vera
Milt, Miss HenryEtter
Milt, Mary Lewis
Moore, Lena
McCalley, William L.
McClelland, Cora L.
McClelland, J.E.
McClelland, John Spence
McCulloch, Mrs. R.M.
Ogden, Dunbar Hunt, Jr.
Ogden, Eliza
Ogden, Grace Augusta
Ogden, Margaret TenEyck
Ogden, Warren Cox
Palmer, Leila Savannah
Peterson, J.T.
Rawson, H.T.
Ross, Herbert G.
Sams, Herbert Charles
Sams, Mrs. M.H.
Saxe, Mrs. George Henry
Scott, Carrie Irvine
Simmons, T.H.
Skinner, Alvin E.
Skinner, Anna Corine
Skinner, Eugenia C.
Smith, Marion
Spurlock, Buford Custus
Sykes, Anna Murdock
Tompkins, Mrs. E.E.
Townsend, Essie Leona
Tuggle, Gertrude Adelaide
Warner, Annie Kennedy
Warner, Nellie
Wells, Marian
West, Mr. & Mrs. Edward H.
West, Mary Madison
White, Mrs. A.A.
White, Albert Matthews
White, Lucile O'Neill
White, Mrs. S.O.
Whitley, Benjamin Morris
Willis, Mrs. A.D.
Willis, Albert D.
Wilt, Henry Etta
Wilt, Mary Lewis
Wright, Walter

1910

Addy, Mrs. J. Alton
Akin, Janet Acie
Anderson, Mr. & Mrs. D.J.
Anderson, May Belle
Axson, Allthea S.
Axson, Carrie Bell
Barfield, Mr. & Mrs. T.J.

THE

SOUTHERN HOUSEKEEPER,

A BOOK OF TESTED RECIPES,

COLLECTED BY THE HOME DEPARTMENT OF THE LADIES' MISSIONARY SOCIETY OF THE CENTRAL PRESBYTERIAN CHURCH, ATLANTA, GA.

MRS. J. N. FAIN, President.
MISS COOIE SLOAN, Vice-President.
MISS BELLE KENNEDY, Secretary.
MRS. JAMES G. McINTIRE, Treasurer.

"The turnpike road to people's hearts, I find,
Lies thro' their mouths, or I mistake mankind."

ATLANTA, GA.
THE FRANKLIN PRINTING AND PUBLISHING CO.
1898.

Barnard, James Devant
Beatie, George
Blackman, Ruth Esther
Burton, Mr. & Mrs. C.H.
Campbell, Lula Groves
Candler, Caroline Grantland
Candler, Myrtis Long
Carlisle, William Rhodes
Cartledge, Carl
Cartledge, Kate
Cavanagh, Mattie
Chapman, Benjamin Hill
Childs, Rebecca B.
Christian, Philip D.
Clapp, Mr. & Mrs. M.G.
Clark, Richard Norman
Clayton, Bessie Harris
Clayton, T.A., Jr.
Cook, Gordon Woods
Cooper, Mrs. Garland
Craig, Edward
Craig, James
Craig, James G.
Craig, Mamie
Craig, Mrs. Willie
Crawford, Mrs. Hugh
Croft, G.E.
Crosland, William A.
Daniel, Mrs. C.B.
Davis, F. Carl
DeLorne, J.E.
Dishron, Oma
Draper, George Albert
Dryman, Estell
Dumas, Miss Dallas C.
Faison, Thomas
Falks, James H.
Falks, Louise B.
Farrar, Jennie
Faust, Conrad Emil
Faust, Gus Harry
Faust, Ormond Emil
Ferris, Florence
Fife, James Alexander
Galloway, J.F.
Gato, Mrs. E.H.
Gay, Frank
Gay, Sara Thrash
Gentry, Maggie
Gentry, Mollie
Gilleland, Mrs. A.J.
Gillespy, Mr. & Mrs. E.H.
Goforth, Elizabeth
Gothe, Max A.
Grace, Amanda E.
Grace, Mary
Grace, Thomas
Happoldt, Mrs. F.A.
Harkins, Clara
Harris, Mrs. R.H.
Harvin, Carlton J.
Hay, Margaret Willis
Hayes, Eva Wilby
Haynes, Carrie Belle
Haynes, George Albert D.
Haynes, Maude Zwilla
Hodnett, Mr. & Mrs. Ambrose W.
Huffman, Hill Robert
Hunt, Eloise Clayton
Hunter, Elizabeth H.
Huse, Mr. & Mrs. F.E.
Langford, Catherine
Langford, James
Langford, Jennie A.
Langford, John
Langford, John Shalor
Langford, Thomas
Lanier, Annie Ames
Lanier, James Sykes
Little, Charlie
Little, Mae
Little, Margaret
Little, Mary
Little, T.M.
MacDonald, Clarence E.
MacDonald, Mr. & Mrs. Herbert
MacDonald, James Duncan
Maclean, Joseph
Meadows, Mrs. L. Belle
Meadows, Mary Belle
Milner, Benjamin C.
Milner, Bessie Grace
Milner, Mrs. Willie J.
Murray, Lena
Murray, Nellie Ruth
Murray, Stewart
McCrea, Thomas H.
McLain, James
Oliver, Cassie Lee
Pearce, Wilbur Young
Pierce, Mrs. L.M.
Russell, Agnes A.
Sawtell, Laura
Saye, Mr. & Mrs. Edward D.
Saye, Sarah
Schofield, Mr. & Mrs. Joshua F.
Setze, Elizabeth Waddell
Setze, Mr. & Mrs. Eugene J.
Setze, Henry
Skinner, Gustavus H.
Slaton, Cassie Battle
Smith, Alice
Smith, Gladys
Smith, Mr. & Mrs. Shelby
Sparks, Martha McClary
Sparks, Robert Ludlow
Steed, Florence
Stout, Mr. & Mrs. Erskine
Stout, Mrs. S.V.D.
Tribble, Cora May
Upshaw, Beulah
Waldroop, L.S.
Wallace, Alexander W.
Wallace, Bruce W.
Wallace, Lawrence E.
Wallace, Mr. & Mrs. Leroy E.
Wallace, Robert Owen
Walters, John D.
Warner, A.W.
Warner, Ila
Warner, Jennie
Whitner, Martha Cobb
Willis, Mr. & Mrs. A.D.
Wilson, Eva Burns
Wolpert, Susie Lenora
Wooten, Mr. & Mrs. W.F.
Wright, Frances R.
Zealey, Mrs. E.O.

1911

Addy, J. Alton
Ashmore, Maude
Ayers, F.P.
Bailey, Willie E.
Bansley, Mr. & Mrs. John David
Barfield, Mrs. Clyde C.
Barry, Andrew B.
Baxter, Sallie Grace
Beatie, Katherine C.
Block, Mrs. E. Bates
Bradley, Amanda J.
Bradley, Laurence M.
Bradshaw, Hattie Bernice
Bradshaw, J. Austin
Bray, H.E.
Brown, Nina Harbin
Buchanan, H.S.
Buford, Evelyn
Buford, Frances Gordon
Buford, Mrs. G.R.
Buford, Gaston Reedy
Buford, James Leslie
Caldwell, Edward Lee
Calhoun, Hugh William
Calhoun, James E.
Cantrell, Mr. & Mrs. E.M.
Carlisle, Isaac Reid
Carlisle, Mrs. M.L.
Cason, Eunis Gilleland
Castles, Anna
Chaffer, Roland F.
Clapp, Mary Helen
Cox, Albert T.
Cox, Minnie Belle
Crawford, Mrs. T.J.
Davis, Lucile
Durham, Frederick Forbes
Elder, Marie Elizabeth
Erwin, Pope B.
Faison, Mr. & Mrs. H.L.
Feebeen, Bessie
Fife, Mause Taylor
Fowler, Lois Angeline
Gean, Mrs. M.L.
Glover, Alice Elizabeth
Greer, Lillian
Griffin, Mrs. C.C.
Grimm, Miss S.S.
Guinn, Mrs. E.S.
Haile, James Ernest
Haynie, Harold C.
Heath, Kate
Henderson, Mrs. E.M.
Hewey, Mrs. H.L.
Hogan, J.D.
Hunter, George H.
Hunter, Maggie
Inglis, George
Ingram, Gertrude C.
Ivey, Annie
Ivey, Maggie
Jervey, Charles
Jervey, Louis
Jervey, Minnie P.
Johnson, Edith Littell
Johnson, William Carlisle
Jones, Maggie

Jordan, Margaretta N.
King, Barrington
Maclegan, R.W.
Mallett, Miss L.
Martin, Mrs. M.A.
Meadows, Walter Harmon
Milner, Charles Whitner
Murry, Mr. & Mrs. J.B.
McCord, Robert B.
McCrea, Martha
McKee, Mary Elizabeth
McLeod, Ada Julia F.
McManus, Edith
McRae, Margaret Marion
Norris, Nancy
Nudrack, Edith N.
Ogden, Dunbar Hunt, Jr.
Ogden, Frederick Wm.
Ogden, Grace Augusta
Overby, Ruby Francis
Palmer, Virgie Lee
Pfaflin, Helen V.
Pollard, Gertrude
Pratt, Mrs. E.C.
Reid, J. Gilmer
Reid, Louise Andrews
Reivers, Mrs. George
Reynolds, Jennie
Rhodes, Boswell B.
Rhodes, Dean
Rhodes, Flora
Rhodes, Harris
Rhodes, Mr. & Mrs. J.F.
Rhodes, Joel Carl
Risse, Robert Wm.
Robinson, Cedrie B.
Sawtell, Estelle E.
Smith, William Murdoch
Stanley, May
Stowe, Mr. & Mrs. E.
Stanley, Florence B.
Thompson, Beatrice
Thompson, Rebecca S.
Todd, Roberta H.
Todd, Victor F.
Tribble, Katie
Tutwiler, Lilian
Tutwiler, Mary
Veazey, Kizzie K.
Walker, Eugene Julian
Walker, Mary Lucy
Wallace, Nellie
Weatherford, Mollie
Welch, Hattie A.
Wells, Esom Albert
Whitmire, Overdown
Williams, Effie Laura
Williams, Victoria C.
Williamson, J.D.
Wilson, Benton C.
Wilson, Ella
Wilson, Sidney Meyers

1912

Adolphus, George M.
Alexander, Herbert C.
Allen, Florence C.
Allen, James D.
Allen, Samuel Arthur
Anderson, Mary E.
Anderson, Sarah B.
Armistead, Frank
Bailey, Ethel Louise
Baldwin, Isabelle
Baldwin, Margaret
Barford, A. Malcolm
Barford, Mrs. F.R.
Barton, Julia May
Bell, Agnes
Bell, Elizabeth
Bell, Irene Lupo
Bell, Mr. & Mrs. Wm., Jr.
Bentley, Francis Evelyn
Born, Gladys Margaret
Bray, Gladys
Brice, Katherine
Briggs, Sarah
Brown, Mrs. Brownie
Brown, Mr. & Mrs. Jacob W.
Brown, Mildred
Busha, Mr. & Mrs. Wm. E.
Caldwell, James N., Jr.
Caldwell, Pearl
Cason, Benjamin Hill
Cheny, M.E.
Davidson, Florence
Davis, Vera Edwina
de Graffenreid, Mamie
Farr, Belle
Ferguson, Mrs. H.A.
Ferguson, Nellie
Greene, Florence Anna
Greelee, Helen
Grinnell, Mrs. Clifford B.
Hall, Jennie
Hall, Mae
Heath, Kate
Henderson, Bessie
Hill, James J.
Hill, William J.
Holloway, Edna Augusta
Jackson, Henry
Jenkins, Adelaide
Jenkins, Charles
Jenkins, Mrs. E.D.
Jenkins, Elberta
Jenkins, Grace
Johnson, Gussie
Johnson, Nora Lula
Jones, Mattie E.
Kaiser, Ruth Brantley W.
Kemp, William M.
Kennett, Mrs. Winfield Scott
Kirby, Eleanor N.
Leslie, Newton
Lewis, J.M.
Massond, Phillip Abi
Mayes, Mrs. Clyde
Morgan, Catherine
Morrison, John E.
McFadden, Laness
McManus, Corrie
Nelson, Lillian Othello
Paddison, A.H.
Parker, Effie Williams
Pendergrast, John B.
Phillips, Thelma
Pope, Walker
Procter, James E.
Procter, Maud
Reeves, Cecil Frederick
Reynolds, Mary
Richey, Jennie Lou
Robinson, Annie
Russell, J.K.
Scully, Annie
Shafer, Frank B.
Shehe, Clara Margaret
Shehe, Mr. & Mrs. L.W.
Tennent, Mrs. W.C.
Tennent, Thomas Hill
Thompson, Alfred Henry
Thompson, Fain
Thompson, Lyda Alexander
Thompson, Robert Charles
Thornton, Elbert L.
Thornton, Lillian W.
Underwood, Charlotte
Walker, Mr. & Mrs. T. Arthur
Walton, Katherine
Wardlaw, James T.
Wells, Susie A.
Whitner, Joseph
Wilson, Annie Maud
Wilson, Miss C.E.
Woods, M.J.
Yekel, Rebecca
Ziegler, Mollie R.

1913

Aiken, Annie
Alexander, Mrs. Elizabeth
Allen, Isabel McRae
Bailey, Henry Alfred
Bailey, Loy Park
Baldwin, Joseph Alexander
Barford, Carey Alexander
Boggs, Ethel
Breedlove, E.G.
Breedlove, Leona Keith
Bridger, Fawn
Bridges, Frank
Brock, Carolyn
Brown, Mrs. Alexander B.
Brown, Alexander Booth
Buford, Frances Gordon
Carmichael, Trel Marion
Carpenter, Edith
Chapman, Nellie Idelle
Chears, Wm. Oliver
Cleckler, Mrs. B.D.
Cochran, Annie
Copock, John William
Cox, Mr. & Mrs. Brooker J.
Cox, Charlie
Cox, Kate Russell
Cox, Mary Claire
Cummins, Mr. & Mrs. Alexander
Cummins, Mary Jessie
Curlee, Mrs. C.B.
Davidson, Newton Edward
Davis, Mr. & Mrs. Arthur O.
De Mars, Mr. & Mrs. J.E.
Dement, Emille Walker
Dement, Robert Lee
Dickert, Gladys Marie
Elder, Lucy
Erny, Annie Mary

Frierson, Mary E.
Gardner, Mr. & Mrs. Wm. G.
Gartrell, Sarah Elizabeth
Gibson, Mrs. J.T.
Gilmer, J.I.
Giltner, Martha Isabel
Goodrich, Mr. & Mrs. David S.
Goodrich, Emma Coyle
Goodrich, Mary
Greenlea, Harold R.
Grimm, Mabel
Hall, Isabell
Heery, Mr. & Mrs. Clarence
Hogan, William Joseph, Jr.
Hollingsworth, A.N.
Humphries, Clinton B.
Hunt, Annie Barnard
Hurst, Nellie
Jackson, Evelyn Parson
Johnson, Emma
Johnson, Miss Haydee
Jordan, Mrs. H.B.
Jordan, Maggie Virginia
Jordan, Nannie Leona
Keith, Mr. & Mrs. Charles
Keith, Charlotte May
Keith, Julian M.
Killiam, T.D.
Lake, Frank Greer, Jr.
Lindsay, Howard Lamar
Lindsay, Mr. & Mrs. I.H.
Lindsay, Tyler Bruce
Lipscomb, Mrs. S.V.
Lockhart, Elizabeth
Lockhart, Helen
Lockhart, Mr. & Mrs. Malcom
Marshall, Lucile
Martin, William Henry
Matthews, Anna W.
Matthews, Julia
May, E.L.
Merony, Lula
Miller, Helen Evelyne
Miller, Dr. O.L.
Moore, Louis Francis
Mum, Arthur Neill
Mum, George Clarence
Murray, Grace B.
McAnliffe, Mary L.
McConnell, Julia
McConnell, Mary
McGaughy, George W.
McIntosh, E.P.
McIntosh, Irene Burns
Nollen, Fram
Ogden, Warren Cox
Paniello, Mr. & Mrs. Santiago
Pinkston, Helen Isabel
Pinkston, Mrs. M.A.
Proctor, Annie Johnston
Proctor, E.B.
Ransome, Mrs. G.F.
Rice, Mr. & Mrs. W.C.
Richards, Bert
Richards, George
Ring, James Lee
Roach, Flora C.
Ruden, Charles Van King
Russell, John Clement
Saye, Mittie Irene
Schrist, Maud
Smith, Lucius N.
Smith, Roy Theron
Stellman, Margaret P.
Stillman, Mrs. Lowe
Stribling, Elise
Sudderth, Clarabess
Sudderth, Carolina
Tannery, Mr. & Mrs. W.P.
Taylor, Mary Gordon
Telford, Ethel Elise
Telford, Margaret Pauline
Thacker, Louise McRae
Upchurch, Dr. & Mrs. W.A.
Wathour, Charles Hulburt
Weimer, Margaret Amelia
Welsh, Henrietta
Welsh, Rosie L.
Wilson, Homer Allen
Winburn, Abel Pound
Winship, Mr. & Mrs. George
Withers, Henry W.
Wolpert, Dollie
Wood, Mrs. J.T.
Wood, Ruth
Wrenn, Harry Lee
Wright, Andrew J.
Wylons, Sarah Alice
Youngblood, Maud E.

1914

Acker, Mabel
Alexander, Lucile Roy
Baker, E..R
Baker, H.D.
Baldwin, Connie G.
Baldwin, Mr. & Mrs. D.H.
Baldwin, D.M.
Baldwin, D. Newman
Barnes, Mary
Born, Mrs. L.C.
Brantley, Edward
Brantley, Ruth
Brantley, Mrs. E.G.
Brown, Myrtice
Brumby, Mrs. Clara H.
Burns, H.M.
Burns, Minnie Alberta
Caldwell, James N.
Cason, Sadie
Chambers, Rebecca Agnes
Christian, J.R.
Clarke, Sarah A.
Coleman, Emma Linder
Coleman, George
Cotton, Nellie
Cunningham, Harold T.
Davidson, Blanche
Davis, Florence
Davis, Vera
DeLorme, Grace Juanita
DuBose, E.A.
Fadden, Mr. & Mrs. R.E.
Force, Charlotte M.
Force, Mr. & Mrs. Philip
Force, Philip H., Jr.
Formby, Clara Henry
Garden, Margaret P.
Garlington, Elsie
Harris, Franklin L.
Haslett, Mrs. F.L.
Hendricks, Lizzie
Hess, W.P.
Heston, Mrs. W.R.
Hicks, Nancy J.
Hodges, William Joseph
Hudson, Mamie Joe
Hutchinson, Mrs. R.L.
Johns, Sadie
Johnson, Kathryn
Johnson, William G.
Keith, Mr. & Mrs. Norman L.
Keith, Sara Elizabeth
Kennedy, John Julian
Kirkpatrick, T.M.
Latting, Bessie B.
Ledingham, Robert A.
Lemon, Mary
Lockhart, Mrs. James B.
Logan, Charlotte A.
MacRae, Mrs. Thomas
Maddox, Mrs. Elsie G.
Marks, Ethel Clayton
Martin, Anna May
Martin, Edward R.
Martin, Mamie
Martin, Samuel John
Mingledorff, B.I.
Mingledorff, Ruth Marie
Moore, Henry McIntosh
McClure, Milton B.
McConaughy, James
McCrackin, Edith
McFadden, Mrs. R.E.
McIntosh, Mrs. John
McIntosh, Kenneth E.
McLeod, Jessie
McLeod, I.M.
Nesbit, Mabel E.
Overby, Lucy Elizabeth
Overby, Marie
Overby, Mrs. Thomas M.
Patterson, Lillie A.
Patterson, Margaret
Rapp, Fredda Eliz
Reese, H.M.
Reeves, Mr. & Mrs. W.H.
Reid, Thelma Jessie
Reynolds, Mabel
Roberts, Mrs. S.L.
Robinson, Geraldine
Rogers, Julia
Rogers, Mary Caldwell
Rushton, Charles E.
Sill, Evelyn
Skinner, Mary G.
Smith, Dr. & Mrs. D.F.
Smith, Evelyn
Smithson, Pearl
Stevenson, R.J.
Stone, Lily
Stringfellow, Mrs. J.R.
Taylor, Margie Bell
Templeton, Esther
Terry, Jimmie M.
Therrel, John F.
Thompson, Clara
Thompson, Herman Lee

Officers of
CENTRAL PRESBYTERIAN CHURCH
75th Anniversary Celebration
Atlanta - March 8th 1933

Thompson, Tasker D.
Van Epps, Mrs. A.C.
Waters, Mr. & Mrs. Tull C.
Watkins, Francis H.
Webb, J.W.
Whitlow, Flora L.
Williams, Mrs. C.C.
Williams, J.C., Jr.
Williamson, Rosa May
Wisiter, Mrs. M.W.
Zealy, Mrs. E.O.
Zell, George Ames
Zell, Mr. & Mrs. Robert L.
Zimmerman, Fred L.

1915

Akin, Ellison
Allen, Arthur
Allen, Mabel Merle
Bailey, Olive
Baker, Mrs. William
Bangham, Minnie
Bansley, John David, Jr.
Barley, Clire
Beckman, Sophia
Benson, Margaret
Boons, John Amos
Booth, Mors C.D.
Brandes, Lucy
Brant, F.S.
Bratton, Louise J.
Bray, Henry W.
Brisendine, Mrs. T.M.
Brisendine, T.M., Jr.
Brooks, Mrs. R.L.
Brown, Nora
Buford, Evelyn
Butler, Edna
Carlisle, Harry Lewis
Carson, Rebecca
Carter, Alice
Cartledge, Lula
Cartledge, Vera
Castles, Mr. & Mrs. P.M.
Castles, Mr. & Mrs. S.W.
Castles, Mrs. W.H.
Christian, Boyce
Clark, Annil L.
Clayton, Pearl Dempsey
Coffin, Dorothy
Cox, Adda Eugenia
Cox, Ernest
Cox, Robert
Crane, Meade
Crawley, Tommie Pearl
Crenshaw, Ed Price
Darracott, F.S.
DeLorine, Robert E.
Dickson, Hugh Carroll
Dimmock, Bertha
Daughty, May
Dyson, Earl
Edmondson, Homer
Folds, Guy
Girtner, Emory
Goodrich, David
Greene, Roy Thomas
Greenlee, Mr. & Mrs. Harold R.
Hadley, Hilda May
Hairston, Flossie
Hall, Mrs. J.G.
Haywood, Cora
Henderson, Marie
Hendricks, Alline Mae
Herring, Bryon W.
Heston, William
Hill, Debra May
Hills, Dorothy
Hills, Mrs. Georgia B.
Hodges, Mary B.
Holcomb, Mrs. W.L.
Holman, Verda
Holt, G. Warren
House, Mary E.
House, T.F.
Hudson, Frank
Jackson, Daisy May
Jones, Mrs. Reps
Johnson, Addie E.
Kendrick, Edward
Kendrick, Martha
Kendrick, Mary Clarise
Kennedy, Elizabeth Lee
Laramore, James
Lindsay, Charles
Lindsay, Junius J.
Long, De First A.
Long, Mrs. Preston
Lyon, Mary
Maclagan, R.W.
Martin, Belle
Martin, Louise
Mathews, Julia M.
Mathewson, L.G.
Meade, Crane
Merritt, G.T.
Mills, Mr. & Mrs. C.W.
Mitchell, Abraham
Mitchell, Mr. & Mrs. George
Mitchell, Jacob
Mitchell, Pauline
Moon, Anna
Moore, Henry Clay, Jr.
Morgan, Marjorie
Moss, Howard Marshall
Murray, John
McAfee, Charles
McClelland, J. Ralph
McClesky, Mr. & Mrs. J.C.
McConnell, Emma
McConnell, Howard Isaac
Oglesby, Fannie
Oglesby, Martha
Parker, Junius H.
Patrick, Mr. & Mrs. P.H.
Patterson, Dr. & Mrs. G.W.D.
Petters, Edwin Winfield
Phillips, Marion Hull
Phillipson, Ethel
Poe, Linton Joseph
Porter, Mr. & Mrs. L.H.
Pratt, Eugene Clinton
Puckett, Hazel
Reeves, Annie
Rumph, George W.
Sawtell, Richard
Shafer, Mrs. Effie
Sheats, Ella Mabel
Sherlin, Mrs. G.A.
Simmerman, Mrs. R.V.
Slider, Earl R.
Smith, Charles A.
Smith, Esther
Smith, Howard
Smith, Mrs. L.B.
Smith, William P.
Stafford, Frank A.
Stalker, Harriet G.
Stall, Meade
Stanley, Luisor
Stewart, Lena
Stewart, Louise
Stockton, Frank
Stockton, I.C.
Stockton, Ruth
Summers, Fred S.
Tedder, John Lee
Templeton, Frances
Thacker, William L.
Thrash, James Burton
Tidwell, LeRoy
Upchurch, Wilborn
Wallace, Pearl Fowler
Wallace, Robert Leroy
Westcott, Glenn
Westcott, Julia W.
Whitton, Estelle
Whitton, Dorothy Mary
Williams, Mrs. C.C.
Willingham, William T.
Wilson, Benton
Wilson, Chessley B.
Wilson, John T.
Wilson, Joseph
Wolfe, Henry
Wolfe, Michael
Woodbury, Roy
Woods, George Newton
Word, Louis Rhett
Yarbrough, James W.
York, Mrs. John H.
Zealy, Eugene O.

1916

Alexander, Mrs. J.E.
Allen, Lucy
Arnold, Fay Elizabeth
Bailey, M.K.
Baker, R.P.
Barfield, Eola
Barnett, Gladys
Bass, Wayne H.
Beale, Robert Hanson
Bell, Jeannie
Bentley, Mrs. H.C.
Bentley, Mary Elizabeth
Bentley, Neta
Bradley, Caroline
Brent, Joseph
Brim, Mrs. W.W.
Brown, Mrs. E.T.
Bryson, Catherine
Buchanan, Lulie P.
Buchanan, William F.
Burroughs, D. Hoyt
Caldwell, E.L.
Calif, James
Carter, Mary Adams

Cartright, J.C.
Castles, Margaret Elizabeth
Christian, Mary Duval
Christian, Mr. & Mrs. P.D.
Christian, P.D., Jr.
Clark, Mrs. L.A.
Cooney, Robert Lee
Coppock, Mrs. Ellie R.
Coppock, Johnston
Cumming, Erle
Davis, Frances
Dodson, Thelma Pauline
Donaldson, Abbie
Dorsey, Mrs. Stella W.
Elliott, Olivia
Equen, Murdock
Erwin, Martha
Fancher, J. Kenneth
Farrar, Mrs. Frank
Fields, William Henry
Finley, Hallie Reese
Finley, J.T.
Fleming, Stella B.
Green, Raymond Eugene
Green, Ruth Victoria
Griffin, Barbara
Griffin, George Clayton
Guilliam, Nellie
Hairston, Janie
Hamell, E.M.
Hamell, Mary
Harrell, Mr. & Mrs. E.N.
Harris, Jennette
Hollis, Irene M.
Hollis, M.O.
Hyndman, Thomas N.
Ivah, Josephine
Irvine, Dixon
Irvine, Harris
Irvine, Mrs. W.H.
Johnson, Ella M.
Kline, Mary
Lanier, Sallie
Lankford, Ollie Belle
Long, William Groves
Lynch, Catherine
Lynch, Patrick
Lyon, Gayner
Lyon, Mrs. L.
Maclagan, Mrs. Robert W.
Manahan, Mrs. C.H.
Martin, Mattie Su
Mayes, Margret
Meadows, Julius Olney
Miller, Julian Edward
Miller, Miss Louie
Millie, A.D.
Milner, Burson
Milner, James
Milner, Mrs. John R.
Milner, Sara
Milner, W.A.
Milner, Mr. & Mrs. W.T.
Milner, W.T., Jr.
Moore, Mrs. W.M.
Morrow, Fred R.
Morrow, Paul
Moseley, Ida Allen
Moseley, Mrs. J.A.
Moseley, John Anthony

McAfee, Charles Little
McAllister, Helen
McAllister, Lucy
McCallie, Margaret
McCammon, Louise Elizabeth
McDonald, H.P.
McDowell, Gertrude
McLeod, Marion
McManus, Walter
Nicolassen, Agnes T.
Nicolassen, Augusta G.
Nicolassen, Dr. & Mrs. G.F.
Nicolassen, Trueheart
Nottingham, J.J.
O'Bryan, Mrs. Eola Barfield
O'Callaghan, Catherine
O'Callaghan, W.J.
Ogden, Elizabeth
Ogden, Margaret
Osborne, Mr. & Mrs. A.R.
Ous, George
Paisley, Mr. & Mrs. J.A.
Perkins, Mr. & Mrs. J.B.
Radford, Garland S.
Ransome, Elizabeth Lou
Reeves, E.G.
Reinhardt, Ruth
Rigutti, Josephine
Riley, Ellie
Roberts, Frances Jurdine
Russell, Duane A., Jr.
Sellers, Nannie B.
Seltzer, Charles
Settzer, Flora Hughes
Shirlin, Catherine Irene
Smith, Alice V.
Stanley, Mrs. Annie L.
Stanley, Mrs. W.W.
Stevens, Eddie I.
Stillman, King, Jr.
Stillman, Lilly
Tatum, Mrs. J.W.
Tatum, Katherine
Tennent, Miss Willie Lea
Thompson, Allison M.
Thompson, Edna Emma
Thompson, Joseph Daniel
Thurman, Ida
Tribble, Ida F.
Turnage, Trixie Wymon
Ward, Mr. & Mrs. R.J.
Wardlaw, James
Webbis, Rita
White, Mr. & Mrs. J.A.
White, Ruby E.
Williams, M.J.
Williamson, Christine
Williamson, Mrs. G.M.
Williamson, Henry
Williamson, Marie
Willis, Agnes Love
Willis, Dr. Charles A.
Willis, Charles M.
Willis, Jennie E.
Willis, Stella E.
Wilson, Fay
Wilson, Viola
Young, Mr. & Mrs. Elmer I.
Young, Lula M.

1917

Allen, Mrs. F.P.
Arnold, Fay Elizabeth
Ashmore, Vesta Jeanette
Barnes, Frank
Barnett, Hattie
Barth, Raymond
Beale, Annie D.
Beale, Ernest Pennington
Beale, Henry C.
Beale, John C.
Beale, Marjorie Anita
Beall, S.O.
Becker, Mr. & Mrs. Fred
Bell, Agnes
Bell, Miss Elizabeth
Bell, Mrs. Elizabeth
Bell, Isabel
Bell, Margaret
Bell, William
Bell, William, Jr.
Born, Ethel
Bostain, Edwin
Bradley, Pauline Louise
Brisendine, Lurwood
Brittain, Mary Louise
Brown, Berta
Brown, Minnie L.
Brown, Samuel Y.
Bruce, Florence Beaman
Bryson, Willie
Butler, Theodore
Campbell, Virginia Orme
Carey, Florida Lee
Carter, Rebecca
Clayton, Adelaide
Clayton, Mrs. E.P.
Clifton, Lyman
Clinstian, May Duvall
Clinstian, Mr. & Mrs. P.D.
Clinstian, P.D., Jr.
Connally, Mrs. Paul D.
Coogler, Jessie
Cook, Amos
Crouch, Alpher May
Daber, Nick
Davidson, Kenneth Bruce
Davis, Molly
de Four, Alberta
de Yamfert, Lillian
Dickert, Mr. & Mrs. D.M.
Dickson, Alice Mary T.
Dickson, James Hill
Dodson, Thelma Pauline
Dorsey, Stella M.
Duckett, Howard C.
Easterwood, Annie
Edmondson, Louise
Eichelberger, Fleta
Elyea, Elizabeth
Estes, Mr. & Mrs. J.M., Sr.
Estes, J.M., Jr.
Estes, Mrs. John M., Jr.
Estes, Leila C.
Estes, Lucy B.
Estes, Myrtis
Faw, J.E.
Fearing, Nana
Finley, Hattie Reese

Fuller, Roy L.
Fuller, Susie
Garrie, Mary Eloise
Garthright, J.C.
George, Taft
Grant, Dorothy
Haden, William Watkins
Hager, Henry Jordan
Hall, Charles Edward
Harrison, William P.
Hart, Lessie
Heard, Harrold Allen
Heard, Mary E.
Heem, Clarence Wilmer, Jr.
Henry, H.L.
Hillings, Minnie E.
Holbeck, Dr. William A.
House, Jessie M.
Hoyt, Julia B.
Huie, Ralph A.
Humphries, Franklin
Jackson, Marion, Jr.
James, John W.
Johns, Sam
Johnson, Clarence B.
Johnson, Dr. & Mrs. Harry B.
Johnson, Theodore
Jones, Marvin
Jordan, Mr. & Mrs. Methvin W.
Kendall, Mary T.D.
Kern, Mary
Kirk, Charles
Knox, Mary
Lake, Julian
Ledbetter, Agnes
Lennard, Louise
MacRae, Mrs. Thomas
Mason, Mrs. Fred
Mason, Fred Charlton, Jr.
Mason, Sarah Ellis Estes
Mathews, Colandus
Mathews, Mary
Mauldin, Berta
Meacham, John Wright
Meriweather, Mary M.
Merriweather, Bertha
Moss, Margart
Mott, Frances
McAllister, Amos Hustler
McCullough, Marian
McKinney, Ruby
McLelland, Ellis Forsyth
McMillan, Laura
McNabb, John A.
Nelson, Edith
Nolan, Mr. & Mrs. George
Pinkston, Mary
Primrose, May Noble
Reeves, Adelle
Reeves, Louise
Rhodes, Blanch
Rice, Lillian
Robbins, Luellyn
Robinson, William
Sams, Katherine
Scruggs, Wirtley Peel
Setze, Henry Rosynol
Simpson, Mary Kate
Sims, Jennie
Smith, Mary Nell
Smith, Morman
Smith, Nellie H.
Sparrenberger, Wm. A.
Strickler, Givens B.
Thomas, Chibaba
Thornton, Alice Louise
Thweatt, Jean Kendall
Vernoy, Bessie
Vogt, Albert
Vogt, Ferdinand
Vogt, Wm. Simpson E.
West, Edna May
White, Ida M.
Wilkie, Eulice
Williamson, Ada Bell
Williamson, Elsie
Wilson, Martha Frances
Wood, M.C.
Wright, George Prioleau
Zeigler, Miss M.R.

1918

Alexander, Millard S.
Anderson, Mr. & Mrs. W.S.
Arnot, William David
Bailey, Bessie
Bansley, Louise
Boyd, Ruth
Brooks, Josiah Franklin
Brown, Frances
Browne, Virginia
Buhler, Majorie Ernestine
Cadenhead, Nadine
Clayton, Susan
Cole, Elizabeth
Crusselle, Elizabeth
Digby, Caroline Belle
Dorroh, Ralph Fuller
Downs, Sarah Kate
Dyson, Mrs. W.G.
Estes, Nannie C.
Foster, Mr. & Mrs. Louis Z.
Fudge, Miriam Clare
Greene, Lucile
Harden, Mrs. H.H.
Hicks, Ethel Evatt
Hightower, Mary Lizzie
Hills, Kathryn Kenmore
Hodo, Mr. & Mrs. Ordga P.
Hoffman, Bertha
Kimberly, Aline Navita
Kirk, Mary C.
Lankford, Grace
Lavery, Addie Virginia
Lavery, Charles Norton
Lewis, Laurence
Long, Mrs. W.G.
Lynn, William Daniel
Lyon, Dollie Myra
Morris, Mrs. A.E.
Muller, Frederick Louis
Murphy, Mr. & Mrs. George E.
Murray, Dorothy Elizabeth
McCammon, Lillian
McDowell, Lucy
Nesbitt, Mrs. R.T.
Padgett, Annie
Pannell, Mrs. Hollis
Patterson, Julia Dent
Philips, Leroy
Ransome, G.C.
Reichel, Edwin Roy
Robertson, Earl Theodore
Robertson, Selena Blanch
Russell, Mary Belle
Sims, Columbus Turner
Slappey, Alice
Stacha, Otto James
Stiles, Agnes Jacob
Strube, Martha
Sydenstricker, Alma Willis
Taylor, Blanche
Taylor, Margaret
Tindall, Mr. & Mrs. Joseph D.
Wall, William John
Weeks, Martha
Willis, Fred L.
Willis, Lydia M.
Winn, Elizabeth
Winn, Elizabeth C.
Winn, James A.
Winn, John Currie
York, Kathleen

1919

Allen, Annie
Armour, Calhoun
Armstrong, Mr. & Mrs. G.P.
Bachman, Jonathan W.
Baggett, Mrs. W.E.
Barnhardt, Charles E.
Bateman, Lucile
Belcher, Ella Mae
Brantley, Chistabel
Brantly, Mr. & Mrs. Edgar P.
Braswell, Beatrice
Braswell, Mr. & Mrs. James B.
Brumley, Elizabeth
Burns, Helen
Burns, Ruth
Burns, Mr. & Mrs. T.A.
Carlton, Evelyn
Chambers, Marie
Chance, Rossetta Wyche
Cleveland, Nellie
Couch, Mr. & Mrs. A.L.
Dennington, Katherine
Drew, Joseph Frederick
Duncan, Ruth
Dwyer, Ethel G.
Estes, Margaret
French, Grace
Gasson, Virginia
Gilliam, Mr. & Mrs. E.H.
Glenn, Mable
Goodwin, Rachel
Hail, Gertrude L.
Hallman, Louise
Harris, Annie Blanche
Helton, Earle
Hicks, Elsie
Hills, Virginia N.
Hodnett, Margaret Jan
Hubbard, Ethel
Inglis, Mrs. George
Ivey, Grace
Jeffcoat, Lùla Bell
Jett, Emily Stacy
Johnston, Mrs. Philip A.

Jones, Mrs. D.C.
Jones, Ruby
Jordan, Agnes
Jordan, Grace
Keath, Bertie
Kendrick, Mrs. John T.
Kendrick, Margaret C.
Lacy, Mrs. B.R., Jr.
Leath, Allie
Mabbett, Mabel
Miller, Abbie
Mills, Mary Evelyn
Moss, Virginia H.
Mullins, Walter A.
McGill, Avis Eufaula
McKibben, Mrs. E.L.
McKibben, Jeanette
McKnight, Linda
Neer, Samuel Kendall
Owen, Hannah
Patterson, Louise
Payne, Clara Edna
Petree, Mrs. Houston K.
Ray, A.A.
Rodgers, Mary
Russey, Marian Janet
Salley, Leon
Samples, Mable
Sams, Martha
Sanders, Ralph Henry
Sawyer, Leona
Scott, Ethel
Sewell, Eudora
Smith, James Donald
Smith, Ruby
Speece, Ave
Speece, Katherine
Speece, Rufus
Starr, Laura Blanche
Steigall, Mrs. Birdie
Taylor, Lois
Telford, Mr. & Mrs. J. Lee
Thomas, Rachel Louise
Thompson, Charles M.
Thompson, Clinton P., Jr.
Vandergriff, Mrs. J.W.
Vandiver, Althie
Way, Mamie Lila
Webb, Lydia Esther
Wells, Carrie Lou
Wells, Margaret
Williams, Evelyn May
Willie, Mrs. A.B.
Willink, Thelma

1920

Adams, Mrs. W.P.
Alexander, James Edgar
Armstrong, Wm. Buckingham
Armstrong, Wm. Robert
Atkinson, Mr. & Mrs. Burwell
Bagby, Arthur Lacy
Barfield, Benjamin C.
Bowen, Mrs. T.L.
Bowmen, Roselle
Brock, Mrs. H.L.
Brown, Callie G.
Browne, Wade
Browne, Mr. & Mrs. Wm. B.
Bumstead, Charles Marion
Burns, Helen
Carlisle, William Rhodes
Cason, Elizabeth C.
Castles, Lonnie Janes
Chambers, Willie Dean
Christian, Irvine
Clayton, Corrine Wharton
Coburn, Buelah
Collins, Martha
Corley, Dorothy
Corley, John
Cowan, Lillian
Cowart, Annie Snider
Craig, George A.
Craig, Nettie Jean
Crowe, J. Fred
Dale, Jane
Denham, Lura
Dennington, Jennie Louise
Dickson, Mr. & Mrs. James H.
Dixon, David
Dockstader, Mrs. C.A.
Dodd, Harry W.
Eikel, Maggie
Estes, Sarah Ellis
Fleming, Helen Margaret
Freeman, Vera Ola
Fulton, Hattie
Gay, Mrs. Frank
Gilleland, Andrew Jackson
Gilmer, Mrs. J.I.
Glover, George, Jr.
Godwin, Rebecca
Grimes, Annie Lee Wilhoit
Haney, Mrs. A.M.
Haney, Sarah
Harkins, Charles Carson
Harris, Mrs. S.B.
Henderson, Alma
Hicks, Leila
Hills, Henry Inman
Hills, Richard Albert
Hudson, James Edward
Hudson, John Marion
Hyndman, Mrs. Thomas L.
Ivey, Bessie
Jeter, Mr. & Mrs. F.H.
Johns, Johnie
Jones, Cecil
Jones, Mrs. Herman
Jones, Herman, Jr.
Jordan, Cora Pound
Jordan, H.H.
Kendrick, Clara
Kendrick, Ellen J.
Kieshian, Vahan G.
Lacy, Mrs. J.B.
Lamb, Thelma Lettie
Long, Robert V.
Lowry, Mr. & Mrs. James I.
Lupton, Mrs. J.T.
Marshall, Frances Epsie
Mason, Mr. & Mrs. Fred
Meacham, J.M.
Millard, Mrs. R.C.
Miller, Mrs. C.F.
Miller, Robert Parks
Moore, Gladys
Moseley, Bessie
Moseley, Francis
Moseley, Lulie
McClure, J. Clarendon
McIntosh, Fowler
McManus, Lucy
Mcneill, Daniel Bowie
McRae, Frances Kate
Nelson, Mrs. W.A.
Oglesby, J.G.
Payne, Varnie I.
Percival, Mrs. J.A.
Percival, Mrs. J.V.
Phelps, Mr. & Mrs. Asher W.
Philips, Minnie
Phillips, Ralph Earle
Phillips, Mr. & Mrs. W.A.
Polley, Wm. Gillespie
Porter, Ruth
Powell, Maxine
Rand, Mr. & Mrs. Fred Leon
Rankin, Helen
Rankin, Marion
Rapp, Clemmie Elizabeth
Reeves, Katherine E.
Reeves, Margaret Louise
Robinson, Myra T.
Rosborough, Edward P.
Rumbold, Allan H.
Rumbold, Jean Willa
Rumbold, Virginia
Russell, Margaret Louise
Schofield, Frances Houk
Scott, Thomas
Seibens, Mr. & Mrs. Arthur R.
Sewell, Dr. & Mrs. J.A.
Shafer, John
Singleton, Elonia
Smith, James Glenn
Snider, Martha Ruth
Spicer, Mrs. Zulima R.
Stokes, Major Charles A.
Strickler, Cyrus Warren, Jr.
Suttles, Arthur
Taylor, Mr. & Mrs. J.H.
Tucker, Dimples
Upshaw, Charles Clifford
Upshaw, Mrs. J.S.
Vernoy, Louise Chase
Vernoy, Mrs. W.A.
Vinzant, Fannie R.
Walker, Annie Lucy
Wells, Jasper Rea
White, J. Bonar
Wilhoit, Elizabeth T.
Wilhoit, Loyd A.
Williamson, Isaac B.
Withers, Edith L.
Wolpert, Annie
Wolpert, Mrs. S.L.
Yopp, Corrine
York, Mr. & Mrs. J.H.
York, Mrs. Steele Otis

1921

Agricola, Charles Philip
Aikin, Janet Acie
Almond, Mrs. W.M.
Bailey, Roy
Bansley, Margaret Cecilia

THE PEOPLE WHO STAYED (1858-1978)

Barclay, Ruby
Barnes, William Franklin
Barry, Carolyn T.
Bass, Hellen Lucille
Bass, Mary Edna
Bedford, Vivan Irene
Berry, Daniel M., Jr.
Blair, Johnny Louise
Bowie, Robert Watson
Boyd, Lucile
Bradley, Hugh Carlton
Britt, Mrs. C.S.
Brown, Edward Thomas
Brown, Paul Frederick
Caldwell, Andrew Calhoun
Cameron, Essie Duckett
Cameron, Robert Ridley
Campbell, Florida
Campbell, Sarah P.
Cardwell, Beulah
Cason, Benjamin H., Jr.
Caudell, Corra
Caudell, John M.
Chance, Elsie
Chandler, Hugh
Cheatam, Alabama Mae
Clapp, Mary Helen
Clark, Richard Norman
Clower, Minnie Love
Coggin, Ethel
Coggin, Sarah Caroline
Cole, Charles Boynton
Collier, Meredith Morgan
Cook, Pearl Dixon
Crawford, Marion B.
Daniel, Mr. & Mrs. John H.
Davis, Corrie E.
Denton, Mrs. Homer C.
Dickerson, Sarah Madeline
Dixon, Ethel May
Dockstader, Charles A.
Duckett, Mrs. H.C.
Easterwood, Mrs. J.T.
Edmondson, Augustus M.
Edmondson, Jewell Estelle
Elder, James Harvey
Fisher, Leonard Stephen
Foster, Agnes Lowe
Foster, Damaris T.
Freeman, Lawrence W., Jr.
Gaddy, Ruby B.
Gaines, Alexander P.
Gault, Horace
Gillespy, Ella Catherine
Green, John Dophin
Greene, Mrs. E. Lelia
Greene, Mary Virginia
Greene, William Fain
Griffin, Jesse B.
Grimm, James Franklin
Haden, W.W.
Hager, Marie Herbert
Hall, Walter Tucker
Haney, John Thomas
Harris, Kathryn Maud
Head, Oscar T.
Hewett, Lula
Hewett, Mrs. J.M.
Hickman, Ollie E.
Hillbraith, Mrs. Henry
Hogan, Frank E.
Hogan, Sibyl
Hogan, Mrs. W.J.
Holmes, Alpheus Simmons
Holmes, Louise
Hoyt, Harry
Hubner, W.W.
Hughes, Edith Helen
Hughes, Leonard Virgie
Jacbos, J.L.
Jansen, Frederica Amelia
Jones, David C., Jr.
Jones, Edward Groves
Jones, Mrs. H.S.
Jones, Harry Jefferson
Kellam, E.P., Jr.
Kelley, Elbert Earl
King, Mary Elizabeth
King, Norah Annie
Kirk, Miller Cameron
Knapp, John Crosby
Lacy, J.S.
Lake, John E.
Langolf, Clara Louise
Lavery, Charles Norton
Leavitt, Mr. & Mrs. Thomas B.
Lee, Corintha
Lee, Nell Lorena
Lee, Walker T.
Lennard, Dixie
Lowe, Alice F.
Lowe, Emily Elizabeth
Main, Mr. & Mrs. G.C.
Mikell, T.B.
Moore, Edith May
Moore, W.N.
Morris, Bernard Linton
Murphy, Olive Virginia
Myers, Mary McAden
Myers, Pickett Lee
McCarley, John Paul
McCrary, Zola
McGeeney, Connie
McKibben, Charles H.
Nix, Francis C.
Norris, William E.
Oastler, Mr. & Mrs. B.R.
Oastler, Thomas
Olson, Alice Earline
Osburn, Elmo
Osburn, Katherine
Owens, Ve Ora
Parrish, R.B.
Patterson, Mrs. Francis
Patterson, Francis Burke
Pogue, Maeola Gwendolyn
Ragin, H.L.
Rhodes, Kenneth
Roberts, Emmie Mae
Roberts, Thomas W.
Rodgers, Albert Anthony
Russell, Fred Homer
Russey, George S.
Russey, Hugh Wesley
Sartor, Mr. & Mrs. James
Schlamp, Rosalie
Schofield, James Herman
Sekanati, Leon
Shadix, Tullalah
Sharp, William Marvin
Shellenberger, Mr. & Mrs. John
Slider, Claire Lucy
Slider, Mrs. Earl R.
Smith, Harold C.
Smith, Martha Marguerite
Smith, Mary Lou
Spitler, R.A.
Stephens, Roger Albert
Stewart, Luna
Swan, Mr. & Mrs. W.B.
Taylor, Alex Selkirk
Templeton, Irvane
Thompson, William Howard
Tillander, Mrs. O.W.
Tillander, Oxel W.
Trammel, Rosalie T.
Trammell, Edna Mae
Tull, J.M.
Turnell, Mrs. J.T.
Turner, Marie
Upchurch, Frances
Vernoy, Samuel Edward
Warner, Louis Stanley
Watson, Ella
Wells, R.C.
White, Sterling Emory
Whitner, Mrs. J.C.
Whitworth, Lillian Mabel
Williams, Marian E.
Wilson, Margaret
Wright, Mr. & Mrs. George P.
York, Eleanor Madge
York, Johnnie Mae

1922

Adams, Mary Frances
Allen, Irene
Ashley, J.T.
Baxter, Mrs. J.O.
Beaty, D. Waldo
Billings, Ruth Marion
Blumberg, Zelick
Bowles, Louise
Bridwell, Lucy
Brooks, T. Evans
Brooks, Mrs. T.H.
Brown, Jesse Carlton
Brown, Mr. & Mrs. Joseph R.
Brumby, Mr. & Mrs. E.H.
Campbell, Mr. & Mrs. Arthur
Chadwick, Albert A.
Clark, George A., Jr.
Clayton, Jane Shumate
Clements, Audrey Gertrude
Clower, Coke
Collins, Mr. & Mrs. Walter A.
Cone, Evelyn
Cone, W.B.
Cone, Warner
Cooper, Annie Agnes
Cosgrave, Pearl
Crandall, Oro Marion
Crenshaw, Mattie Lou
Croft, Ley L.
Dean, Lovick
Dennington, Mrs. R.S.
Derrick, Essie Maye
Dickey, Mrs. L.J.

Church Night Supper in 1948. "Cooks of the evening" are standing in the far corner. There were 5-7 ladies for each week of the month who did the cooking. Sunday School classes rotated in setting the tables and in serving.

Dillard, Evelyn Lois
Dillard, Mr. & Mrs. James Hall
Dillard, Julia Adele
Dillard, Marg. Zanobia
Duncan, Miss Willie May
Dyche, Eugene
Ellis, Mary Idell
Elrod, Awtry Solomon
Feather, Lillie May
Field, Agnew F.
Field, Ella W.
Field, Dr. Frank H.
Field, Frank Kells
Field, Mason D.
Fisher, Mrs. Cincinnatus S.
Fletcher, Carroll
Fletcher, Mr. & Mrs. L.J.
Fletcher, Marion Emma
Floyd, Resina
Friddell, Lorine Ross
Gibson, Gertrude Walker
Gist, Nathaniel, Jr.
Gossett, Louise
Green, Effie Velma
Green, Dr.Samuel
Gresham, Charles Druillard
Griffin, George Clayton
Hamrick, Mary
Haney, Walter Paul
Harris, Sydney
Harvey, Bessie
Hatcher, Ruby
Heery, Arthur Benjamin
Hendricks, Margaret Alice
Henry, Evelyn
Herring, Mrs. Bryan
Higdon, Flora
Higdon, Polly
Howe, Lang Ludwick, Jr.
Howell, Mrs. E.S.
Howell, Robert Spencer
Hubner, Mary
Hubner, Mrs. W.W.
Hunter, Nina Russell
Ivah, Joseph Charles
Ivy, Stella Pearl Adella
John, Charles
Jordan, Mr. & Mrs. George P.
Keen, George L.
Keen, Iris
Keith, Ruth H.
Kelly, Alice Smith
Kendrick, Anna E.
Knapp, Reginald Herbert
Lee, Charles C.
List, Mabel
List, Marie Alice
Locke, Daisy
Locke, Miss Jesse B.
Locke, Mr. Jesse Marion
Love, Charles S.
Love, Mrs. N.E.
Lovelace, Clyde T.
Lowe, Mr. & Mrs. W.H.
Lowry, Aquila Jones
Lowry, James Isaac, Jr.
Lynn, Mrs. C.W.
Lynn, Charles William
Mallard, Clara Jones
Malone, Corrine Fisher
Martin, William B.
Martin, Mrs. Willie B.
Mason, Fred Charlton
Miller, Mr. & Mrs. R.P.
Miller, Reuben C.
Mills, Mr. & Mrs. W.W.
McGaughey, Mrs. A.D.
McGaughey, Andrew D.
McGaughey, Pansy Spencer
McGaughey, Ruth Mary
McGaughey, Miss Spencer
McGill, Mrs. Odell
McNaughton, Dr. Wm. Jones
Nelson, W.R.
Norris, Mr. & Mrs. W.E.
O'Neal, W. Byron
Osborne, Martha Jean
Paiseley, Margaret
Parnell, Mrs. L.A.
Peck, Nettie
Perkerson, Annie Ivah
Perry, Mr. & Mrs. Marion G.
Prewett, Thomas A.
Quarterman, Lucile
Rainford, Henry Herbert
Rigutti, Edward
Rippon, Charles S.
Roberts, Mr. & Mrs. Horace W.
Rothen, Charles J.
Sands, Glenn
Saye, Mrs. C.W.
Saye, Mr. & Mrs. E.D.
Saye, Mittie
Schultz, Vivian Elmore
Sergeant, Mrs. George W.
Shaw, Mr. & Mrs. Angus R., Jr.
Sheppard, Dr. Hubert
Shields, Catherine
Shields, Mrs. Rosser
Smith, Mr. & Mrs. B.H.
Smith, Bernardine E.
Smith, Dorsey Louise
Smith, Eugene Cathrall
Smith, Grace Rupert
Smith, Mrs. L.H.
Smith, Randolph Tutwiler
Smith, Vernie
Smith, Vollie
Spencer, Mr. & Mrs. Macon B.
Stanley, Mrs. H.S.
Stephens, Mrs. A.E.
Stephens, Myrtice
Taylor, Mr. & Mrs. Ed
Telford, John Ross
Telford, Robert E.
Thomas, Mrs. C.
Turner, Mary
Turner, Onree
Turner, Mrs. W.A.
Walker, E.H.
Walker, Mary
Warner, Mr. & Mrs. Hugh A.
Watson, Athalene K.
Watson, Evelyn
Watson, Marie
Whelchel, Aaron A.
Whelchel, Vera
Whitehead, Robert Clifton
Whitten, Theron Rice
Williams, Harold McGregor
Williams, Mrs. J.L.
Williams, Marion Lovene
Wilson, Florida
Wolpert, Dellie
Wolpert, Walter S.
Woodbury, Roy A.

1923

Agnew, Georgia May
Allen, Elizabeth W.
Allen, Mrs. W. H.
Almand, Minnie Lou
Anderson, Almon Estes
Anderson, Mr. & Mrs. W. S.
Arwood, Floyd
Arwood, Walterette
Baker, Estelle
Barfield, Wm. Edward
Barnes, Jessie Lee
Barnes, Mary C.
Baxter, Andrew Harvey
Bedenbaugh, Mrs. C. D.
Billings, Elizabeth
Blair, Erin
Boon, Harry M.
Brannon, Wm. Levi
Brumby, Wallace McPherson
Burns, Mrs. D. M.
Burns, Ethelyn
Burns, Martha B.
Burruss, Mrs. Fred W.
Cain, Ollie
Camp, George Elliott
Campbell, Rosa
Cassady, Harry Arnold
Cates, Earl William
Chapin, George
Clark, Mrs. George A.
Cleveland, Marie
Craig, Mrs. J. L.
Crawford, J. H.
Croft, Ley L.
Crow, George Emanuel
Crusselle, Elizabeth
Dennington, Robert S.
Dickson, Mr. & Mrs. T. C.
Duke, Bessie Estelle
Dupin, Dorothy
Elrod, Awtry J.
Embrey, James Thomas
Erwin, R. A.
Ewing, Rebecca Virginia
Faust, Elizabeth Thomas
Gilleland, Mr. & Mrs. Guy W.
Goodrich, Wilkins
Green, Charles A.
Greene, Sarah Eleda
Greene, Wm. Jack, Jr.
Griffin, Dr. O. J.
Harden, Claire
Harrelson, Mrs. E. B.
Harrelson, Isham Joseph
Higgins, Minnie S.
Hill, Hines L.
Hobbs, Mary Emma
Holbeck, Georgia Laureta
Irvine, R. A.
Ittner, Frances Campbell
Ittner, Frank D.

Johnston, Martha
Jones, Dora Hazel
Jones, Mr. & Mrs. H. C.
Kennedy, Ada
Kennedy, Frank Cowan
Kennedy, Heyward
Knapp, Wm. Spencer
Lewis, Mr. & Mrs. A. L.
Locke, Sealie Virginia
Logan, Louis Morrow
Long, John C.
Lynch, Clara Josephine
Martinos, Marion
Millard, Jeannette
Milner, Mrs. C. Glenn
Morris, Bernard
Morrow, Dorothy
Morse, Mrs. John H.
Myers, Fern Elizabeth
McAllister, Kate Lloyd
McAllister, Ralph Vivan
McNaughton, Alexander B.
McNaughton, Annie E.
McNaughton, Charles Wm.
McNaughton, Dr. W. J.
McNeil, Ola Middie
McNiece, Estelle M.
Napier, R. F.
Neidlinger, E. L.
Nesbit, Mary Lee
Ness, Margaret
Norton, Samuel D. H.
O'Neal, Mrs. Ola M.
Parks, Mr. & Mrs. C. A.
Parks, Hugh
Payne, Vannie
Perkerson, Oda
Philips, James Pierce
Phillips, Asa R.
Phillips, Ezra E.
Phillips, William A.
Reed, Catherine
Reese, H. C.
Richardson, Eugene Horace
Richardson, Mrs. S. P.
Richardson, William V.
Rives, William M.
Roberts, H. E.
Roquemore, Walter
Rutley, Mabel J.
Sargent, George W.
Saye, Claude DeWitt
Saye, Clifford Wilson
Saye, Elmo William
Scholl, Lida May
Scott, Mr. & Mrs. W. W., Jr.
Shand, James Black
Smith, Mrs. M. U.
Smith, Maggie Mae
Smith, Polk Watson
Smythe, Mr. & Mrs. A. Neal
Sparks, W. C.
Stevenson, D. F.
Stewart, Clara
Stewart, Mrs. W. B.
Stow, Mr. & Mrs. E. C.
Sullivan, Mr. & Mrs. D. W.
Sullivan, Martha
Sullivan, Mattie Pelham
Sullivan, Pelham
Suter, Mr. & Mrs. Edward S.
Thatcher, Mary West
Thatcher, Samuel Eugene
Thompson, Mary Cliff
Vandiver, Annie Bell
Vernoy, Eugene Arrington
Warner, Ralph Howard
Watson, Kate C.
Watts, Fannie
Webber, Mr. & Mrs. Frank F.
Williams, Mrs. C. L.
Wise, Amelia
Wright, John Lee
Wright, Joseph C.
Wright, Mildred
York, Mr. & Mrs. Steele O.
Zimmerman, Mr. & Mrs. H. R.
Zwicker, Pauline Camp
Zwicker, Stanley B.

1924

Adams, Mr. & Mrs. C. F.
Bartlett, Dora
Blackwell, Joseph Kemp
Blackwell, Martha Frances
Blackwell, Mr. & Mrs. Walter Lee
Bridges, Frances McAllister
Brimm, Mrs. H. W.
Campbell, Clarence C.
Campbell, James LeRoy
Campbell, William C.
Clark, Obie Lee
Clotfelter, Ruth
Cone, Elizabeth Mary
Davis, John
Davis, W. Stacy
Downs, Rossie
Garren, Bernice F.
George, Ruby
Grau, Mr. & Mrs. Ruseell Price
Groves, Mr. & Mrs. Clifton
Hambrick, Janette Grace
Happoldt, Albert
Harbuck, Mrs. J. H.
Harrison, Jesse E.
Hill, Mrs. Frank G.
Hills, Grace
Holmes, Lucile
Hoyt, Mr. & Mrs. S. B.
Hughes, Mrs. Leonard
Hubner, Charles W.
Hubner, Mrs. Frances
Hubner, Helen Frances
Hubner, Robert Whitney
Icenogle, Karl L.
Ingraham, Mrs. Harry L.
Jansen, Mr. & Mrs. Joseph
Jeffords, Ralph Leon
Keen, Mrs. Willie
Kinnear, Edith
Knapp, Mr. & Mrs. J. C.
Knapp, Maud Elizabeth
Kornegary, Bertha Case
Landiss, Charles
Landiss, Nora Johnson
Leadingham, Harry Pearce
Leadingham, Dr. & Mrs. R.S.
Macrae, Mrs. H. F.
Macrae, Henry Forrester
Magruder, Edith
Magruder, Mrs. R. E.
Malone, Hansell Bryan
Matthews, W. Curtis
Miller, Mrs. Augustus Taylor
McAllister, Dr. & Mrs. J. A.
McCalley, Raymond Dickert
McIntosh, Sarah
Nolan, A. A.
Oakes, Jessie May
O'Callaghan, Wm. Lawrence
Olson, Lela
Parks, Virginia
Perkins, Belle
Perkins, Merle
Philips, Mary Grace
Pilat, Mrs. L.
Pogue, Jennie
Rice, Ethel
Roberts, Mrs. Thomas W.
Runion, Lucy
Russell, Mr. & Mrs. E. H.
Sanders, Brannon Idus
Schultz, Lillian
Sharp, Mrs. L. McGregor
Shepherd, Mrs. Hubert
Sims, Velma
Sims, Wilma
Smith, Myrtice
Spitler, Mary Wight
Stewart, Mrs. W. A., Jr.
Stillman, Dr. & Mrs. W. King
Strickler, Mary R.
Thornton, Mary Jim
Waldrop, Mary Clementine
Waldrop, T. M.
Walker, James C.
Watts, Joe
Whiting, Paul
Wilcutt, Katherine
Wolcott, Margaret Hall
Wolcott, Mr. & Mrs. Robert
Woodbury, Mrs. R. A.
Wright, May

1925

Alexander, Elizabeth Call
Alexander, Eloisa Baker
Andrews, Kate A.
Baker, Mary Frances
Banderson, Miss I. V.
Baxter, Virginia Harriet
Bayol, Charlotte Elizabeth
Bayol, Katherine Lea
Bennett, Lelia
Biddy, Herbert
Biddy, Joseph Moses
Bishop, Charles Henry
Bowles, Emmie
Brannon, Mrs. L. A.
Brannon, Lewis Albert
Bray, Bernice
Bray, Miss Willie Browning
Brooks, Ohlan Robert
Brown, Miss Eleazer
Brown, Minnie
Brown, Miss Ottis
Bryant, Stanhope
Buffington, Ida Margaret

THE PEOPLE WHO STAYED (1858-1978)

Buffington, Martha Louise
Buford, James Leslie
Butler, Lille Belle
Cartledge, Louise
Chambers, N. T.
Cheatham, John R.
Chevalley, Annette
Cheves, Mr. & Mrs. Dan S.
Cleckler, Elizabeth
Cox, Mrs. Robert
Craig, Arthur Alexander
Cumming, Mr. & Mrs. Alex
Davis, John Hume
Deal, Margaret
Deans, Mrs. W. O.
Dorsey, Sanford
Edwards, Robert R.
Edwards, Mrs. Robert Ray
Estes, Jafries
Eubank, Hannan Elizabeth
Evans, Hannah M.
Fisher, Mrs. Carl
Fisher, Mrs. L. S.
Fleming, Mrs. Andrew
Gaines, Virginia Ethel
Gentry, Mrs. George L.
George, Mary Winnie
Gartrell, Augustus Blair, Jr.
Gilleland, Reba Armetia
Gilleland, Willie Leonard
Glaze, Carrie Lou
Gresham, Charles D.
Hairston, Nellie Heiss
Hairston, Summer Lincoln
Hall, Ruby Colman
Harbuck, John H.
Harrelson, Evelyn Zeline
Harris, John Sanford
Harrison, Lillian Leola
Harvey, Mr. & Mrs. J. M.
Hays, Mrs. C. S.
Hays, Calvin S.
Hazelrig, Dorothy
Hazelrig, Mr. & Mrs. E. B.
Hazelrig, Harry Hill
Henson, Mr. & Mrs. Wm. C.
Hickey, Marie Boggs
Hickman, Ollie Eugene, Jr.
Hildebrand, Pearl
Hills, Henry Lyman
Hillyer, Mary Hurd
Hinton, Frances
Hoyt, Winn C.
Hubner, Rose Elizabeth
Huie, Dorothy
Huie, Mrs. Ralph
Huie, Ralph, Jr.
Hughes, Mr. & Mrs. John W.
Hull, Miriam Josephine
Hyatt, Irvin
Hyatt, Jessie
Icenogle, Inez Allen
Johnson, Mrs. L. C.
Jones, Mr. & Mrs. E. A.
Jones, Margaret
Jones, Mary Elizabeth
Kendrick, Wm. Richard
Kidder, S. D.
Kirk, Mr. & Mrs. Charles E.
Lance, James Arthur

Langford, Vick Loraine
Langford, V. R.
Linam, Vera
Logan, Mr. & Mrs. Joseph A., Jr.
Maddox, B. H.
Maddox, T. P.
Mason, Mrs. J. L.
Massey, Jackson Lidell
Miller, Augustus Taylor, Jr.
Miller, Helen Oakley
Morgan, Charles R.
Morgan, James Bartow, Jr.
Mullins, Elizabeth Ione
Murat, Miriam
McClure, Sarah Dimmock
McDowell, Mrs. George M.
McIntyre, Charles P.
Nelms, Sarah Joe
Nelms, Sue
Norris, Edward
Owens, V. E.
Parker, Bennie Merle
Patterson, Wilmer Fay
Pentecost, Maltbie
Petty, Oscar
Pfeiffer, John
Philips, Frances
Phillips, Helen Evelyn
Pitchford, Louise
Pritchard, Mary
Pritchard, Ruby Jones
Rebb, Otis Miller
Reed, Cleo Teenie
Register, H. E.
Reeves, Claude B.
Savitz, Benjamin Norman
Simms, Bertha Annette
Simms, Mary Vaught
Smith, Dorothy Lucia
Smith, Willie Hearn
Swann, Harry
Swaringen, Catherine Virginia
Thomas, Elsie Juanita
Thomas, Mr. & Mrs. J. Frank
Thomas, Joe
Turner, Beatrice
Veal, Mr. & Mrs. Eldridge S.
Walker, Charles Respess
Way, Eva
Wells, George H., Jr.
Werner, Elizabeth Cowles
White, Kate
Wigley, Murnic Louise
Williams, Maymie
Willis, Eugene Fletcher
Wilson, Ethel
Winship, Emily
Woodhead, Dr. Amos Martin
Wooten, Evelyn
Wray, Clifford Daniel
Young, Clifford Anderson
Young, Janie
Young, Victor Dawson

1926

Adams, Wm. Pearse
Adcox, Annie Leola
Alexander, Essie M.
Amis, Alice W.

Andrews, Zeb Vance
Appleby, Edwin Thomas
Appleby, Scott Bascom, Jr.
Barbour, Henry Wey
Barden, Leila Lois
Beaty, Mrs. D. Waldo
Bond, Harry Kellor
Brand, Monteen
Brine, Woodruff Werner
Brown, Mr. & Mrs. Charles W.
Brumby, Dorothy Rudicil
Buford, Alice Walker
Buford, Mrs. C. S.
Butler, James Brown
Calhoun, Alpha
Chapman, Mrs. W. H.
Clapp, Mrs. Miller
Clark, Annie Lou
Clark, Dr. Evert Edward
Cook, Samuel Woods
Cooper, Margaret
Crawford, Jean
Cruselle, Guy H.
Daughtry, Annie Stone
Deans, Dr. W. O.
Demere, Mrs. E. H.
Dickson, James Hill
Dorsey, Louie Lamar
Dunn, Wm. John, Jr.
Durden, Joe Respress
Durden, Mary Elizabeth
Estes, Mr. & Mrs. John M., Jr.
Estes, Vivan Elizabeth
Gilleland, Mr. & Mrs. W. J.
Gilmer, Dorothy Louise
Gossett, Frances Elizabeth
Gray, Mildred Louise
Gregory, Ross
Haney, Mary Jim
Harris, Henrietta Frances
Harris, Sara Lois
Head, Mary Ruth
Head, Mr. & Mrs. Oscar T.
Hightower, Homer
Hill, Albert Whitel
Hill, Emma Mae
Hills, Margaret
Houk, Herbert O.
Hoyt, Agnes Alexander
Jones, Douglas Rupert
Jones, Mr. & Mrs. James Slaughter
Jones, Katherine Alice
Jones, Margaret Olive
Kesler, Blanche
Kiishian, Lucy
Knox, Roscoe Charles
Kolakowski, Carl
Lake, Emma
Lewis, Alma
Lindsey, Wm. Harbey
Malone, Frances Lane
Manry, John Ardis
Marchetti, Victor, Jr.
Mason, Daisy Pearl
Maxwell, Louise
Meadows, Mrs. M. W.
Merritt, Lawrence T.
Metcalfe, Samuel Littler
Mills, Sarah Evelyn
Mobley, Hazel Mills

Christmas in the 40's, celebrated by pageants and offerings to Thornwell Orphanage.

Moor, Henry Howland, Jr.
Moore, J. Gordon, Jr.
Moss, Burnley M.
Myers, Ona Mae
Myers, Thelma Louise
Mynatt, Joseph L.
McKeen, Wm. B.
McRae, Mr. & Mrs. Richard F.
Neel, Vera M.
Nelson, Lillian Othella
Newell, Cleveland Pounds
O'Callaghan, James
O'Neal, Avis Marguerite
Osborne, Millicent
Parks, Mr. & Mrs. Claud A.
Parks, Virginia
Pentecost, Mrs. M. K.
Procter, Anna Mildred
Proctor, Mr. & Mrs. James E.
Ragin, Julia Jenkin
Ragin, Mary Caldwell
Ray, Pearl
Richards, Mrs. Paul R.
Riviere, Mr. & Mrs. J. A.
Russell, L. P.
Russell, Nellie Elizabeth
Schumann, Mr. & Mrs. Wm. Hiram
Selph, Archie Melvin
Shaw, Rubin Rudolph
Sims, Mary Odell
Sims, Naomi
Smith, Katie Elizabeth
Smith, Marion St. Leon
Smith, Max Crawford
Spurlock, Mrs. Blueford Custer
Sweat, Eugenia Ruth
Vivrett, Walter Koellein
Vogt, Mrs. Albert
West, Mr. & Mrs. E. H.
Wheeler, Elizabeth Sue
Wilhite, Alice
Wood, Hugh
Wood, Maria Robinson
Wray, James Fred
Young, Catherine Bell
Young, Mary
Zimmerman, Clifford

1927

Abbott, Fred S.
Allen, William
Allen, Viola
Bailer, W. A.
Bently, Daisy
Bolton, Mr. & Mrs. George T.
Bolton, Hugh Jack
Bolton, John Weldon
Brown, Wm. Caskey
Bruce, Mrs. John W.
Buchanan, Kathleen
Buchanan, Wm. F., Jr.
Burns, Mrs. D. M.
Cates, E. W.
Cates, Mrs. L. W.
Chambers, Mrs. Ruth
Colvin, Catherine McKeehan
Cox, Mrs. Leon J. (Louise Calhoun)
Crosland, Dell (Mrs. Wm. J.)
Crow, Lou A.
Davidson, Laura
Davis, Catherine Moore
Drew, Hazel Dozier
Drew, Olen
Duke, Julia Mae
Ewing, Mrs. L. G.
Ewing, Margaret
Fischer, Leonard Stephen
Flournoy, Josephine G.
Fooshee, George Leroy
Fooshee, Joseph Leon
Fooshee, Mr. & Mrs. Robert L.
Francis, Maybelle
Freeman, Marion
Gailey, Theodore

THE PEOPLE WHO STAYED (1858-1978)

Gibbs, John Newton
Gossett, Mrs. Denie H.
Gossett, John W.
Greene, Wm. Jeff
Gunn, Edgar W.
Gunn, Edgar Woodson
Higgins, Adra L.
Hoke, Rebecca
Hood, Mr. & Mrs. W. H.
Hoyt, Sam Bogle
Johnson, Ray Selvin
Jones, Gertrude West
Kendrick, Jack
Macgruder, William Ranson
Marques, Earnest Daniel
Marques, Isabelle
Martin, Janet Valentine
Moore, Frank Wilson
Myers, Sophia S.
McClelland, Mrs. Ellis F.
McCown, Effie Ellen
McCown, Elsie Louise
McDonald, Walter S.
McIntyre, Carmon
McIntyre, Ercelle
McIntyre, Evelyn
McNeil, Homer Henry
Newman, Mr. & Mrs. J. W.
Penagee, Jeanette
Pinkston, Marvis
Redwine, Mrs. A. J.
Rodgers, Walter Norton
Sampson, Frank W.
Shaw, Lee Laurence
Sims, Bessie
Sims, Wilson
Snyder, Helen
St. John, Claude Wm.
Stokes, Maj. & Mrs. Charles
Tennant, Janie
Thomas, Harriet
Tuzeneau, Lorena
Vivrett, Mr. & Mrs. G. L.
Vivrett, Mary Catherine
Vivrett, Sarah DeLane
Watts, Ida Mae
Watwood, Mrs. Lambert
Werner, Harriet Eleanor
Whiting, Guy
Williams, Charles Jackson
Wingard, Carl F.
Wood, Vera Elizabeth

1928

Alexander, Annie
Baker, Bryant
Baker, Howard Lewis
Bedford, Wm. Glenn
Bentley, Velma Clara
Bradshaw, Jesse Austin
Bridges, Elizabeth
Burbank, Mrs. E. W.
Cunningham, Cornelia
Doyal, Mrs. Paul M.
Doyal, Thelma
Feldman, Viola
Fitts, Mrs. B. O.
Glenn, Mrs. N. R.
Glenn, Thelma
Griffin, Mrs. O. J.
Hagen, Evelyn Louise
Hames, J. N.
Hickman, Paul Roland
Jones, Anna
Jones, John Ashley
Little, Frances Elizabeth
Luce, Mrs. Charles B.
Mabry, Mattie
Miller, Edwin
Milliams, Mr. & Mrs. Frank A.
Milliams, Wm. A.
Mills, Clarence Wilbur
Morgan, Miriam Elizabeth
McAllister, John Robert
Phares, Beula
Philips, Dorothy
Philips, Robert Stanley
Rayburn, Mr. & Mrs. F. T.
Rayburn, Mildred Evelyn
Rhodes, Janie Flourney
Roberson, Bessie Mozelle
Russey, Daisy Smith
Saleba, Eloise Lucy
Sherard, Esther
Singleton, J. H.
Smith, Bernardine Edwards
Speer, Lee Roy
Tanksley, Corrine Phillips
Taylor, Lena
Viser, John Graham
Watrous, F. W.
Watrous, Lucy Angeline
Webb, Annie May Tanksley
Webb, C. W.
Wells, Elizabeth Frances
Wilhelm, Mrs. C.
Willis, A. B.
Wilson, Cora Odell
Wray, William
Yarbrough, Roy
Yarbrough, Mrs. V. J.
Yarbrough, V. J., Jr.
Young, Leah Kate
Zimmerman, Kennett

1929

Bedford, Mildred Enola
Bellingrath, Avis Mae
Bradley, Sara Rebecca
Brown, Wm. Ernest
Buchanan, Elizabeth Porter
Castles, Annie Lee
Chapelle, Mrs. J.L.
Chapelle, Thomas
Chapman, Mary Frances
Cleveland, Mildred
Dillard, Nancy Young
Ellerson, Francis
Greene, James Wm.
Hagan, Wm. Joseph, III
Hardin, Gladys Enla
Henning, Katherine Rose
Hunt, Georgia Everhart
Johnson, Fred Wm.
Johnston, Harry Buckanon, Jr.
Jones, Edward Tyler
Kendrick, Ann Elizabeth
Kendrick, Virginia Claire
Kent, Harry W.
Knapp, Jane Davidson
MacGaughey, Barbara
Moore, Alvin Palmer
Moore, Wm. Sherwood
Myrick, Clarence Clifford, Jr.
McCalley, Catherine Etiole
Parker, Emma Marie
Proctor, James, Jr.
Shepard, Eugene Thomas
Stewart, Ruth Charlotte
Taylor, John Thomas
Warner, Beatrice
Warner, O.F.
Wells, Gladys Josephine
Wigley, Mrs. James Frank
Winship, George, Jr.
Woolf, Thomas Harley
York, Elsie Reeves

1930

Aiken, Mr. & Mrs. Ellison
Alexander, Evelyn
Almand, Charles Marvin
Almand, George Ira
Amend, Mary E.
Barber, Geraldine Annette
Barth, Mrs. Carl
Baxter, Charles H.
Beech, Allen Ashley
Bentley, Sara E.
Bessemer, Clarice Akins
Bessemer, S.M.
Boswell, Leslie
Brown, Eldredge Edmunds
Burns, Joseph Wiley
Burns, Shelby Dennis
Cameron, Sarah
Chance, Mrs. Ira
Cheves, Howard Scott
Clark, Jack Campbell
Clark, Lei Everett
Collins, Mr. & Mrs. Wm. A.
Crafts, Harry Gibbs
Craig, James Edward
Crawford, Margaret
Davis, A.O., Jr.
Demere, Edward
Dickson, Mrs. J.C.
Dickson, Jack Duncan
Dickson, Robert Willis
Donahue, Cynthia
Estes, John Minor, III
Ewing, James Grant
Fincher, Joseph Olin
Fields, Mattie
Fowler, Myrtle Dow
Fowler, Raymond Ezra
Goodwin, A.H.
Goodwin, Daisy Dean
Gravitt, James Aldine
Hagan, Edward James
Hayes, Moses Sim
Henry, Mr. & Mrs. C.A.
Hickman, John Williams
Hills, John
Hindman, Thomas L., Jr.
Holland, Ella J.
Holland, Robert Marion

Holmes, Eloise Nipper
Honea, Mrs. P.H.
Hornsby, Alonzo Ringer
Ingraham, Virginia L.
Irvine, Emma Agnes
Irvine, Mrs. Wm. Preston
Jackson, Aubrey
Jones, A. Tim
Jones, Elma Lee
Jones, Martin L.
Jordan, Hunter Nevin
Keen, Edward F., Jr.
Kelly, Marie
Kendrick, Doris
Knox, Charles
Lang, James Roan
Layton, Mr. & Mrs. H.W.
Leach, Robert Lynn
Little, Billie
Maddox, B. Herbert
Matthews, Mrs. Curtis
Miller, Augustus T.
Miller, J.T.
Morris, Mrs. H.R.
Muckenfuss, Emily
Muckenfuss, Julian
McDonald, George
McKee, Burruss
McKee, Mrs. John
McKee, Lydia
McKee, Mary
MacRae, Thomas
Nelms, Lamar Hall
Newman, James Wm.
Noland, Mabel Wells
Oglesby, Frances
Oglesby, Stuart, III
Oglesby, Mrs. Stuart R.
Patterson, Leila
Patterson, Sue
Peavy, Mary
Peek, Marie
Perry, G.E.
Pettit, Bertie
Pettit, Mary Ruth
Pettit, Stephen I.
Ramsden, Harold
Ramsden, Mrs. J.E.
Rand, Mildred Jessie
Reynolds, Ned
Roan, Leila Carrie
Roland, Harold Eugene
Shulenberger, Mr. & Mrs. J.H.
Singleton, James Franklin
Singleton, John Henry, Jr.
Slider, Isabelle Logan
Smith, Mrs. L.N.
Stalker, Ian Fraser
Stalker, Marie
Stephenson, Polly DePass
Stephenson, Robert Maffett
Stewart, Jane
Stewart, Luna
Stewart, Thomas Hill, III
St. John, Margaret Sue
Sullivan, Daniel, Jr.
Taylor, Mr. & Mrs. J. Homer
Terrell, Augustus S.
Terrell, Edward Arthur
Thompson, Margaret Elizabeth
Thompson, Thomas Walker
Underwood, Harold
Underwood, Lillian
Waldrop, Mrs. Larrie
Webb, John Wesley
Wells, May
Wells, Mary Frances
Wicks, Jack
Wicks, Mr. & Mrs. John
Woodberry, Stella
Wooding, Nathaniel Jackson, Sr.
Workman, Robert

1931

Alexander, Carrie Allen
Baskin, J.L.
Baskin, Lydia Wheeler
Brantley, Anne
Brown, Jennie Lela
Burnett, Margaret
Burruss, Edwina Walker
Burruss, Mary Kate
Carlisle, Harry Lewis
Chance, Ira, Jr.
Chandler, William Hugh
Chase, James E.
Christian, Lucile
Clotfelter, Henry Lewis
Collum, Mary Sue
Crafts, Claudia
Curry, Rufus Randolph
Durett, Joseph A.
Eagan, Anna Young
Eagan, William Russell
Edmondson, C.J.
Frazer, Mr. & Mrs. J.B.
Hall, James Adkins
Henderson, John Augustus
Henderson, L.V.
Hickman, Susan Lucy
Higgins, Mrs. M.S.
Huff, Mr. & Mrs. W.F.
Huie, Dorothy
Jackson, Henry
Jansen, Frederica
Johnson, Fred C.
Keel, Mr. & Mrs. E.E.
Kennedy, Mrs. M.D.
Kreeger, Frances
Kreeger, Robert Everett
Leach, R.L.
Leavitt, Mary Elizabeth
Locke, William Leslie
Long, Mrs. George W., Jr.
Lowe, Mr. & Mrs. W.H.
Mable, John Alexander
Mable, Rose Edwards
MacRae, Douglas Griffin
Mathis, Mr. & Mrs. SC.
Mathis, S.C., Jr.
McClain, Opal Allen
McGrath, Mrs. William Richard
Norris, Wallace E., Jr.
Oglesby, Richard
O'Neal, Otis Newnon
Parker, Mary Louise
Peacock, Virgil Edward
Percival, Mrs. Jessie A.
Shaw, Dr. Ray Y.
Smith, Noel
Underwood, John Terrell
Underwood, Shannon
Wallace, Mr. & Mrs. E.D.
Watkins, Flora Lyle
White, Mr. & Mrs. Sterling E.
Williams, Dorothy
Williams, Mr. & Mrs. J.C.
Williams, Dorothy Margaret
Williamson, H.P., Sr.
Wise, Amelia
Wolcott, Margaret
Young, Anne
Young, Thelma

1932

Allen, Gertrude Florence
Anderson, Walter Edward
Astin, Alice
Astin, Mrs. J.S.
Astin, Julian Sherwood
Astin, Lillian Alma
Astin, Louise
Astin, Roland Merle
Astin, Roy
Barbour, Mrs. Wey
Benner, Mrs. R.C.
Biddy, George Wesley
Biles, Jack Benjamin
Butler, William Henry
Castles, Mamie
Chance, James William
Chapman, Mary Crusselle
Cheves, Dorothy Marion
Collum, Mrs. Ed
Converse, Mrs. Icie Wolfe
Coulter, Myrtle
Cowan, Mr. & Mrs. Robert E.
Entriken, Selma Penegar
Fetzer, Jacob Frank
Fisher, Guy Gilleland
Fisher, Mrs. William T.
George, Marguerite E.
Griffeth, Claire
Horton, Ruby Lorene
Howell, Julia
Howell, LeRoy
Howell, Margaret Geneva
Howell, Wilmer Lloyd
Huie, Ralph
Keener, Ervin Leon
Kennedy, Dorothy Louise
Kennedy, Myrt D.
Knapp, Marion McNaught
Leach, Daniel Pritchard
Lennard, Mr. & Mrs. J.M.
Lennard, Julius, Jr.
Lennard, Lois
Mays, Agnes
Moody, Tommie
Muckenfuss, Ruth Barbara
Muckenfuss, William
Mullins, Mr. & Mrs. W.E.
McCalley, Mrs. Raymond
McCalley, Mrs. Robert
McGill, Mrs. B.D.
McGill, Margaret E.
McGill, Robert L.
Nessling, Augustus Cornelius

O'Callaghan, Richard Hayes
Parker, Mr. & Mrs. S.W.
Peacock, Edward
Proctor, Mary
Sanders, Arthur Norman
Sanders, Ruby
Shaw, Lawrence
Shearer, Mrs. Langley P.
Singleton, Mary Eugenia
Smith, Mrs. James G.
Sprague, William Henry
Stewart, Horace Carlton
Stribling, Lemuel D.
Sullivan, John Hansell
Swaringen, Charlotte
Swaringer, Mrs. J.B.
Terrell, William M.
Tribble, Frances Virginia
Tribble, Mrs. James T.
Tribble, Majorie Elizabeth
Turner, Earl
Walker, Anna Harriet
Walker, Nita
Walters, Mrs. A.J.
Wells, Tommie Luther
Whitmire, Thomas W.
Wilhelm, James W.
Williamson, Mr. & Mrs. J.E.
Yarbrough, Georgia

1933

Abercrombie, Van
Barber, Fred
Boyd, Margaret Howell
Brown, Mr. & Mrs. J.G.
Brown, LeRoy Charles
Burn, Mellie A.
Carpenter, Christine
Carpenter, Edward W.
Carter, Mrs. Lewis Wm.
Carver, Charles E.
Castleberry, Juanita
Chafin, Mr. & Mrs. Herman
Chapman, Dover Mae
Chapman, Pleasant Smith
Clark, Everett Edward
Clarke, Mrs. M.C.
Clarke, Samuel Edward
Cleveland, Jean
Cox, Elizabeth
Cox, Eva S.
Craft, Martha Delphia
Crenshaw, John Walden
Davis, Caroline
Davis, Dorothy
Duke, Mr. & Mrs. H.E.
Dunford, Mr. & Mrs. J.W.
Easterwood, Annie
Estes, Bettie
Estes, Mr. & Mrs. M.P.
Estes, Marion
Fant, Margaret
Florence, Mr. & Mrs. George A.
Freeman, Mr. & Mrs. Milton O.
Fuller, Emily
Fuller, Martha Ann
Glover, George Z., Jr.
Graddy, Faith
Graddy, Martha Faith
Hall, Harry
Hall, Mary Lee
Hammock, Howard
Hammock, Louise
Hannah, Caroline
Hanson, Howard Gray
Haynes, Mrs. J.H.
Haynes, John Henry
Haynes, Sarah
Hornby, Alice Louise
Irvine, William
Knight, Mamie K.
Kritzler, Emaline
Kritzler, Fred
Kritzler, Mrs. Fred A.
Lambert, Clayburn Leon
Lambert, Estelle
Landers, Arthur
Layton, Davis
Leach, William
Leavitt, Leona
Luce, Sara Barbara
Lunsford, Rosella
Miles, Charlotte
Morris, B.L.
Morris, Jack
Morris, Sadie
Morris, Mrs. Roy Olson
Muckenfuss, Rose
McCowan, Effie Ellen
McCowan, Elsie Louise
McKee, Catherine Brantley
McMullen, Carrie Lena
Norman, Thomas Hall
O'Callaghan, Katherine
Peacock, Nell Marie
Pope, Mr. & Mrs. Neal Q.
Rainford, Charles
Rainford, Mary
Rankin, Mrs. Robert
Ransone, Emily Elizabeth
Rich, Mr. & Mrs. Thomas T.
Richards, Mrs. J.M.
Roberts, Doris
Roby, Mildred
Roby, Robert Allen
Rocker, Mr. & Mrs. Glen
Rocker, Glen
Scruggs, Mrs. A.J.
Shelnut, Clifford Bernard
Shelnut, J.C.
Shields, Robert
Snyder, Mrs. C.O.
Stewart, Paul Harold
Tanner, Dorothy
Terry, Nora Bell
Thrash, Mrs. Gordon
Todd, Mary Hubbard
Todd, Myra
Turner, May
Turner, Ozella
Upchurch, Katherine M.
Waters, Ida
Wilhelm, Dorothy Ann
Williamson, Mrs. H.P., Jr.
Williamson, Jack Lanier
Wolcott, Benjamin Hale
Wolcott, Mr. & Mrs. R.H.
Wray, George Madison
Wright, Mary

1934

Askin, Mrs. W.B.
Barfield, Mrs. A.A.
Barrzell, Ida
Bartlett, Mr. & Mrs. A.C.
Beale, Robert H.
Born, L.C.
Brooks, Miriam Cornelia
Bruner, A.E.
Califf, Mr. & Mrs. J.G.
Calkins, Mr. & Mrs. James W.
Cleveland, Mrs. L.R.
Cotts, John D.
Cox,Sarah Evelyn
Edmondson, H.W.
Fowler, Joseph Roy
Freeman, Milton Oliver
Hall, Walter Joseph, Jr.
Harden, Mr. & Mrs. H.H.
Harden, Harper H., Jr.
Hayes, Mrs. Thomas Swift
Hunter, Janie
Hunter, Mary L.
Kelley, Dorris Elizabeth
Linn, John Venable
May, Betty White
Minish, Mrs. V.B.
Mobley, Mollie
Morgan, Mirriam
Nicholson, Mr. & Mrs. Paul F.
Owen, Clure Halman
Owen, Elizabeth Smith
Pascal, Florrie Ethelyn
Russell, Anna Scott
Scott, Florence Evelyn
Smith, Mrs. James D.
Swaim, Carey G.
Thrash, Gay
West, Paul D.
Widener, Dorothy Jane
Young, Leah

1935

Akers, Isabel
Barmettler, Anee
Beale, Mrs. Robert H.
Beech, Mr. & Mrs. Allen A.
Boyer, Carl
Boyer, Ralph Alvin
Brown, Mary Virginia
Buchanan, Mary Ann
Calkins, Maribelle
Cone, Evelyn
Cone, William B.
Cowan, Robert E., Jr.
Craft, Allen C.
Crenshaw, Minor Estes
Eichelberger, Mamie W.
Estes, Sarah
Fraser, Conradine
Garner, Jones E.
Green, Florence
Hanson, Mary Frances
Humphries, Mrs. W.F., Jr.
Johns, Charles Edward
Johns, Mattie Louise
Johnson, Addie E.
Jones, Mr. & Mrs. Cecil

Kendrick, Edward Storey
Kennedy, Mert David, Jr.
Kirkus, Mary Ellen
Knapp, Helen
Lankford, Dan L.
Lunsford, Reader
MacLagen, Roberta Emma
Miller, Ethel Erma
Miller, Robert
Miller, Stevie Andrew S.
Morrow, Lorene
Mott, Mrs. E.W.
McCalley, William L., Jr.
McCarley, Mrs. John P.
McCroskey, Bettie Marie
McCurry, Robert
McIntosh, Mrs. M.L.
Nisbet, O.M.
Norman, Julia
Oglesby, Micajah Lamar
Paine, Mary
Peddicord, Mr. & Mrs. Samuel R.
Perry, Laura
Peterson, Mrs. Annie
Radford, Bettie Jean
Radford, Frances
Radford, Mr. & Mrs. G.S.
Rand, Edgar
Russell, Annie K.
Sanders, Jack
Shelnutt, Mary Louise
Shillinglaw, Mr. & Mrs. Robert
Smith, Lorene
Stanton, Arthur
Stewart, Dorothy Jean
Stewart, Paul Harold
Sweat, Dorothy
Thompson, Henrietta
Thompson, Mr. & Mrs. J. Homer
Thompson, John Fraser
Traylor, Mr. & Mrs. Forest
Traylor, Forest, Jr.
Turner, Susie
Whitner, Elizabeth
Whitner, Virginia
Wilson, Hugh Amos
Wolcott, Robert Henry

1936

Abraham, Jimmy
Allen, Mrs. J. A.
Benham, Vernon W.
Bentley, Douglas F.
Biles, Mary
Blaich, Adeline
Blaich, Benjamin
Blaich, Sadie
Brewer, H.A.
Brewer, Lois
Brewer, Olive Mae
Brown, Elizabeth
Brown, Mrs. Samuel Y.
Byrd, Mrs. Erin C.
Carroll, Bertha
Carroll, Charles A.
Cary, Grace
Cary, James
Cary, William
Cary, Mr. & Mrs. Wm. T., Sr.
Cason, Anna Belle
Chapman, Homer
Cheatham, Mrs. John R.
Chestnut, Mr. & Mrs. J.M.
Collins, Sybil
Craig, Elizabeth
Craig, Mr. & Mrs. W.E.
Cunningham, Mrs. C.C.
Embry, Rosa
Estes, Eugene
Estes, Lila
Farmer, Julia
Farmer, Roy
Golden, Rosa Pitman
Gunn, Few Alonzo
Gunn, Mrs. Willie Ross
Gurley, Willie
Harper, Thelma
Harris, Edith
Haynie, Walter
Herzberg, Isabell
Holland, Mrs. Fred
Hollingsworth, Mary Belle
Houck, John B.
Hubbard, Mary E.
Hyndman, Mary Ann
Hyndman, Mary Elizabeth
Ittner, Ann Campbell
Layton, Harvey M., Jr.
Lee, R.E.
Lemon, Mary Alice
Logan, Virginia Dare
Mitcham, Mrs. B.H.
Morrow, Mildred
Moseley, Frances Earle
Moseley, John Arthur
McCowan, Charles Earnest
McGloughlin, Florence Ann
Nelson, Rosa
O'Callaghan, Ben Lacy
Rankin, John Robert
Robinson, Mr. & Mrs. C.R.
Robinson, Carline
Robinson, Donald
Robinson, Nannie
Russell, Rowena
Ryan, Mrs. Mattie
Scott, Harry
Shedd, Annie
Shedd, Nell
Simmons, Alfred
Smith, Grady
Smith, Harold
Smith, Katie
Stribling, Louise Jackson
Sweat, William Landers
Taylor, Ewell
Taylor, Rosa Lee
Thompson, Mr. & Mrs. Walter C.
Toler, Grace
Torrance, M.L.
Via, Harold
Waters, Ed
Watts, Mrs. Harvey
Weed, Morris
Weed, Mr. & Mrs. James R.
Wilson, Mr. & Mrs. Homer
Wray, Lola

1937

Allen, Mrs. P.R.
Baggett, Mr. & Mrs. R.T.
Beatie, William David, Jr.
Black, Virginia
Blair, J.L.
Boatwright, Ralph
Boatwright, Louise
Browder, Evelyn Crawford
Brown, Mrs. Carl
Brown, Mrs. Paul, Jr.
Burnett, Nell Fowler
Butler, Mr. & Mrs. Ben M.
Butler, Jean
Camp, George E., Jr.
Chance, Ira
Clark, Elizabeth Carlisle
Cobb, Annie
Cole, Mrs. Boynton
Craft, Mary Antoinette
Crenshaw, Lucy Boyce
Curran, Edgar E.
Dawson, Mrs. Thomas E.
de Mourelle, Mrs. J.L.
de Mourelle, Joseph L.
Dennison, Frank V., Jr.
Dial, Lillian
Dumphy, Dorothy
Embry, Charlie
Ficken, Mrs. E.S.
Fraser, Hazel Anne
Futch, Emily
Gaines, Mrs. Alexander
Gilbert, Glendola
Gilbert, Jean
Glaze, Charles
Glives, Mozelle
Goldwire, Mr. & Mrs. J.O.
Gowan, J.P.
Greene, Mr. & Mrs. James A.
Griffin, Ethel
Griffin, H.S.
Gunter, Katherine
Hanson, Marion Louise
Harris, Marshall
Hinton, Sallie
Hollingsworth, Mr. & Mrs. R.L.
Hollingsworth, R. Roy
Holtzlaw, Mr. & Mrs. Richard
Hudgins, J.B.
Huff, Joyce
Huff, Mrs. W.R.
Huie, Eleanor
Hunter, Mrs. Walter A.
Jackson, Henry
Johnson, Birdie
Jones, W.T.
Keen, Edward F., Sr.
Kennedy, Bernice
Kennedy, Louise
Klassett, Andrew
Klassett, Katie L.
Klassett, Mary Belle
Layton, Dorris
Layton, Mr. & Mrs. Harvey W.
Lemon, Cecil Moorefield
Lemon, Jeanne Elizabeth
Luther, Peggy Murphy
Luther, Walter Adams, Jr.

Dr. Lacy, Dr. Oglesby, Dr. Richards

Maddox, Mrs. Herbert
Maddox, Mr. & Mrs. T.P., Sr.
Marler, Edgar Darby
Mason, Fred C., Jr.
Myers, Mr. & Mrs. Giles McA.
McDaniel, Grace
Peddicord, Samuel Robert, Jr.
Penner, Elizabeth
Pennington, Elizabeth Etta
Perryman, Annie B.
Phillips, Mrs. Owen
Roberts, Mrs. B.E.
Roberts, Boyce
Rowland, Harold Eugene
Rumble, Douglas, Jr.
Steiglitz, Evelyn Jeanette
Smith, Harold Frank
Smith, John, Jr.
Spears, Mrs. S.T.
Stillman, Dr. & Mrs. Wm. King, Jr.
Stonecypher, Horace
Stroup, Bettie Jane
Turner, Leon
Walls, Augustus
Webb, Mr. & Mrs. G. Davis
Williamson, Isabel
Williamson, Mrs. J.W.
Williamson, Westwood
Wilson, Robert E.

1938

Arnold, Mrs. S.J.
Baker, Fred
Baker, Louis
Baker, Mamie Lee
Barbour, Millicent Eugenia
Beeler, Dr. J. Moss
Bell, Mr. & Mrs. A.W.
Bell, Mrs. Alex
Bell, Mary Jane
Bigham, Mary
Bishop, Joe Lee
Bradshaw, Mrs. J.A., Jr.
Calhoun, Mrs. Martha
Carter, William Maynard
Childers, Mr. & Mrs. J.L.
Clark, Mrs. Samuel
Coyle, Ella
Crosland, Joyce
Crosland, Wm. Alexander, Jr.
Dacus, Mrs. Claudia
DeFoor, Andrew Lynn
Dennis, Emma
Doyle, Ray
Duncan, Edward J.
Elliott, John
Estes, Frances Elizabeth
Farmer, Julia
Farmer, Roy
Fletcher, Helen
Fletcher, John
Fletcher, Mrs. L.S.
Garrard, Mrs. E.A.
Godwin, Marie Elizabeth
Goldwire, Esther Agnes
Goldwire, Frances Eris
Goldwire, James Cochran
Hall, Lorene
Hansell, Mr. & Mrs. Wm. A.
Hansell, William A., Jr.
Harris, Charles Wm.
Haynes, Margaret Brand
Hendrix, Sara
Herbertson, Betty
Hills, Mrs. Richard A.
Hobbs, Audrey
Howell, John
Hubbard, Nell
Johnson, Mrs. Fred
Jones, Alice Elizabeth
Jones, Myles C.
Keel, Mr. & Mrs. Edward E.
Kendall, Mr. & Mrs. J.S.
Kendall, Jennings S., Jr.
Kendrick, Daniel F.
Kendall, Mary Clem
Kieth, Ruby
King, Mr. & Mrs. Early
Knox, Mrs. Ben
Laurence, Sara
Leach, Bud Oliver
Lee, Charles Russell
Lennard, Mrs. Julius, Jr.
Lindsay, Mr. & Mrs. Lamar H.
Marler, Mildred
Moore, Madelyn
McDaniel, Betty Frances
McDaniel, Grace
McElroy, Eugene Lee
Pannell, Robert Dewey
Persons, Mrs. Harvey F.
Persons, John Pat
Phillips, Edith Elizabeth
Poss, Nena Louise
Radford, Anne
Reckels, Guian
Reckels, Reba
Roberts, Lenie
Rust, Donald
Sanders, Kathryn
Scanling, F.W.
Sills, Ruth
Smith, Mrs. Harold C.
Smith, Mary Emma
Soell, Mr. & Mrs. Albert W.
Stafford, Mrs. L.M.
Stillman, Annie Laurie
Streater, Wallace
Tarleton, W. Bruce
Upton, Margaret
Wallace, Mr. & Mrs. R.L.
Waller, Mr. & Mrs. Stuart
Whitfield, Joseph Hoyt
Whitman, David S.
Wilhite, Mrs. W.P.
Wills, Irene
Wills, Jean
Wyatt, Pauline
Wynn, Joseph Dean, Jr.

1939

Allen, Dorothy
Allen, George Ralph
Allen, Mary Frances
Anderson, Caroline May
Bethune, S.J.
Boles, Alexander Patrick
Boles, Mr. & Mrs. S.P.
Brisendine, Garrett M.
Brisendine, Kathryn
Brock, Charles Elbert
Clark, Wm. Augustus, Jr.
Cochran, Charles
Coleman, Lillian
Copeland, Mrs. Charles

Cox, Sarah
Cranford, Peter G.
Cranford, Mrs. Peter G.
Curry, Mr. & Mrs. J.A.
Davis, Ruth E.
Derrick, Mrs. L.C.
Dickson, Mrs. J.H., Jr.
Duke, W.C.
Dunford, Bootsie
Eubank, H. Fred
Fletcher, Mrs. John
Fountain, Eva Sue
Fowler, Herbert
Franklin, John Quincy
Franklin, Mrs. John Quincy
Franklin, Wm. Thomas
Garland, Dorothy
Godwin, Louise Ann
Godwin, Mildred Frances
Graham, George P.
Hardin, Ida Kenney
Harrell, Betty Jo
Herriman, Mrs. Perry Lee
Hess, Clarice Sophia
Hess, Samuel
Hollingsworth, Mr. & Mrs. Charles G.
Hollingsworth, J. Hope
Karston, Mrs. Emmett
Kennedy, E. Harris
Key, Verna Lee
Key, Verda Ruth
Leiter, Melba Perry
Marler, Dempsey Charles
Miller, Irma Rose
Mosley, Frances Mildred
McGregor, Mr. & Mrs. C.T.
McKibben, Mrs. C.H.
Nardin, Frederick William
O'Callaghan, Mrs. W.L.
Plott, Mrs. Robert
Plott, Robert R.
Pope, Emily Lowe
Pound, Josephine Leah
Ragland, Dr. Fred
Rawlins, James Calvin
Roberts, Mrs. Lessie
Rogers, Kenneth
Rowland, Mary Louise
Ryan, Jessie E.
Ryan, Mattie Louise
Ryan, Mrs. Timothy E.
Shearer, Langley, Jr.
Sinkoe, Mrs. Abe
Smith, Clyde O.
Smith, Raleigh Littleton
Upton, Margaret
Waters, Mrs. Tull C.
Weldon, Elijah M.
Weldon, Margaret Estelle
Weldon, Mrs. Ruby E.
Weldon, Ruby Joyce
Weldon, Thomas Burnell
Whitman, Mrs. D.S.
Whitner, Joe Coffin
Wittes, Helen
Wright, Frances P.
Yancey, Mr. & Mrs. W.L., Jr.

1940

Anthony, Claud Lee
Archer, A.H.
Archer, Mrs. Jimmie J.
Benner, Robert Earl
Bradley, Katie
Branch, Mr. & Mrs. R.D.
Bright, Mr. & Mrs. Norris
Burton, Lois
Chafin, Herman Keith, Jr.
Cheves, Mrs. D.S.
Cochran, Mr. & Mrs. Sterling L.
Cole, Mr. & Mrs. R.W.
Coleman, Dr. R.C., Jr.
Craig, Mrs. M.S.
Crenshaw, Mr. & Mrs. B.L.
Dunlap, Louis E.
Eady, Mrs. W.S.
Eady, William Stevens
Edwards, Mr. & Mrs. V.L.
Eskew, Henry
Franklin, John Quincy
Gardner, Juanita Wanda
Garland, Paul E.
German, Mr. & Mrs. R.F.
Graddy, Faith
Hambrick, Pearl
Hammond, Ruth Mathilda
Hickman, Mrs. Paul R.
Hills, Mrs. A.L.
Holmes, Maude Philips
Howard, Beverly Jo
Hoyt, Mrs. S.B.
Johnson, Evelyn Jewell
Johnson, Joe Willie
Johnson, Julius C.
Johnston, Mrs. Don K.
Jones, Mrs. Weston
Karston, Emmett
Kennedy, Frank Edward
Knight, Mrs. Cleveland
Lovern, Grady Lamar
Lovern, Thomas G.
Lovern, Mrs. Thomas G.
Ludl, Mrs. F.A.
Magee, Jessie
Mayo, Jimmie Harriett
Mayo, Laura Ellen
Mayo, Martha Irene
Mobley, Thomas
Montgomery, Mrs. F.J.
Morris, Peggy Louise
McCurry, Ruth Jean
Poole, Mr. & Mrs. Harry G., Jr.
Proctor, James Harvey
Rayburn, Mr. & Mrs. F.T.
Rogers, John H.
Scott, Wm. Washington, III
Sowell, Charlie Emmit
Shaw, Mrs. Lee
Shaw, Tom Gordon
Shepherd, Mr. & Mrs. A.C.
Shepherd, Gloria Eugenia
Shepherd, Ida Martha
Shepherd, Mrs. Ryman
Sheppard, Arthur Charles
Spigner, Madoleen
Tickner, Frederick A.
Turner, Marion Gilder
Van Orden, Edna Thompson
Verhine, James L.
Warren, Eulalia Blackstock
Waters, Betsie
Waters, Marie
Winterbotton, Mrs. Harold
Wynn, Addie
Wynn, Richard

1941

Anderson, Walter E., Jr.
Anderson, Wilmer
Atkinson, Caroline Mallory
Atkinson, Lee Olin
Barber, Bertie Florence
Beale, Mr. & Mrs. E.P.
Beale, Frances
Beale, Joseph D.
Beale, Ray Howland
Benner, R.C.
Billingsley, Jennie
Blair, Mrs. B.F.
Blair, Helen
Champion, Kate
Cheves, Mr. & Mrs. Ralph T.
Cochran, Deryl
Collins, Arthur Wood
Crawford, Janie
Crosland, Jean Claire
Daniel, Harold Eugene
Daniel, Paul Milton
Daniell, Leonard C.
Daughty, Kathleen
Dickens, Mr. & Mrs. R.S.
Dill, Lillie
Duke, Susie
Ellison, Mr. & Mrs. Hairston
Freeman, Mary G.
Gardner, Reginald Astor
Hammond, Wm. Edward
Hammond, Mrs. J.M.
Hayden, Dorothy Lee
Heaslett, Lillian
Hennon, Wm. Franklin
Hollingsworth, Mrs. Robert
Hoskins, Winifred
Howard, Katherine Nimo
Huck, Dr. William
Humphries, Wm. Franklin, Sr.
Jackson, Mrs. Marion J.
Johnson, Mrs. Herschel W.
Johnson, Noble Junior
Masters, Evelyn M.
Merrell, Alice Elizabeth
Morgan, Mr. & Mrs. David B.
Morrow, James Arthur
Mosely, Mona Louise
Murray, Jessie
McDaniel, Betty Frances
McDaniel, John
McDaniel, Sarah Rudin
McFalls, Anna Ruth
McIntosh, Edna Neff
McIntosh, Lewis Cumbie
McLean, Nancy
O'Neal, Mrs. Otis
Pierce, Clyde T.
Pinnell, Betty Jane
Pinnell, Marian Louise
Porterfield, Barbara Jean
Powell, Mrs. W.L.
Purcell, Josephine
Rawlins, J.C.
Reynolds, Eugene Roy
Reynolds, Martene
Roberts, Mrs. Boyce E.
Ross,Alice
Russell, John Scott
Schmidt, Mr. & Mrs. Wesley
Shaw, Marie Lucile
Smith, Vivan Margaret

Stalker, Mr. & Mrs. Ian
Stephens, Mrs. Henry A.
Stickney, John Cobb
Stokes, Mr. & Mrs. Burt
Taylor, Alexander S., III
Taylor, Eva Louise
Taylor, Lillian
Traer, Mr. & Mrs. Wyne S.
Turner, James Walter
Webster, Alexander
Webster, Mrs. Bella Scott
Webster, Mr. & Mrs. Peter S.
Whiteside, Ruth
Widener, Johnny C.
Wilkinson, Mrs. J.F.
Wilkinson, R.F.

1942

Akers, Hubert L.
Anthony, Mary Anne
Bansley, John David, III
Barker, Gloria Nell
Barringer, Lottie Margaret
Berryhill, W.R.
Bessemer, Carolyn
Boggess, Mr. & Mrs. R.D.
Boggs, Beth
Boggs, Dr. & Mrs. Lake S.
Boyd, Dr. & Mrs. Hartwell
Brantley, Mrs. E.G.
Brooks, Ethel
Byrd, Mr. & Mrs. Thomas L.
Chesnut, Peggy Ann
Childers, Mrs. Annie Bell
Childers, Eugene Edwards
Childers, James Levi
Clay, Mrs. Johnson
Conarro, Mr. & Mrs. R.M.
Cook, Bobby W.
Couey, Albert Simpson
Cripe, Mr. & Mrs. E.E.
Cross, Betty Joyce
Daniell, Marvin Lee
Davis, Mrs. R.C.
Davis, Roger Charles
Davis, Raymond Charles
Davis, Reginald Lewis
Davis, Ronald Coleman
Davis, Shirley Frances
Davis, Sidney Marjorie
Decker, Lorene
Edwards, Carol
Franseth, Jane
Fraser, Mildred Bruce
Gossett, Mr. & Mrs. J.W.
Graham, Mr. & Mrs. Brantley G.
Graham, Marjorie Gay
Haden, Maxie
Haden, Riley
Harrington, Mrs. H.R.
Henson, Mr. & Mrs. John M., Jr.
Holland, Mr. & Mrs. David C.
Holley, Louise Elizabeth
House, Mrs. Oscar C.
Huck, Terrence
Ittner, Frank Darlington, Jr.
Johnston, Emma Eloise
Kemp, William Hansel
Latham, Agnes
Leach, Elmer H.
Lee, Mrs. J.E.
Lemming, Ivy Louise
Lowry, Mrs. John D.
Martin, Joan
Martin, Louise
Mason, James
Mason, Margaret
Matthews, Margaret
Matthews, Wm. Curtis, Jr.
Middleton, Mr. & Mrs. Wm. S.
Moore, Mr. & Mrs. Claude P.
Morgan, Mrs. J.B., Jr.
Moss, John Robert, Jr.
Moss, Thomas
Mozley, Mary Katherine
Mullinax, Flora Edna
Mullinax, Jack Nathaniel
McClure, Mary
McDaniel, Sarah C.
McGlonn, Anne
O'Callaghan, Mr. & Mrs. Wm. L.
Plunkett, Thomas L.
Powell, Leonard
Rebb, Mrs. Otis M.
Richards, J McDowell, Jr.
Rowland, Gloria Dawn
Rogers, Wm. Gibson
Rylee, James Edward
Sheppard, Jacqueline
Spaanbrock, Jacqueline
Spitler, Mrs. Wm. A.
Spivey, Mrs. K.E.
Stewart, Blanche
Stewart, C. Wallace
Stillman, Wm. P.
Stockton, Mr. & Mrs. R.E.
Stowers, Joel
Sullivan, Mrs. Jack
Taylor, Clarabell
Taylor, Hubert V.
Vogt, Erma
Walker, Mr. & Mrs. Charles R.
Whiteside, Howell L.
Williams, Rosemary J.
Wilson, Mr. & Mrs. Archer
Wilson, Beatrice Farmer
Wilson, Janet Juanita
Wilson, Katherine Inez
Wilson, Leon
Young, Mrs. T.W.

1943

Anderson, William C.
Attaway, Ronald
Attaway, Mrs. S.B.
Barr, Mrs. Wm. J.
Bentley, Lilly
Boggs, Janna
Bradley, Mrs. Walter E.
Bradley, Walter E., Jr.
Bramblett, Bessie Lee
Brittle, Virginia Helen
Brown, Georgia Anne
Brown, Mrs. H.P.
Buchanan, Gordon Lewis
Buchanan, Mr. & Mrs. Thomas S.
Carver, Betty Gloria
Cason, Mr. & Mrs. Jack G.
Conarro, Carlton Milford
Crenshaw, Albert D.
Crenshaw, John W.
Cross, Ruth May
Crump, Lola Ruth
Curley, Tycia
Curley, James Gus
Dabney, Ruth
Denmark, Samuel Wister
Elliott, Barbara Ann
Falk, Mr. & Mrs. Joseph A.
Fritz, Eugene
Greene, Catherine Virginia
Greene, Mrs. Thelma
Hall, Frank Shirley
Hawkins, Mr. & Mrs. Sherman B.
Hopkins, John Robert, Jr.
Horton, Helen Catherine
Hughes, Pauline
Jenkins, Barbara Ann
Jenkins, Lillian Jean
Ladley, Marie
Lanier, Rebecca
Leach, Mrs. E.H.
Lemming, Mrs. W.B.
Lemming, Wm. Burton, Jr.
Long, Harry J., Jr.
Long, Mr. & Mrs. Harry J., Sr.
Long, Ruby Frances
Mason, Carl Harrie
Mason, Mr. & Mrs. M.B.
Mason, Margaret Williams
Milam, Mrs. L.B.
Mitchell, Mrs. E.C.
Moore, Jessie
Moore, Mrs. W.T.
Moss, Jean
Mott, Mrs. E.W.
Muckenfuss, Margaret E.
Muckenfuss, Ruth Harris
Muirhead, Mrs. William E.
Mullinax, Eddie Ruth
Murphy, Robert Bruce
McCallie, Edith
McDaniel, Pauline Marie
McKee, Mary Louise
Peacock, Jane
Pope, Neal Quitman, Jr.
Price, Mrs. Charles Lee
Price, Juanita Barbara
Rayburn, Mr. & Mrs. Morris B.
Rayburn, Patrick Maurice
Scott, Mr. & Mrs. Harry V.
Smith, Virginia Ann
Stewart, Thomas James
Suter, Barbara Jean
Swartz, Clair Ritchie
Tate, Mrs. Donald H.
Thompson, Edward A.
Thompson, Mr. & Mrs. J. Homer
Thompson, T.W.
Thrasher, Andrew Jackson
Thrasher, Peggy Louise
Tyre, Mr. & Mrs. T.C.
Voyles, Gene Homer
Voyles, June Evelyn
Voyles, Mrs. J.R.
Wallcott, Mrs. B.H., Jr.
Watson, George L.
Wenger, William R.
Whitner, Dorothy Grace
Willis, Martha Ann
Wilson, Homer James
Wilson, Mr. & Mrs. Sydney M.
Woods, Dorothy Anne
Woods, Mrs. M.J.
Woods, William J.

1944

Barringer, Mr. & Mrs. C.A.
Barringer, Castle A.
Barringer, Helen
Beale, Hugh
Beasley, Carroll

Bell, Mr. & Mrs. Edward L.
Bradshaw, Annie Lee
Bradshaw, Martha Louise
Brantley, Annie Laurie
Brook, Drew Thompson
Brook, Mrs. W.B.
Brown, Mrs. Charles D.
Brown, Mr. & Mrs. W. Grier
Bryant, Carl Milton
Butler, Mrs. Herman Wesley
Carter, Mrs. Wm. Maynard
Clayton, Thomas A.
Connally, Emma Calhoun
Crenshaw, Mrs. Albert D.
Daniell, Earl Franklin
Daniell, Roy
Doby, Wm. Clifford
Donehoo, Richard Eugene
DuBois, Mrs. Don, Jr.
Eagan, Mrs. William R.
Floyd, Resina
Franklin, Carl Edward
Freeman, Mrs. M.O.
Glover, Mrs. George Z.
Goines, Emmett
Goines, Henry
Goines, Mrs. L.N.
Goines, Sarah Louise
Goodhue, Wistar Evans
Hammond, Robert Henry
Heath, Mr. & Mrs. Gordon Adair
Hewitt, John Edward
Hollingsworth, Mr. & Mrs. Horace
Houseal, James W.
Howard, Jerry Franklin
Hunt, Paul Williams
Irvine, Mr. & Mrs. Wm. Thomas
Jackson, Henry
Jansen, Joseph Nicolas
Johnson, Barbara Moore
Johnson, Madeline Dickson
Kennedy, Annitte Marie
Kennedy, Caroline Elizabeth
MacRae, Harry Forrester
Mason, Marion B., Jr.
Mason, T.C.
Mayo, Carlton Earl
Mayo, Delores Ann
Mayo, Mr. & Mrs. Earl Harrison
Mayo, Nettie Elizabeth
Merritt, Ida
Merritt, L.T.
Miller, Frances
Miller, Mrs. Marion R.
Moore, Anna
Morris, Clara
Muckenfuss, Dorothy Mildred
Mullinax, Bettie Sue
Murray Frances
McDaniel, Wm. Vergil
McGahee, Charles A.
McLain, Annie Lee
McNair, Louise Champion
Oastler, Bertram Robert
Orr, Jack Oglesby
Page, Lewis B.
Palmer, Mrs. Alvin
Parks, Mr. & Mrs. C.A.
Parrish, Lunita
Pass, Mrs. D.T.
Phillips, Elizabeth Carmen
Phipps, Rollin E.
Plunkett, Mr. & Mrs. A.F.
Roberts, Thomas P.
Satterwhite, Thomas Clayton
Sawyer, Edna Gannaway
Small, Oscar Dotteridge
Smith, Clyde O.
Smith, James Donald
Smith, Milton Morton
Smith, Sarah
Stephens, Mrs. A.E.
Stern, Leon David
Stern, Louis Allen
Stevens, Mr. & Mrs. Wm. F.
Stowers, Edward James
Stowers, Mrs. Hubert
Stribling, Mr. & Mrs. L.D.
Summers, Ralph LeRoy, Jr.
Thrasher, Barbara Ann
Thrasher, Essie Lee
Tiller, Doris
Tyre, Teddy Carlos
Voyles, John R.
Warren, Lawrence Grover
Warren, Rosalie Thelma
Waters, Mr. & Mrs. C.H.
Weatherford, Mrs. J.S.
Weldon, Elijah Merrill
Whitner, John Addison, III
Whittaker, Mrs. T. Lowry
Wigley, Sarah Barbara
Williams, Mrs. J.B.
Wilson, Mrs. D.W.
Wilson, Sam W.
Wilson, Mr. & Mrs. Thomas W.
Wolcott, Mrs. Robert H.

1945

Allen, Hazel Evaland
Allen, Ontra Arlene
Autry, Samuel Hugh
Bansley, Mary Grace
Beale, Floral Beverly
Beatty, Bernice
Beatty, Paul
Boss, Reba Lois
Brandon, Frances
Brantley, Mr. & Mrs. Hugh C.
Brantley, Hugh Clifford
Brogdon, Mr. & Mrs. W.M.
Brown, Charles D.
Brown, Hubert P.
Carson, Jessie
Carson, Mrs. M.B.
Carver, Mary Frances
Clark, John C.
Cobb, Mr. & Mrs. I.O.
Darrington, Annie Fetzer
Davies, Evelyn Longino
Dunn, William K.
Ellington, Jack Wesley
Engers, Mr. & Mrs. Charles L.
Etheridge, Mamie Jane
Fargason, Wm. Franklin, Jr.
Ferrogattie, Mrs. Guido
French, Mrs. E.R.
French, Edward Rogers, Jr.
French, Theodore Roberts
Gardner, Mrs. W.G.
German, Mr. & Mrs. Robert F.
Greene, Mrs. Wm. Jeff
Hale, Mr. & Mrs. G.B.
Hale, Hal M.
Hale, Marion F.
Hale, Nancy J.
Hamilton, Harold Hull
Harkins, Mrs. Charles
Hawk, Lorraine
Head, Charles Grady
Hightower, Mr. & Mrs. J.C.
Hightower, Lula
Hogan, James Cedo
Hogan, Mrs. W.J., III
Hollingsworth, Charles G., Jr.
Kennedy, Mary Jones
Koto, Mr. & Mrs. Fred Tatsuo
Lamb, Wayman Cam
Leach, Mrs. J.R.
Leach, John Robert, Jr.
Martin, Monirea
Mason, James T.
Mauldin, Evelyn Mason
Michael, Sarah Jane
Mitchell, Beverly Ann
Mock, Hazel Coleman
Oastler, Carmen
Oastler, Mrs. Thomas W.
Parham, Barbara Joyce
Pass, D.T.
Rhodes, Mr. & Mrs. James Edgar
Rhodes, James Edgar, Jr.
Rogers, Myrtle Louise
Schleimer, Mildred
Schleimer, Richard K.
Singleton, Mrs. H.S.
Snead, Lucile Marion
Smith, Mrs. Max C.
Stearns, Mr. & Mrs. Clyde L.
Streater, Carol Elizabeth
Streetman, Mrs. B.L.
Streetman, Dorris
Swaringen, Charlotte
Swint, Harvey Lovester
Tannah, Mrs. J.W.
Tatum, George A., Sr.
Tatum, Lucy M.
Tatum, Margaret M.
Testard, Mr. & Mrs. Hugh A.
Turner, Jesse C.
Upchurch, Mary Katherine
Uselton, Betty Jean
Van de Voort, Anita
Van de Voort, Mr. & Mrs. Horace
Villeneuve, Sara Clark
Wadsworth, Mrs. C.R.
Walker, Ruth Z.J.
Wenger, Mr. & Mrs. Ernest A.
West, Mrs. Paul D.
Whiteside, Otis Donald
Yancey, Mrs. W.H.
Zimmerman, Mr. & Mrs. H.R.

1946

Alexander, Mrs. John M.
Alexander, John M., Jr.
Alexander, Matilda Caroline
Alexander, Victoria Holladay
Allen, James Arthur, Jr.
Allen, Vera Lee
Atkinson, Lee Patrick
Barber, Mrs. Fred L.
Bardsley, Gerald Calvin
Barnes, Mrs. William F.
Barnett, Alma Dawson
Bellinger, Mr. & Mrs. Fred
Bray, Mrs. Hal W.
Bray, Hal W., Jr.
Brown, Dr. & Mrs. Paul F., Jr.
Burns, Mrs. Virginia
Chisholm, Anne Christine
Clayton, Aline
Cornett, Mrs. Mary M.

Cox, Mrs. Barney L.
Cox, Barney Lee
Crowe, Robert Lee
Davidson, Edwin Lloyd
Davidson, Mr. & Mrs. Lloyd W.
Davidson, Philip Wallace
Dillard, Mrs. Clara
Doby, Silas Clifford
Dorsey, Mr. & Mrs. G.A.
Dorsey, Robert Rha
Erickson, O.V.
Faucette, James Edward
Fernandes, Stanley A.
Fetzer, Mrs. J. Frank
Fitzgerald, Dr. Robert Banks
Florence, Lula Belle
Gibbs, Roberta Louise
Gibbs, Sarah Elizabeth
Gordy, Mrs. Frances Steele
Hale, Mrs. C.L.
Hamby, Robbie Lucile
Hamilton, Mr. & Mrs. Lawrence R.
Hansell, Mrs. William A.
Hill, Martha Ann
Holland, Warner P.
Howell, Mrs. H.A.
Howell, Mrs. T.O., Jr.
Joines, Joseph Walker
Jones, Mrs. C.H.
Kendrick, Mrs. Edward, Jr.
Killebrew, Edna M.
Knight, Hugh Edward
Kraus, Mrs. G.W.
Kraus, George W., Jr.
Lemming, Frank Edgar
Lloyd, Mrs. Grover
Maddox, John Herbert
Martin, William DeWayne
Mixson, Mr. & Mrs. H.L.
Mullinax, Barbara Ann
McCord, Theresa
McElroy, Mrs. Ralph B.
McKee,Charles
McLain, Robert Lee
McMahan, Mr. & Mrs. John H.
McMahan, Marjorie Lynn
Nelms, Mrs. Maude
Newman, Mrs. James W., Jr.
O'Callaghan, Mrs. L.J.
O'Callaghan, Mrs. R.H.
Oglesby, Mrs. Stuart R., III
Olgetree, Linda May
O'Neal, William Howard
Owens, Mrs. John H.
Parker, Mrs. Hugh Fred
Price, Charles Howard
Puckett, O.C., Jr.
Pullen, Virginia
Riddle, Cornelius G.
Rogers, Ollie Mae
Romedy, Alice Claudia
Romedy, Mr. & Mrs. J.W.
Ruffner, Mr. & Mrs. Glen
Savage, Walter H., Jr.
Schliemer, John A.
Sharpe, William Coppedge
Shirley, Lillian
Singleton, Mrs. James F.
Spaanbroek, Jacqueline
Stalker, Mr. & Mrs. J.A.
Starnes, Robert A.
Stephenson, Robert Luther
Stevenson, Robert
Stillman, Lois
Sullivan, Mrs.Charles E.
Trimble, Ben Andres
Trimble, Mr. & Mrs. Ben P.
Trimble, Jessie
Walker, Mrs. Charles M.
Walker, Mr. & Mrs. E.P.
Wall, Barbara Ann
Wall, David Bennett
Wall, James William
Warren, Mr. & Mrs. Roy D.
Webb, Mr. & Mrs. William B.
White, Robert E.
Wilson, Sidney M., Jr.
Wiman, Martha Anna

1947

Allen, Mr. & Mrs. Charles H.
Allen, Mr. & Mrs. Harry E.
Anderson, Mrs. William C.
Bell, Mr. & Mrs. Arthur E.
Black, Mr. & Mrs. C.D.
Blair, B.F.
Blaser, Frances M.
Boles, Mrs. Samuel P.
Brittle, Helen
Brown, Bessie Evelyn
Brown, Mrs. P. Rufus
Brown, T. Hugh
Bruce, John W.
Caldwell, Mr. & Mrs. R.J.
Carpenter, Mr. & Mrs. David
Carver, Charles Edward
Collins, Mr. & Mrs. E.L.
Collins, Gracie Mae
Crenshaw, Edwin E.
Crenshaw, Joseph Don
Crenshaw, Mr. & Mrs. Joseph R.
Crenshaw, Patsy Delois
Crowe, Mr. & Mrs. Ralph B.
Curley, Mrs. George Z.
Daniels, Horace L.
Dendy, Mr. & Mrs. W.C.
Dowdy, Mrs. Clyde
Eddings, Mr. & Mrs. Patt E.
Eining, Emma
Fessenden, Capt. & Mrs. Allen S.
Fessenden, Barbara Ellen
Fessenden, Mary Virginia
Folds, Betty Catherine
Gear, Mrs. Felix B.
Gear, Muriel
Glover, Mrs. George Z., Jr.
Goodale, Mable
Gowan, Ruth Elizabeth
Green, Mr. & Mrs. Curtis
Green, Janice Karen
Hale, Barbara
Hall, Mrs. C.E.
Hammond, Edna
Hanevold, Robert B.
Hanson, Harold Carlisle
Hanson, T.R.
Happoldt, Mary Louise
Harkins, Mrs. I.E.
Heath, Gordon Adair
Hill, Mr. & Mrs. O.L.
Hills, Frances Stuart
Hippy, Mrs. W.T.
Jansen, Ernest Weimer
Johnson, S.M.
Kilgo, Frank D.
Knight, Helen Imogene
Knight, Hubert Lamar
Knight, Mrs. J.L.
Kraus, George W.
Lee, John Lorton
Leftwich, Janice Elizabeth
Lesesne, Max M.
Lewis, Mary Elizabeth
Lumsden, Thomas Newton
Meadows, Mrs. R.W.
Miller, Clyde
Moncrief, Ada Kay
Moody, Ruben R.
Moss, Mrs. J.R.
Mullinax, Mrs. A.D.
Mullinax, Mrs. Cleo
Mullinax, Robert
McCowan, Mrs. Clay, Jr.
McCowan, Julian Clay, Jr.
McElroy, William Ray
McGill, Bush Daniel
Nelms, Howard
Nelms, Mrs. Howard M.
Nelms, Mr. & Mrs. Lamar Hall
Nisbet, Mr. & Mrs. John W.
Norris, James A.
Norwood, Mrs. John F.
Osborne, Vivan Ann
Pannell, Mrs. Robert D.
Pannell, Mrs. Vera
Parker, Mrs. J.R.
Parr, Marilyn Gertrude
Parr, Mr. & Mrs. Thomas L.
Parr, Thomas Myron
Peoples, Norma June
Proctor, Talmadge H.
Pursell, Frances Jeanette
Pursell, Frances Lucille
Randall, Henry H.
Scanling, Joan Valodin
Skinner, Mrs. C.W.
Skinner, Charles W.
Smith, Mrs. S.N.
Sparks, Doris Annette
Sparks, Norma Jean
Sprague, Mrs. Lottie
Sprague, Lynn Beverly
Sprague, William Chris
Sprowl, Dr. Bradley Dent
Stalker, Gertrude
Stearns, Jesse Frank
Stieglitz, Mr. & Mrs. Fred H.
Stieglitz, Nain Elizabeth
Taylor, Mrs. George Aiken
Thomas, Barbara Ann
Thomas, James Charles
Thurman, Charles B., Sr.
Thurman, Mr. & Mrs. Charles B.
Thurman, John K.
Todd, Jakey Albert
Underwood, Dorothy
Walden, Mrs. Ora M.
Walker, Mrs. B.D.
Wall, Hardy Andrew
Wall, Maxine Kellog
Walters, Mr. & Mrs. R.O.
Wheless, Mary
Willis, Eugene Fletcher, Jr.
Windsor, Mr. & Mrs. J.L.
Yearwood, Janie Sue
Yearwood, Juanita Eugenia
Yearwood, Julia Ann

1948

Allen, Mr. & Mrs. R.L.
Allen, Richard
Baker, Robert Clinton
Barr, William John, Jr.

The sanctuary in 1943 with the "old" organ. The antique brass urn containing floral arrangement is still in use.

Barrett, Ann Elizabeth
Beavers, Lucy
Biles, Betty Anne
Bradshaw, Beverly Elaine
Brice, Lucille N.
Bridges, James Roy
Carter, Mr. & Mrs. Frank
Causey, Barbara Louise
Chapin, John Hunt
Crenshaw, Mary Harriet
Dickens, Roy
Dickey, Mrs. Jesse B.
Dunn, Robert Carl, Jr.
Dunn, Shirley Anne
Fant, Margaret H.
Fargason, Richard Fowler
Gaines, Mary Virginia
Glasco, Barbara Ann-
Green, Sonja Nona
Griffin, Mrs. H.S.
Hanson, Mrs. Harold Carlisle
Happoldt, Fred A.
Happoldt, Willie Boyce
Hardin, Flora Estelle
Hiatt, Marcia Elizabeth
Hickman, Mrs. John W.
Kelley, Mrs. Mamie W.
Kelly, John Bradley
Kendall, Mr. & Mrs. J.S.
Kendall, Mr. & Mrs. J.S., Jr.
Kendall, Mack Carlyle
Kendall, Sarah Lucile
Kendrick, Mrs. Jack
Kendrick, Lynn Willene
Kraus, Mrs. George W., Jr.
Lambert, Mrs. Estelle
Leftwich, Wytona Helen
Lewis, Mr. & Mrs. Samuel Wm.
Lloyd, Barbara Jean
Logue, Mr. & Mrs. D.A.
Mayfield, Robert Walter
McCroskey, Mrs. Tom
McFall, Ann Victoria
McKee, Lydia
Newton, Elbert Perrin
Norman, Margaret J.
Norman, Mrs. Thomas J.
Nunn, Mr. & Mrs. Ben Thomas
O'Neal, Dorothy Louise
O'Neal, Mary Frances
Ormond, Mr. & Mrs. Leary Lamar

The sanctuary twenty years later.

Osborne, Louis N.
Palmer, Clarence
Peacock, Mr. & Mrs. Wm. Luther
Peacock, Wm. Luther, Jr.
Pigg, Mr. & Mrs. Thomas V.
Price, Doyle Aaron
Pritchard, Wm. Latham
Ragan, Mr. & Mrs.James A.
Rivenback, Mrs. George Lee
Singleton, Mrs. John H.
Slay, Mrs. Albert L.
Slay, Lessie Grae
Smith, Frances Louise
Spivey, Albert G., Jr.
Sprague, Jessie
Stalker, Gertrude Kyle
Standridge, Dr. Robert Wren
Stephenson, Joseph Edmond
Stephenson, Martha Anne
Stephenson, Mr. & Mrs. Morris H., Sr.
Stephenson, Morris H., Jr.
Stephenson, Stanley Doane
Stevens, Shirley Jelean
Stillman, Margaret P.
Strickler, Mrs. G.B.
Turner, Onice Myrl
Underwood, Mrs. Shannon
Walker, Mrs. Charles Respess
Wallis, Jack Whitfield
Warren, Bernice Jossie
White, Mary Hines
Williams, Mary Roy
Wright, Mr. & Mrs. Pattillo S.
Wynn, Mrs. Joseph Dean, Jr.

1949

Adams, Mrs. Horace George
Andres, Mrs. Benjamin
Atkinson, Betty Jean
Bell, Mary Lee
Besch, Evalyn Ruth
Bridges, Beulah Mae
Bridges, Eva M.
Bridges, Joseph Walter
Brown, Anne Marie
Brown, Joanne
Brown, Samuel Y., Jr.
Bruce, Mrs. Edward H.
Bruce, Sue
Chesser, Lillian Lucile
Chickering, Mr. & Mrs. F.W.

Childrey, Mr. & Mrs. Garlend L.
Collins, Hary Richard Fain
Davis, Mr. & Mrs. Jerrell R.
Dendy, Ann
Duckworth, Carolyn Jane
Dunn, Mr. & Mrs. R.C.
Elliott, Mr. & Mrs. Henry H.
Evans, Margaret Loverne
Greene, Louise
Gunter, Mr. & Mrs. Guy T.
Hall, Mrs. Raymond E.
Hamilton, Barbara Ann
Hamilton, Etta R.
Happoldt, Kay
Harrell, Ethel Hutcheson
Heath, David
Henry, Sammie Jane
Hills, Richard A., Jr.
Hinson, Jean Downes
Holt, Margaret
Howell, Betty Louise
Ivey, William David
Jones, Thomas Lon
Jordan, Mr. & Mrs. John F.
Kelly, Mr. & Mrs. Lawrence L.
Kemp, Clarence Evans
Kemp, Mr. & Mrs. Clyde D., Sr.
Knight, Mrs. R.J.
Lee, Lorton
Lennard, Sara Jane
Lewis, Mr. & Mrs. Brewster
Lindsay, Mary Caroline
Lumsden, Dr. & Mrs. Thomas N.
Medlock, Mr. & Mrs. James E.
Miller, Betty Lou Jenkins
Miller, Ralph C.
Monfort, Mary E.
Mulligan, Alice
Mullinax, Edward
McCleskey, Dorothy Elizabeth
McCleskey, Mrs. T.A.
McKeown, Mrs. W.L.
Norris, Mrs. Wallace E.
Patterson, Ann Elizabeth
Peddicord, Nancy Margree
Phipps, Mrs. Charles D.
Pigg, Bennie Sue
Pigg, Vella Marie
Porter, Mr. & Mrs. James Lee
Proctor, Albert Lee
Pullen, Robert Ray
Quillen, Mrs. Charles A.
Richards, Mary Makemie
Rotch, Anna Belle
Smith, James Harold
Smith, Laura Wilson
Taylor, Alleane
Taylor, Frank Hart
Taylor, Mr. & Mrs. W.H.D.
Thomason, Frances Juanita
Warner, Mrs. Hattie Jones
Warren, Bertie Drucilla
Warren, Betty Jean
Webb, Elijah Melvin
Wellner, Albert T.
Wellner, Mrs. S.W.
Wells, Mr. & Mrs. H.G.
Wells, Patricia Sue
Whittington, Charles Wesley
Whittington, Mary Louise
Williams, Mr. & Mrs. Allen S.
Windsor, Roy
Young, Mr. & Mrs. Wm. Madison

1950

Adams, Horace G.
Allen, Anita Louise
Allen, Elinor Jane
Ballard, Mr. & Mrs. Winthrop J.
Beale, Virginia Marie
Bize, Felicia Ann
Boulware, Marijane
Braden, Betty
Braden, Bill
Braden, Mrs. Blanche
Braden, Bobby
Braden, Larry Dean
Brinson, Mrs. George C.
Brown, Jerry Norman
Brown, Perry Davis
Brown, Rebecca Ruth
Carroll, Orra M.
Carter, James Luther
Carver, Patricia Arlene
Clarke, Mr. & Mrs. Morris M.
Cole, Martha Lillian
Cole, Ramona Fran
Cooke, Barbara Elizabeth
Cooke, Mr. & Mrs. John W.
Coughlan, Mr. & Mrs. James H.
Daniell, Raymond
Elliott, Merrell Collier
Fambrough, Don Wayne
Frye, John Spence
Giffen, John Crowe
Giffen, Phoebe Jane
Giffen, Mrs. Robert B.
Glover, Beverly Jean
Green, Dr. Loula Margaret
Guffin, Ruby Olive
Hale, Mrs. Hal
Hancock, Mr. & Mrs. E.C.
Harris, Mrs. Gloria H.
Harris, Mr. & Mrs. Lawreston H.
Heirs, Reginald Hubert
Henry, William Laurence
Higgenbotham, Alma Frances
Horton, Maxwell Leroy
Howell, Mr. & Mrs. Roland A.
Huber, Mrs. Pauline K.
Huie, Mrs. Ralph A., Jr.
Jackson, Mr. & Mrs. James E.
Jakes, Anne Radford
Jordan, John Franklin
Kelley, Jeanne Alice
Kelley, Linda Katherine
Lambert, Mrs. Ruth
Lambert, Sara Jane
Lenger, Mr. & Mrs. Russell W.
Looney, Mrs. Ardella
Marchman, Dorothy Gertrude
Mayson, John Evans
Merrell, Ricky Earl
Miller, Patricia Ann
Morris, Mrs. Henry A.
McIntyre, Mr. & Mrs. Eustice C.
McMahan, Mr. & Mrs. John H.
McMahan, Marjorie
Neel, Betty Jean
Norton, Mr. & Mrs. Jean G.
Nunn, Martha Ann
O'Callaghan, Mrs. Ben Lacy
Osborne, Mr. & Mrs. Lewis N.
Page, Mrs. Lewis B.
Pinner, Mrs. Emma Kite
Pinner, Rebecca Louise
Polk, Mr. & Mrs. J.M.
Polk, Virginia
Proctor, Mr. & Mrs. Earl D.
Rankin, William
Reynolds, Charles G.
Richburg, Charles M.
Roby, Sidney C.
Rodriguez, Mr. & Mrs. Rafael
Rogers, James Homer
Rogers, Mrs. John H.
Romedy, Cornelia Mary
Scanling, Helen
Sewell, Maude H.
Sharpe, Buna Harold
Shaw, Mrs. Lee L.
Shaw, Mary Virginia
Sheehee, Mr. & Mrs. Leidy W.
Shouse, Mr. & Mrs. John R.
Sickler, Beverly
Sosebee, Mrs. W.N.
Thomas, Robert William
Tolbert, Mr. & Mrs. Louis E.
Van de Erve, Janet
Verhine, Carolyn Virginia
Verhine, Mr. & Mrs. James Lester
Verhine, James Lester, Jr.
Webb, Jo Ann
Webb, Shirley Sandra
Whidby, Mrs. Lois W.
Williamson, Minnie
Wilson, Mrs. Sam W.
Wolpert, Mrs. W.J.

1951

Arnold, Mrs. Ernest J.
Arnold, Philip
Ball, Mr. & Mrs. Samuel T.
Ball, Samuel Thomas, III
Beatty, Frank William
Bradshaw, Brenda
Brown, Toinette Dorman
Brown, Walter Lee
Cheves, Patsy
Clayton, Patricia Anne
Cooke, Mary
Corriston, Agnes W.
Crosby, Mrs. W.J.
Dendy, James Spalding
Deneke, Ernest Andrew
Duffy, T.F.
Elliott, Charlotte
Fairleigh, George D.
Fambrough, Mrs. Donald W.
Fausset, Joseph Carl
Fisher, Mr. & Mrs. Leonard S., Jr.
Forrest, Mr. & Mrs.Charles L.
Fuller, Doris
Gear, Albert Richard
Giffen, Robert Bruce
Grant, Mrs. Mattie
Hamilton, Mr. & Mrs. Harold H.
Haynes, Mary Helen
Heath, Mrs. W.T.
Hopper, Mrs. Gloria Smith
Hopper, William Clayton
Hurd, Mrs. W.G.
Johnson, Mr. & Mrs. Dan
Kane, Mr. & Mrs. Edward R.
Kelley, Mr. & Mrs. John B.
Kendrick, Mrs. John
Leftwich, Charles Henry
Leftwich, Lucy

Leftwich, Mrs. Madeline Walters
Lentz, Mrs. A.D.
Leroy, Ruth
Lewis, Mr. & Mrs. H. Clay
Liu, Wei-Chin
Logan, Mr. & Mrs. Joseph A.
Mashburn, Jimmy
Mauldin, Marian Linn
Miller, Zemula
Milner, Mr. & Mrs. I. Carl
Murphy, Mr. & Mrs. Rupert L.
Nicholson, Barbara Alice
Ohl, Charles Nelson
Ohl, Mr. & Mrs. Fred
Ohl, James Frederick
Ohl, Martha Ann
O'Neal, Mrs. Alton
O'Neal, Claude
Palmer, Bonnie
Pinney, Mrs. H.B.
Pruitt, Louise A.
Pullen, Mrs. R.R.
Rogers, Charles Howard
Rogers, Mr. & Mrs. Frank W., Jr.
Rogers, John Alfred
Sage, Mrs. Herbert A.
Salem, Capt. & Mrs. Joseph
Scott, Mr. & Mrs. Harry V.
Smith, Mrs. B. Lee
Smith, Mr. & Mrs. Bertice H.
Smith, Mr. & Mrs. Morris F.
Snyder, Judge John D.
Stevenson, Aline
Streater, Wallace Fletcher, Jr.
Taylor, Frederick Benjamin
Taylor, Hubert Vance, Jr.
Thomas, Mrs. Charles A.
Thomas, Eddie Joseph
Thomson, John C.
Trimble, Ben A.
Van de Erve, Mrs. John
Varnadoe, Ruby Irene
Walsh, Mrs. Robert F.
Wells, Carolyn
Wells, Mrs. Paul L.
Winfrey, Mrs. W.S.
Wisham, Robert
Wynn, Mr. & Mrs. Joseph D., Jr.
Yancey, Mr. & Mrs. W.H.
Yarber, Mr. & Mrs. Stanley G.

1952

Adams, Beverly Fay
Adams, John W.
Andres, Mrs. Benjamin
Appel, Mrs. Ruby Ann
Arnold, Judith Van Attie
Barnes, Jeffrey Allen
Barnes, Mrs. Ralph H.
Barnes, Scott Ralph
Beale, Robert C.
Blankenship, Larry A.
Blankenship, Mrs. M.L.
Blankenship, Patricia Ann
Bowen, Mattie Lou
Brady, Paul W.
Brady, Mrs. Verna
Brown, Evelyn Cornelia
Brown, Patterson Wynne
Brown, Tony Rudolph
Bruce, John L.
Calhoun, Mrs. Malcolm P.
Carlson, Harold Theodore
Carroll, Bessie
Carter, Wm. Maynard
Chase, Lulye B.
Cobb, Isaac William
Dacus, W.E.
Dean, Carl Wayne
Dean, Mrs. Christine
DesChamps, Dr. Margaret Barr
Elliott, Mrs. George
Elliott, Mary Louise
Endicott, Mr. & Mrs. Lucian J., Sr.
Endicott, Lucian J., Jr.
Fairleigh, Kathryn Frank
Fisher, Lydia
Foley, Jane Esther
Freeman, Harriett Jo Anne
Gerhardt, Robert Owen
Gunter, Mr. & Mrs. Guy, Jr.
Harbuck, Robert Harold
Harris, John E.
Heath, Betty Jean
Heath, James Michael
Hinkle, Mrs. Nell Mae
Hoover, John Wesley
Hyndman, Mrs. Thomas L.
Johnson, Tomlinson Fort, III
Kellam, Mr. & Mrs. Sydney S.
Kennedy, Bernice E.
King, Norah Annie
Large, Mr. & Mrs. Joseph W.
Lazenby, Mrs. Carl
Lennard, Susan Carol
Lorenz, Charles Benjamin
MacRae, Martha
Macy, Mr. & Mrs. Wm. Hall
Mendonsa, Arthur Ad.
Messer, Frances
Miles, Mrs. Lurline B.
Miles, Norman Harper
Miller, Mrs. Edward O.
Miller, Edward D., Sr.
Miller, Edward Duke, Jr.
Mitchell, Stephen Morris
Morgan, Martha Jean
Morris, William Jack
Morrison, Mary
Mullinax, Sandra
McGee, Mr. & Mrs. Samuel R., Jr.
Nix, Mr. & Mrs. B.R.
Nix, Joe Martin
Nix, John
O'Callaghan, James Howell
O'Callaghan, Mary Katherine
Ohl, Mary Susan
O'Neal, Alton D.
Orr, Mrs. Agnes
Proctor, Mrs. James E., Jr.
Pugh, Mrs. Janie
Rankin, Mrs. William G.
Romedy, James W.
Sims, Claude William, Jr.
Smith, William Max
Stalker, Susan Oliver
Steinkamp, Mr. & Mrs. Albert L.
Taylor, Mr. & Mrs. Benjamin H.
Thurman, Seaburn Michael
Turner, Annie Laurie
Turoff, John
Turoff, Mr. & Mrs. L.W.
Turoff, Robert
Varnadoe, Ruby Irene
Wachter, Paul
Walker, Lillian
Williamson, Mrs. James W.
Zoll, Mrs. Oliver
Zoll, Mr. & Mrs. Richard Daniel
Zoll, Rosemary

1953

Bivins, Mr. & Mrs. Grover G.
Bradford, Thomas Raymond
Childre, Jane Elizabeth
Cook, Susan Ada
Cowan, Mr. & Mrs. Robert E., Jr.
Dennard, Blanche
Downing, Araminta
Elder, James A.
Elder, Margaret L.
Fairleigh, Henrietta Penny
Fesperman, Mr. & Mrs. Wm. B.
Frick, Carl Louis, Jr.
Garwood, Sam Griffin
Garwood, Mr. & Mrs. Thomas C.
Graham, Janice Anita
Hammack, Mr. & Mrs. Wm. D., Jr.
Harper, Earline Laura
Harper, Laura M.
Hicks, Frederick Samuel
Hills, Thomas Derrill
Jackson, John C.
James, Mr. & Mrs. Wm. Hardin
Jones, Mr. & Mrs. Edward
Jones, Martha Annette
Koto, Mrs. Carl
Kuchler, Mrs. Eula
Linch, Laura Elise
Linch, Samuel Albert
Lindsay, Martha
Mahlin, Edward H.
Mason, Syliva Cynara
Merritt, Ida
Mitchell, Mrs. E.C.
Murray, Mr. & Mrs. Walter C.
McFarlin, Dennie Warren
Nelson, Mary Frances
Oglesby, Frederick Charles
Parr, Mr. & Mrs. Albert F., Sr.
Parr, Barbara Anne
Price, Charles Howard
Pruette, Julie Ann
Roberson, Patricia Sue
Rogers, Mr. & Mrs. Frank W., Sr.
Rogers, Frank W., III
Roland, Mrs. Harold E., Jr.
Saunders, Saralyn
Scott, Beverly Dean
Shepherd, Mrs. Earl
Sowell, Mrs. C. Emmit
Spruell, Dennis Steven
Spruell, Floyd Gilford
Styron, Mrs. I.F.
Tweedy, Don Wesley
Upchurch, Margaret Elizabeth
Veldhuis, Mr. & Mrs. Jerome A.
Visnor, Mary Ann
Williams, Mary Ann
Windsor, Madeline Louise

1954

Adams, Jacqueline Aliene
Adams, Larry
Addison, Barbara Viola
Adkins, Mr. & Mrs. Harry T.

Allen, Roberta
Anderson, Mr. & Mrs. D.V.
Ball, Patricia Dean
Beard, Billy
Boswell, Mr. & Mrs. William F.
Brooks, William Stanley
Bryan, Mr. & Mrs. George W., Jr.
Buffington, Virginia
Burns, Mrs. Virginia
Caldwell, Evelyn
Caldwell, Marlene
Calhoun, Margaret Cromatic
Chastain, Linda Anne
Couey, Mrs. Albert S.
Cross, Edgar Clayton
Davis, Margaret
Dickson, Dr. & Mrs. Robert W.
Edwards, Mr. & Mrs. Wm. E.
Farr, Jesse Floyd, Jr.
Fawley, Charles Walter
Fawley, Mr. & Mrs. Norman E.
Fincher, Mrs. James Rebie
Foley, Thomas Henry, Jr.
Gaines, Alexander P., Jr.
Garwood, Thomas C., Jr.
Gerhard, Mr. & Mrs. Chris H.
Gerhardt, Catherine Barnhart
Giffin, Mrs. Robert B.
Glenn, Roy
Graham, Mrs. C.A.
Harper, Raymond
Harris, Buddy
Heath, George William Thomas
Hill, Robert C.
Honiker, Mr. & Mrs. Charles D.
Honiker, Eddie Fox
Honiker, Julie Fox
Hornsby, Dawson L.
Housworth, Evan H.
Hutchins, Mrs. Carl W.
Hyndman, Dr. Thomas L.
Johnson, Eva C.
Johnson, Mrs. Lewis E.
Johnson, Wesley
Johnson, Wilda
Kennedy, Carol Elizabeth
Kerley, Mrs. Juanita S.
Kersey, Janis Blanche
Kohler, Robert William
Kuchler, Irene
Laverette, John G.
Leman, Mrs. Marie Tuggle
Lowe, Mrs. W.H.
Mauldin, Luther Robert
Moseley, Mrs. F.D.
McElroy, Kenneth Lester
McGee, Samuel Russell, III
McIver, Mr. & Mrs. J.B.
McRae, Brent Allen
Oakle, Jean
Osborne, Billy Joe
Ray, Mrs. Archie C.
Ray, Richard Archibald
Ray, Timothy Britt
Romedy, Ralph Moser
Shutley, Mr. & Mrs. John T.
Slagel, Mr. & Mrs. Ronald V., Jr.
Smith, Harold R.
Stanton, Mrs. Arthur P.
Summers, Larry David
Taliaferro, Hampton Drake
Talley, Wilhelmina O.
Taylor, Jan Clark
Walsh, Michael

1955

Adams, David James
Alford, James E.
Allen, Lewis Cleveland
Blosfield, Jerry Wm.
Brady, Mr. & Mrs. Roy G.
Brady, Mr. & Mrs. Thomas R.
Brooks, Joanne
Brown, Paul F., IV
Bruce, John Louis
Burch, Mr. & Mrs. Marvin C., Jr.
Carroll, Mrs. H.F.
Carroll, Ronald Cleveland
Carter, Lucile
Carver, Mrs. Charles E.
Chappell, James Perry, Jr.
Cobb, Mr. & Mrs. James Venner, Jr.
Collier, Mrs. L.F.
Collins, John Stewart
Coulton, William Frederick
Cowan, Mr. & Mrs. Robert E.
Crenshaw, Mr. & Mrs. Walter J.
Dupree, Mr. & Mrs. Alban W.
Edwards, Cora J.
Fortson, Mr. & Mrs. William J.
Foss, Mr. & Mrs. G.A.
Freeman, Charlotte Louise
Gerhard, Jeffery Lee
Girouard, Capt. & Mrs. T.J.
Goudelock, Dr. & Mrs. W.J.
Hahn, Mr. & Mrs. Carl Joseph, Jr.
Hale, Priscilla Lea
Hanson, Mrs. Thomas R.
Hereford, Joanna Knight
Holbrook, Mr. & Mrs. Clifton W.
Howser, Julia Hoyt
Hudson, Mr. & Mrs. Henry Wm.
Jones, Mr. & Mrs. A. Tillman
Karston, Mr. & Mrs. Carl Emmett
Kelley, Mr. & Mrs. John B.
Kerley, Gloria Geraldine
Knox, Mrs. Ben
Lane, Dr. & Mrs. John Cook
Lenger, Mark Duane
Lenger, Mr. & Mrs. Russell W.
Lenger, Whitney Fields
Mahlin, Mr. & Mrs. Edward A.
Martin, Mr. & Mrs. James Lester
Mauney, Martha Evelyn
Mills, Michael C.
Mills, Richard C.
Muckenfuss, Ruth
McDermott, Mr. & Mrs. John K.
McKee, Mary Louise
O'Callaghan, Richard Hayes, Jr.
Palmer, Gerald Alvin
Palmer, Kim Winslow
Piper, Idus R.
Pittman, Mrs. W.C.
Rankin, Bruce
Rankin, Judith Gardner
Richards, Charles Malone, III
Richards, Cora J.
Roche, Mrs. R.J.
Shuler, Mrs. William L.
Singleton, Sarah Anne
Smith, Caroline Belle
Smith, Mr. & Mrs. Charles C.
Smith, Fraser MacRae
Smith, Mary Nell
Smith, Stephanie Marie
Stockton, Marilyn
Summers, Sharon Annette
Sutton, Kay Bryann
Taylor, Martha Helen
Thomas, Bryan Wesley
Thompson, Mrs. W.H.
Thurmond, Mrs. A.K.
Toombs, Mrs. Henry J.
Trimble, Jessie Romney
Turner, Marilyn Adella
Velazquez, Constance
Walling, Robert Harold
Walsh, Thomas Monroe
West, Mrs. A.J.
Williams, Nancy Jane
Yarbrough, Georgia

1956

Abbott, Mr. & Mrs. George P., Sr.
Armstrong, Henry Crawford
Ayliffe, Alice Roberta
Ayliffe, Mr. & Mrs. David D.
Ayliffe, John Charles
Beale, Capt. & Mrs. Robert C.
Bellinger, Barbara Lynn
Blankenship, Mrs. Barbara B.
Boswell, William F., Jr.
Bradley, Sara
Bretch, Mr. & Mrs. John K.
Buffington, Paul G.H.
Buice, Mrs. Helen
Calhoun, Ann Black
Calhoun, Malcolm P., Jr.
Clark, Mr. & Mrs. David C.
Cobb, Francis Elizabeth
Crow, Mr. & Mrs. John M.
Dalton, Robert Thomas, Jr.
Dean, Madeline Coral
de LaRue, Mr. & Mrs. Marcel G.
Dickson, James H., III
Fife, Mr. & Mrs. William M.
Garwood, John Glover
Grimes, James H.
Grimes, John W.
Grimes, Mrs. Robert H.
Hale, Ernest Samuel
Hawkins, Bobby Kenneth
Hawkins, Gerald Hugh
Hawkins, Mrs. Loy
Heath, Marabel
Hernandez, Mrs. Alma Mae
Hernandez, Lucile
Herring, Mrs. H.G.
Hoover, J.W.
Howard, Mr. & Mrs. Harry O.
Hudson, William Henry
Ladshaw, Mr. & Mrs. Thomas Gordon
Lamb, Wayman Cam
Lanier, Mr. & Mrs. James Robert
Large, Betty Jo
Limbaugh, Ellen Faye
Limbaugh, John Forrest
Limbaugh, Mr. & Mrs. L.O.
Limbaugh, Louis David
Magill, Dell
Mills, Mr. & Mrs. W.A.
Montgomery, Mr. & Mrs. James H.
McCarty, Mrs. Lola Steed
McCarty, Madeline Carol Dean
McCutchen, Leighton M.
McElroy, Mae
Nelms, Mr. & Mrs. Frank D.
Nelms, Stephen Lamar
O'Callaghan, Karen St. Clair
Petty, E.W.

Dr. Oglesby, Miss Dorothy Woods and Dr. Taylor on the occasion of Dorothy's 25th anniversary as church secretary.

Petty, George Frank
Petty, Jack Weston
Proctor, Elizabeth B.
Rodriguez, Mary Ann
Shuler, William L.
Smith, Mrs. Grace
Smith, Jack Ralph
Stalker, Sally Fraser
Starnes, Thomas Lee
Stevens, Judith Lynn
Still, Mr. & Mrs. James E.
Styron, Sheila Anne
Thomas, Barrie Lane
Underwood, Sharon
Wall, Eric Hardy, Jr.
Warren, Gerald Glenn
Watson, Wayne Joseph
Wilkinson, Mr. & Mrs. Fred T.
Williams, John Kenneth

1957

Anslow, Lt. Col. & Mrs. Ralph O.
Beachy, Mr. & Mrs. Robert G.
Beachy, Robert W.
Bolen, Mr. & Mrs. Wm. Edward
Boswell, Chrysis
Bothwell, Kathy L.
Bradshaw, Judith Anne
Brooks, James J.
Brown, Susan Marie
Buchanan, Mrs. W.F.
Caldwell, Rita Jean
Chandler, Dorothy Frazer
Chandler, Jerry
Chandler, Robert Bruce
Cheatham, John Rhymes
Christian, Stanford Clark
Cook, Mrs. Walter Granger
Cooling, Howard
Davis, Robert Gene
Doss, Mr. & Mrs. William C.
Farrior, Louise
Fife, William M., Jr.
Foss, Victoria Ann
Gray, Mr. & Mrs. Ben B.
Hawkins, Jimmy D.
Head, Hoyt George
Hessler, Mr. & Mrs. George H.
Hickman, Nancy Renee
Hills, Henry Lyman, Jr.
Hoover, Mrs. John W.
Hopkins, Mr. & Mrs. James Henry
Howard, Harry David
Howard, John Kennedy
Hutchinson, Julia
Johnson, John Van
Jones, Anne C.
Kea, Mr. & Mrs. J.C., Jr.
King, Mrs. Ruby
Kuchler, Charlotte Elizabeth
LaSalle, Mrs. Ivalee
Meadows, Esther Ruth
Meadows, Robert Emory
Mosher, Brenda Gail
Murray, Mrs. Wm. Theodore
McCall, Mr. & Mrs. James M.
New, Mary Linnie
Nicolai, Mike
Powell, Mr. & Mrs. Wm. Robert
Richard, Robert Lee
Rogers, Robert Tucker
Savage, Linda Dianne
Schneider, Mr. & Mrs. Guy H.
Schrimper, Mr. & Mrs. Frederick G.
Sharpe, Mrs. William C.
Singleton, Mary Eleanor
Smith, Laura
Smith, Mickey Rolland
Stribling, Mr. & Mrs. Lemuel D.
Stribling, Mary Jane
Stribling, Sarah Ellen
Strouss, Mr. & Mrs. W.S.
Taylor, Mrs. Frank H.
Thomas, Jo Ann
Thomas, Melvin
Thomas, Vernon
Thompson, Mr. & Mrs. Lewis P.
Thornton, Eugene Thomas
Tripp, Mr. & Mrs. Richard R.
Tuten, Mary Elizabeth
Tuten, Nola Mae
Ward, Mrs. Leatha
Wells, Katie Elizabeth
White, Robert Eugene, Jr.
Wilson, John Winfred
Wilson, Marjorie
Winburn, Julia E.
Wood, Carl E., Jr.
Worley, Mrs. Bertha
Worley, Elva Sue

1958

Adams, Linda Sue
Adams, Ronald Brent
Addison, Diane Evelyn
Anthony, Mr. & Mrs. Calvin L.
Baker, David William
Barnes, Mrs. William F.
Belcher, Carolen
Black, Mr. & Mrs. J. Edgar, Jr.
Borden, Judith Lee
Bratcher, Linda Irene
Chapman, Mr. & Mrs. Judson Wm., Jr.
Chapman, Russell William
Croft, Dorothy Diane

Cronan, Mildred Geraldine
Cummings, Bradshaw
Cummings, Mr. & Mrs. Silas D.
Cummings, Vincent B.
Cummings, Walter H.
Donehoo, Richard Eugene
Donehoo, Mrs. Ruth Fordham
Duncan, Mrs. Henry Grady
Gaines, Delia Upchurch
Hansard, William Lewis
Hernandez, Brenda
Hills, Mary Anna
Huck, Mrs. William
Kea, Karen Holland
Landrum, Edward Owen
Layton, Mr. & Mrs. James L.T.
Leach, John, Jr.
Leach, Richard
Leach, Roy
Limbaugh, Robert Harrison
Myers, Mr. & Mrs. Robert L.
Nix, John Arthur
Nix, Mrs. Sherman
O'Callaghan, Cynthia Anne
O'Callaghan, Susan Ellen
Oglesby, Dina Suellen
Oglesby, Susan Elizabeth
O'Reilly, John Patrick
Patterson, James Franklin
Riddle, Hazel Annette
Smith, Ronald
Spruell, Brenda Jane
St. John, Claude William
Stovall, Mrs. W.S.
Stovall, Walter Steven
Strickler, Elizabeth Anne
Summers, Pamela
Thornton, Jackie Patricia
Wells, Shirley
Wells, Will Tom, Jr.

1959

Adams, Mrs. C.L.
Eller, Lynn E.
Fisher, Mrs. L.S.
Gaddy, Tommy Elaine
Gray, Charles Roy
Gunter, Nancy Jean
Hernandez, Lois Ann
King, Nora Annie
Knowles, Billy Dewayne
Knowles, Bobby Lee
Kohn, Norman Scofield
Loden, Mr. & Mrs. Harry C.
Lowry, Paul M., Jr.
MacKay, Mr. & Mrs. Douglas A.
Moore, Teddy Lynn
Morris, Coley G.
McAteer, Mrs. T.P.
Oglesby, Mrs. Richard Archer
Ryburn, Jean
Smith, Audra
Stair, Mrs. Fred R., Jr.
Stair, Mary Miller
Terrell, Martha Frances

1960

Allen, Mrs. Richard W.
Anslow, Joy Elizabeth
Baerman, Mr. & Mrs. Malcolm C.
Baker, Mr. & Mrs. H.L.
Bradshaw, Brenda Carol
Burns, Mrs. R. Hugh
Crook, Arthur
Crook, Mrs. James R.
Faxes, Edwardo
French, Mr. & Mrs. James M.
Gibson, Lee Ben
Hart, Elinor
Ingram, Mrs. Gary
Jamieson, Mr. & Mrs. Murray
Mazzera, Roger
Medlock, Michael Parks
Milner, Sara
Morton, Jean
McClure, Mr. & Mrs. William J. Sr.
Piephoff, Mrs. C.E.
Pitts, Shirley Ann
Purse, Mrs. Thomas
Scott, Mrs. C.S.
Smith, Joe
Smith, Meredith
Strobel, Phyllis
Underwood, Timi
Warren, Bobby Gene
Willis, Mr. & Mrs. C.W., Jr.
Wood, Mr. & Mrs. George Charles

1961

Baria, Dr. & Mrs. William H.
Bates, Mr. & Mrs. John
Brady, Sharon Dian
Burr, Marilyn
Byington, Mr. & Mrs. Gerald A.
Davis, Mrs. Cecile Mae
Freeman, Mr. & Mrs. Sam
Germany, Mr. & Mrs. John L.
Grider, Mrs. Edgar M.
Hacke, Mr. & Mrs. John R.
Hickman, Mrs. Paul
Hill, Fred E.
Horne, Mr. & Mrs. Robert E., Jr.
Jamieson, Mary Margaret
Kornegay, Mr. & Mrs. H. Street
Mahlin, Mr. & Mrs. Edward A.
Maloney, Dr. & Mrs. George R.
McClure, Elizabeth Dee
Neel, Mrs. J.P.
Neel, Joseph P.
Neel, Richard
O'Brien, Wallace Allen
Phillips, Charles Geoff
Phillips, Mr. & Mrs. Otis, Sr.
Phillips, Otis, Jr.
Phillips, Patty
Reyes, Ana
Stair, Thomas Osborne
Stelling, Robert E.
Taylor, Jacqueline
Taylor, Mabel Agnes
Turner, William M.
Walker, Charles R., Jr.
Walsh, Mrs. J.C.
Whigham, Daniel Brown
Whigham, Mr. & Mrs. Robert S.
Whigham, Robert S., Jr.
Wilcoxon, William G.

1962

Ayliffe, Mary Lou
Ball, Mr. & Mrs. Samuel T., III
Brunton, Francis
Carlton, Mrs. F.S.
Clark, Melissa
Crow, Judith
Dendy, Emily
Elder, Margaret L.
Halter, Mr. & Mrs. Eugene J.
Halter, James S.
Halter, Janis P.
Harris, David M.
Hay, Alfred N.
Hernandez, Jane
Horne, Mr. & Mrs. D.E., Sr.
Kelly, Mr. & Mrs. Charles F.
Kirk, Elizabeth N.
Marchlenski, Frank
Marsh, Mr. & Mrs. Charles H.
Marsh, Rebecca
Mayo, Mrs. Carlton E.
Mixon, Mr. & Mrs. Thomas F.
Morgan, Gloria Lillian
Morgan, Mrs. Jonnie
Morgan, Melanie Lee
Morgan, Norman Hall
Morris, Shirley Anne
Myers, Mrs. Robert L.
McCutchen, Anne C.
Oglesby, Dina Suellen
Oglesby, Col. & Mrs. Stuart R. III
Oglesby, Susan Elizabeth
Pearson, Mr. & Mrs. David W.
Proctor, David
Ragland, Mrs. Virginia G.
Rogers, Mr. & Mrs. William G.
Schaeffler, Mr. & Mrs. Wm. A.
Sims, Mr. & Mrs. Claude W., Jr.
Still, Karen
Styron, Ruth
Taylor, Daniel M., Jr.
Taylor, Mr. & Mrs. Daniel M., Sr.
Thurman, Mrs. Charles B.
Wall, Michael Andrew
Wilson, Dan Frank, Jr.
Wolpert, Wm. Joseph, Jr.

1963

Baria, James William
Brady, Keith
Bretch, John Steven
Brock, David G.
Caldwell, Romona Jeanette
Clark, Marion S.
Couey, Mr. & Mrs. Albert S.
Crenshaw, Carolyn Anne
Crook, Virginia Reed
Dale, William Martin
Drew, John, IV
Fife, Daniel Nelson
Furlow, Frances R.
Greene, Paul Reese
Guthrie, David V.
Hairston, Mr. & Mrs. S.L.
Hillstrom, Daniel Paul
Hudson, Peggy Marlene
Layne, Irvin R.
Miller, Mr. & Mrs. Richard B .
Morris, Diane
McClure, Susan Lacy
McCullough, John J.
McCullough, Robert E.
McCullough, Mr. & Mrs. Robert L.
McGeachy, Margaret Ann
Owens, Mr. & Mrs. Marvin Lee
Price, Alice Leigh
Price, Cynthia Lee
Price, Mr. & Mrs. E. Jack

Pruitt, Sylvia
Rankin, Lois W.
Salem, Donna Jean
Scott, Willie Pearl
Smith, Elizabeth D.
Smith, Kathryn Vaughn
Smith, Mrs. John R.
Smith, Maryellen
Still, Kathryn
Strickler, Mary Jean
Veldhuis, Ann
Walker, Rex Seibel

1964

Allen, Mrs. Richard L.
Bacon, Mrs. Steve
Beachy, Keith
Black, Brenda Catherine
Boren, Gail
Boren, Linda Deanne
Bowen, Barbara Maury
Bratcher, Barbara
Bratcher, Nancy
Bratcher, Paul
Chambers, George Cleveland
Converse, Mr. & Mrs. Milton J.
Coppedge, Dr. & Mrs. L.J.
Crow, Mrs. John M.
Crow, Sara Susan
Diefell, Mrs. John Jey, Jr.
Donelson, Sharon
Donelson, Mr. & Mrs. Wesley
Donelson, Willard
Elliott, Charles Jack
Ford, William Frank
Gibson, David
Gibson, Mrs. Delores
Gittings, Roberta Louise
Hale, Cornelia
Hall, Richard W.
Henderson, Mr. & Mrs. Leonard T., Jr.
Ingram, Gary D.
Isaacs, Dr. & Mrs. James Pershing
Isaacs, James Pershing, Jr.
Isaacs, John
Ivey, Susan Diane
Kane, Edward R., Jr.
Kelley, Sue
Kelly, Carolyn
Lorenz, Katherine O'Callaghan
MacRae, Mrs. Douglas G.
Moore, Mr. & Mrs. James Leonard
Morton, Mrs. Duncan
McCord, James P.
McCord, John J.
McCord, Mr. & Mrs. Ned J., Jr.
McCord, Ned J., III
Nelms, Frank Donald, Jr.
Oglesby, Jill Allison
Ohl, Mrs. James F.
Porter, Mr. & Mrs. Allen
Proctor, Katherine Fairbanks
Reed, Mr. & Mrs. Daniel M., Jr.
Richards, Mr. & Mrs. Clarence H.
Richardson, Mrs. James T.
Richardson, Mr. & Mrs. R.H.
Riddle, Janice Elaine
Slagel, Linda Lorraine
Smith, James G.
Sprayberry, Albert
Summers, Scott Howard
Tallent, Wanda
Tomasovich, Mr. & Mrs. Stephen M.
Wallace, Mr. & Mrs. Franklin D.
Wallace, Mr. & Mrs. J.C.
Wallace, Webster Simon
Wilson, Andrew Bennett
Wingard, Mrs. George Thomas, Jr.

1965

Andrews, Mrs. Ruby Lee Boss
Ard, Mrs. Dillard
Arnold, Mrs. Philip S.
Baird, Eleanor Lynn
Bissell, Mrs. N.D.
Clark, Leila Estes
Colley, Mr. & Mrs. Frank H.
Crook, Sharon Elizabeth
Dotson, Molly
Frye, Sarah Ethel
Gailey, Carolyn
Hollingsworth, Mr. & Mrs. Byron F.
Howard, Capt. John C.
Isaacs, Robert David
Johnson, Agnes Irene
Kane, James M.
Kane, William A.
Kelly, Mr. & Mrs. Gordon
Kohn, Mrs. Norman S., Sr.
Large, Thomas Allen
Lorenz, Charles B., Jr.
Lorenz, Katherine H.
Lovingood, Mrs. Carl H.
Neal, Mary Ann
Nelms, Nancy
O'Callaghan, Ben L., Jr.
Price, Patti
Price, Peggy Susan
Richardson, Mack Steven
Richardson, Sheryl Leigh
Sims, Mr. & Mrs. Carl Franklin
Smith, Annette
Stamey, Judith Ann
Stearns, Mrs. C.L., Sr.
Urbach, Col. Walter
Walker, Marshall
Womack, Mary

1966

Bailey, Betty Anne
Bansley, Mrs. J. David
Bradley, Charles Douglas
Burch, Marc
Caskie, Mr. & Mrs. Hamilton B.
Castles, Mrs. Charles W.
Crenshaw, Nancy
Crone, Douglas C.
Dennis, Dr. & Mrs. Brown W.
Echon, Joyce Lynne
Gilliam, Ken
Head, Mr. & Mrs. C. Grady
Head, Virginia
Holle, Carole A.
Holler, Angeline
Holler, Mrs. A.N.
Justice, John C.
Leach, Anne
Macfarlane, Mr. & Mrs. J. Granger
Moore, Mrs. Lee C.
McClure, Jeff
McCord, Mary
McCord, Michael
McLeod, Mr. & Mrs. Marion E., Sr.
McLeod, Marion Eugene, Jr.
Nysewander, Patricia Jane
O'Callaghan, Carol
Pass, Mrs. D.T.
Patterson, Mrs. M.C.
Quillian, Frances
Riddle, Dale
Sikes, Mary L.
Stenhouse, Louise
Taylor, Arthur Reed
Taylor, Betty Jo
Veldhuis, Mark
Walling, Leigh
Wilburn, Diana Deenbar
Wilson, Alice

1967

Allen, Mrs. Arthur T., III
Beachy, Bruce
Brown, Mrs. Patterson W.
Calhoun, Margaret
Carlton, F.S.
Clark, Mary E.
Covington, Mr. & Mrs. Howard W.
Daniell, Winifred
Glover, Catherine
Greene, Mr. & Mrs. J.B.
Griffin, Eddie Bruce
Hacke, Mr. & Mrs. J. Richard
Harris, Henry E.
Hill, Helen
Jones, Mrs. A.T.
Lowry, Paul
Moore, Josephine
McCarthy, Mr. & Mrs. David E.
McIver, Mrs. Douglas D.
McLoughlin, John B.
O'Callaghan, Knox
Oglesby, Lisa
Powell, Donnie
Powell, Jerry
Richardson, Mrs. James T.
Sprayberry, Carol
Tate, Mr. & Mrs. James R.
Taylor, Mrs. J. Randolph
Thomas, Lillian Dale
Thompson, Mr. & Mrs. Charles B.
Underwood, Mrs. J.T.
Walker, Mrs. Peter G., III
Windsor, Charles Clayton
Windsor, Mr. & Mrs. Clayton C.

1968

Allen, Mr. & Mrs. James T.
Ashmore, Miss Vesta J.
Baker, Mr. & Mrs. Clarence M.
Brockman, Allan A.
Bryan, Clay Hamilton
Cartledge, Louisa B.
Chatman, Mr. & Mrs. Edward
Conklin, Mr. & Mrs. David
Cornes, Mrs. Dorothy H.
Covington, Carolyn Cox
Covington, Catherine Ann
Covington, Mr. & Mrs. Thomas, Jr.
Crosby, Mrs. Ella W.
Daniell, Miss Diane Carol
Daniell, Mr. & Mrs. Richard A.
Dickson, Robert Willis, Jr.
Drath, Col. & Mrs. Wilfred H.
Edenfield, Bruce McCord
Green, Mr. & Mrs. William O.
Hacke, Rebecca Susan
Havice, Harriet Katherine

House, Mrs. Elizabeth Cox
Kehrer, Mr. & Mrs. Elmer Thomas
Kimes, Mr. & Mrs. Wm. Ross
Lamb, Mrs. Lillian Katherine
Lawler, Earl Roger
Leach, Mrs. Louise T.
McLeod, Miriam Terrell
Mitchell, Kathryn Gayle
Moon, Mrs. Allene
Oakley, Mr. & Mrs. Godfrey P., Jr.
O'Callaghan, Wendy Leigh
Parnell, Mr. & Mrs. Albert H.
Patrick, Mr. & Mrs. James H., Jr.
Patrick, Kevin Lee
Patrick, James Cary
Perry, Mrs. Ray H.
Rea, Mrs. Robert J., Jr.
Robinson, Joseph Lee
Ruben, Dr. & Mrs. Frederick L.
Salem, Joseph, Jr.
Sanders, Mr. & Mrs. Walter L.
Satterfield, Mr. & Mrs. Clyde E.
Shedd, Alice Louise
Shedd, Katherine Emily
Shedd, Mr. & Mrs. Donald S.
Shipley, Mr. & Mrs. Norman B.
Sims, Gayle Marie
Singleton, Mr. & Mrs. Oliver W
Sowell, Catherine Elizabeth
Starnes, Susan Marie
Stone, Mr. & Mrs. R.R.
Stone, Patricia Anne
Taylor, Katherine Kerr
Thompson, Miss De Anna
Tucker, Mr. & Mrs. John H.
Turner, Dr. Malcolm Elijah
Turner, Mrs. Charles C.
Walker, Lauren Ann
Walker, Lona Marie
Walker, Peter G.
Walsh, Mr. & Mrs. James Henry
Walters, Mrs. Doris Reaser
White, Mr. & Mrs. Frank D.
Wilson, Mark Hugh
Windsor, John Clayton
Youngs, Allan R.

1969

Allen, James Arthur, Jr.
Amos, Mr. & Mrs. Anthony Lewis
Atkins, Bonnie Norris
Ayliffe, Carol Ann
Bilbro, Dr. & Mrs. Robert H.
Black, Beverly
Boyle, Donald Banks
Bryan, Dr. & Mrs. John A.
Bryan, Josh Alexander
Burch, Cathy Diane
Caplan, Mr. & Mrs. I.L.
Chelette, Dairlyn Jo
Chelette, Jeffrey Denis
Clarke, Carolyn L.
Cox, Mr. & Mrs. Val
Curtis, Janice Dell
Davis, Helen West
Dickson, Mary Alice
Ellis, Mrs. Stewart E.
Fowlkes, Mary Anne
Francis, Joan
Greer, Terry Clifton
Hacke, Michael Carl
Hale, Mr. & Mrs. Grafton B.
Hewell, Mrs. Jerry F.
Hickman, Paula Jeanne
Howard, Helen Ohl
Jones, Ian Dixon
Jones, Jean
Kehrer, Jonathan Thomas
Kelly, James David, Jr.
Kilgore, Mr. & Mrs. Franklin H.
Kiser, Polly Parker
Knight, Mr. & Mrs. Byron
Lancaster, Beth Neville
Lancaster, Lewis Holladay
Longbine, Mr. & Mrs. Frederick Wm.
Longbine, Mary Rose
Mathieson, Mr. & Mrs. Neil B.
Mosley, Jean Bryan
McClure, Susan Lacy
McClure, W. Jeff
McClure, Mr. & Mrs. William J.
McGinty, Margaret Ann
McIlvaine, Mr. & Mrs. John J.
Newsom, Mark W.
Padgett, Frances Louise
Patterson, Sarah Ann
Pickett, Edna Mason
Redus, Mary Edith
Rose, Lucy Atkinson
Schnieder, Deborah Jeanne
Shedd, Laura Jane
Smith, Alice E.
Strickler, Warren Thomas
Styron, Irving Franklin
Summers, Susan
Tatzel, Mr. & Mrs. Norbert C.
Tucker, Mr. & Mrs. Deane C.
Uselton, Mr. & Mrs. Lloyd Wm., Sr.
Weeks, Lt. Col. & Mrs. Howard L.
Weeks, Howard L., Jr.
Whigham, Roger Chris
Wilson, Georgia Greene
Yohan, Edith

1970

Andrews, Mrs. Emmie I.
Barnwell, Mr. & Mrs. Chas. F.
Barnwell, Chas. F., Jr.
Barnwell, Julie F.
Barton, Mr. & Mrs. Teri P.
Beck, Janice Marie
Blake, Robt. Edward
Bowman, Pepe Mestayer
Buchi, Elizabeth
Burns, Virginia Kathleen
Burroughs, Mrs. Keith
Campbell, Mr. & Mrs. Frank C.
Chatman, Sidney Chuch
Coleman, Mrs. Barbara A.
Crais, Capt. & Mrs. David E.
Daughdrill, Mrs. Jas. H., Jr.
Daughdrill, Jas. Harold, III
Daughdrill, Louisa Rish
Fields, Martin C.
Fowler, Mr. & Mrs. Wm. Wyche, Jr.
Friedman, Mrs. J. Lee
Gillespie, Sara Cunningham
Hogue, Carol Margaret
Hoskins, Shirley Horne
Irwin, Alexander McArthur
Johnson, Mr. & Mrs. Walter
Jones, Jean Ellen
Jones, Mr. & Mrs. Richard Carlton
Jones, Mr. & Mrs. Stanley Seburn
Jones, Mrs. William S.
Kefauver, Mrs. Barbara Goss
Kefauver, Karen Reed
Large, Steven Andrew
Longest, Mr. & Mrs. Beaufort B.
McDaniel, Mrs. James M.
McDaniel, Janice P.
McDaniel, Mary Lynn
McElhannon, Mays Clinton, Jr.
McElveen, Claire Elayne
McQuilkin, Mary Cathryn
Morrison, Margaret Sue
Nelms, Susan Elizabeth
O'Callaghan, Elizabeth Anne
Oglesby, Stuart Lamar
Pilcher, Mary Judith
Ritchie, Mr. & Mrs. Wm. B.
Rogers, Mrs. Robt. Tucker
Russell, Mr. & Mrs. Frederick Albert
Rutledge, Mrs. Alene C.
Savage, Linda Diane
Savage, Mr. & Mrs. Walter H., Jr.
Scofield, Mrs. Doris Allen
Smith, Mr. & Mrs. N. Marriner
Sutherland, Mr. & Mrs. Jas. L.
Taylor, Margaret Anne
Walling, Lynne Elizabeth
Waltz, Mr. & Mrs. Warren M.
Wildman, Mr. & Mrs. Jas. H.
Withrow, Berlinda Gaye
Withrow, Donna Sue
Withrow, Mr. & Mrs. Robert C.
Withrow, Sandra Kay
Wunner, Mrs. Jane R.

1971

Allen, Richard Louis
Allen, Mrs. Richard Louis
Barnwell, Cheryl Diane
Bland, Byron Lanier, III
Carpenter, Mary Moreland
Chambers, George Cleveland
Counts, Mr. & Mrs. Reynold M.
Cox, Mrs. William N.
Daniel, Mr. & Mrs. Thos. Richard, Jr.
Dean, Mr. & Mrs. Eugene A.
Douglas, Mr. & Mrs. Stuart
Fleet, Mrs. Mary Grace Bansley
Frase, Mrs. Ronald G.
Gellerstedt, Mr. & Mrs. L.L., Jr.
Gladstone, Mr. & Mrs. Rankin Monroe
Hamilton, Mrs. Lee M.
Harper, Mrs. Barbara Ruth
Hendrix, Mr. & Mrs. Walter Clifford
Hesse, James Edward
Hobson, Jane
Hollander, Mr. & Mrs. Kenneth A.
Horne, Mr. & Mrs. William A.
Hunnicutt, Cynthia
Hunnicutt, Mr. & Mrs. Howard
Kehrer, David Hynson
Krause, Kenneth H.
Lang, Mr. & Mrs. Robt. B.
Leach, Susan Caroline
Love, Mr. & Mrs. Nelson E.
McFarland, Mr. & Mrs. J. Edgar
Moss, George Richardson
Nash, Mrs. David W.
Patteson, Tommy Lee
Pelfrey, Mrs. James W.
Propst, Mr. & Mrs. Floyd E., III
Reed, Dr. Frederick Edgar, Jr.
Ritchie, William Avery
Roberts, Mrs. Paul
Schneider, Alice Elizabeth

Shaw, Anne Elizabeth
Shedd, Alan Christensen
Sims, Keith Alexander
Strickhouser, Margaret Anne
Tatzel, Norbert Anthony
Taylor, Mary Virginia
Theos, Fred Woolbright
Thurman, John Kevin
Tippit, Mrs. A.S.
Tippit, Sydney Elaine
Tucker, Elizabeth D.
von Unwerth, Mr. & Mrs. Frederick H.
Ward, Mrs. Jack H.
Willson, Patrick James
Withrow, Mary Kathleen

1972

Adams, Mary Elizabeth
Andrews, David Lamar, Jr.
Boggs, Wade Hamilton, III
Bruce, Mrs. Lenecia L.
Bryan, Wilkes Holladay
Buckingham, Mr. & Mrs. John W.
Cash, Gary Stephen
Clay, Mr. & Mrs. A. Stephens
Cromartie, Mr. & Mrs. A. Dean
Fisher, Mr. & Mrs. Allan C.
Frisby, Jas. R., Jr.
Gladden, Mr. & Mrs. Jos. R. Jr.
Grider, Margaret Ellen
Hacke, Sarah Jayne
Hale, Mr. & Mrs. Wm. Daniel
Hand, Mrs. W. Lee
Harmon, Mrs. Judith Skaggs
Harris, Mr. & Mrs. C.T.B., Jr.
Howell, Jay
Jones, Cheryl Elizabeth
Kehrer, Heather Ann
Knight, Franklin Randolph
Landrum, Mrs. Mary Louise
Lang, Robert Caldwell
Mabry, Raymond Edward
McCumber, Mr. & Mrs. Alan L.
Moore, James L., Jr.
Morrow, Janet E.
Mundy, Watson Adams
Nemeth, Mrs. Gyuri
Oglesby, John Fewell
Oglesby, William Stovall
Ozmelek, Mrs. Jessie Trimble
Payne, Grace F.
Philler, Mr. & Mrs. Henry
Powell, Mr. & Mrs. John Henry, III
Robinson, Johnny L.
Scott, Mr. & Mrs. Wallace R., Jr.
Sharp, Henry Kerr
Shriver, Mrs. Donald W.
Shriver, Margaret Ann
Sims, Donna Elizabeth
Smith, Mr. & Mrs. Chas. A.
Smith, Donald D.
Strickler, Joan Patricia
Theos, Julie Elaine
Thurman, Edith Laree
Trimble, Benjamin A.
Trimble, Mr. & Mrs. Ben P.
Urch, Mr. & Mrs. Wm. Albert
Uselton, Michele Darlene
VandeBrake, Mr. & Mrs. Lynn
Vining, Alice Marie
Waddel, Mrs. W.F.
Walling, Greg Bruce
Ward, John David
Weltner, Mr. & Mrs. Chas. L.
Willson, Mrs. Patrick L.
Wine, Thos. Clarence

1973

Abernathy, Mr. & Mrs. Robt. C., Sr.
Allen, Mr. & Mrs. Robt. Daniel
Barrow, Madeline Harris
Boykin, Mrs. Lutricia W.
Brown, Mr. & Mrs. Travers G., Jr.
Bryan, Mr. & Mrs. Robt. F., Jr.
Clarke, Legare Warren
Dennis, Brown W., Jr.
Enos, Mr. & Mrs. Richard J.
Etzler, Carole Ann
Evans, Alexander Wier
Evans, David
Evans, Mrs. John B.
Evans, John Borden, Jr.
Evans, Andrea G.
Evans, Christopher Todd
Frase, Michelle Christine
Good, Richard Carter
Graham, David Archer
Green, Martha Evelyn
Gunn, Mrs. Geo. W.
Gunn, Margaret Eugenia
Harp, Jane
Harris, Clifton Tumblen Bud
Hatcher, Mr. & Mrs. Samuel Fox
Hollander, Mark Howard
Holt, Susan Snook
Howell, David Bansley
Ittelson, Mr. & Mrs. John C.
Jung, Jennifer
King, Mrs. Marvin S.
Lancaster, Mrs. Lewis H., Jr.
Lastinger, Mr. & Mrs. Jas. N.
Lehfeldt, Mr. & Mrs. Martin
Logan, Mrs. Chas. A.
Loring, Mrs. Mary Patricia
McChesney, Mr. & Mrs. Sam J., Jr.
Miller, Mr. & Mrs. Wm. A.
Moulthrop, Mr. & Mrs. Edward
Muller, Mr. Wm. John
Nardin, Mr. & Mrs. Fred W.
Perry, Mrs. Pearl Minton Ray
Pickens, Mr. & Mrs. John A.
Porter, Mr. & Mrs. Richard F.
Reed, Mrs. Frederick E., Jr.
Richardson, Mr. & Mrs. Joe A.
Robinson, Mrs. Catherine E.
Sharp, Margaret
Shedd, Alan Christensen
Shedd, Mr. & Mrs. Donald Hodgdon
Shedd, Laura Jane
Shriver, Timothy Donald
Smith, Glynn Garner
Smith, Kathryn Vaughn
Smith, Martin Reed
Stacy, Mr. & Mrs. Donald R.
Stephenson, John Timothy
Stephenson, Mr. & Mrs. Mason W.
Tate, Mr. & Mrs. John Austin, III
Tatzel, Teresa Ann
Taylor, Arline Johnson
Telford, Mrs. Sally S.
Thompson, Alice Carter
Thompson, Mary Elizabeth
Watson, Mrs. Susan Lee
Wells, Ida Maxwell
Wells, Mr. & Mrs. Robt. W.
Weston, Mr. & Mrs. Paul L.
Wilkinson, Daniel Douglas
Wilkinson, Mrs. Douglas
Wilkinson, Elizabeth Henrietta
Wilkinson, John Gilchrist
Wilkinson, Nancy Graham
Wilson, Mr. & Mrs. George F.

1974

Aguilera, Mrs. April M.
Akonchong, Andreas
Allen, Gregory L'heureux
Barclay, Thos. Michael
Benoy, Mr. & Mrs. Ira Clay
Boggs, Mrs. Wade
Bonkovsky, Mrs. Frederick
Brown, Barbara Lynne
Burroughs, Keith Jennison
Culp, Mr. & Mrs. William
Evans, Margaret Thornhill
Force, Ms. Linda Hunt
Gaffron, Camille
Goodhue, Katherine E.
Griffith, Mr. & Mrs. Walter Kimball
Hagan, Mrs. Frank
Holcomb, Richard Bruce
Hussel, Paul James
Hussel, Mrs. Shirley Lanter
Johnson, Dr. & Mrs. A. Emerson
Keller, Mrs. Norma P.
Kohn, Bryan Scofield
Landrum, Paul Berkeley
Lindburg, Dr. & Mrs. Donald G.
Lower, Mr. & Mrs. Robt. C.
McCreary, Fred R.
McGehee, Mr. & Mrs. Frank T.
McWhorter, Ms. Elizabeth Lee
Mobley, Mr. & Mrs. Donald Lyman
Mobley, Marcia Dodd
Montgomery, David Martin
Montgomery, Mr. & Mrs. J. Howard
Moore, Harold Bowman
Moulthrop, Mr. & Mrs. Philip C.
Newsom, M. William
O'Callaghan, Mrs. Richard H., Jr.
Oglesby, Frances Lipscomb
Peery, Mr. & Mrs. Geo.
Richardson, Mrs. R.P.
Richardson, Sydney
Richter, Mr. & Mrs. Eckhart
Richter, John Charles
Roberts, Irene Snow
Rotch, Mrs. Kenneth G.
Sizemore, Mr. & Mrs. Michael M.
Steinberg, Kathryn
Steinberg, Mrs. Lois
Taylor, Mrs. B. Harrison
Taylor, Martha Lela
Ward, Elizabeth Louise
White, Janie
Whitton, Mrs. Grace O.

1975

Allen, Clayton Richard
Ashe, Mr. & Mrs. R. Lawrence, Jr.
Boyce, Mr. & Mrs. James
Boykin, Roderick Keith
Cobb, Margaret McEver
Colladay, Franklin Grimes, Jr.
Davies-Venn, Mr. & Mrs. Prince C.
Dennis, Margaret Puryear
Dobbs, Margaret P.
Duffey, Carol C.
Duffey, Mrs. Freida
Erickson, Ms. Carleton G.

Evans, Edwin Cuttino
Hardge, Miriam Cowan
Harrel, John Allen, Jr.
Hendrix, Walter Clifford
Henry, Mary Virginia
Hollander, Todd Vaughan
Jennings, Wm. Paul
Johnson, Andrew Emerson, IV
Johnson, Rebecca
Lang, Julia Alrich
Lastinger, Barry M.
Layne, Irving Rodgers
Lindburg, Lori Kristen
McChesney, Mr. & Mrs. Samuel J.
McCune, Amy
McCune, Mr. & Mrs. Jack C.
McCune, John Jeremy
McCune, Mary Conner
McCune, Tessa T.
Meacham, Katharine Rothrock
Morgan, John Michael
Oglesby, Jane Martin
Powell, John E.
Reinoehl, Judy K.
Richmond, Robt. L., Jr.
Sanders, Pamela Lavette
Smith, George Marriner
Tatzel, Thos. Christoff
Telford, Geo. Brown, III
Tennis, Mark Hibbard
Wallace, Wm. M., Jr.
Warnock, Mr. & Mrs. Wm. H.
West, Herbert Jahiel, III
Whitley, Mr. & Mrs. Richard Lee
Wilson, Geo. Francis III
Wilson, Jon Thomas
Wilson, Robin Brownlow
Witherspoon, Eugene Daniel, III
Witherspoon, Katherine Ann
Witherspoon, Mrs. Peggy Fitch

1976

Biola, Mr. & Mrs. Joseph L.
Brooke, Mr. & Mrs. Gary T.
Curtis, Mr. & Mrs. Wm. E.
Dennis, Julie Robson
Dickson, Mrs. Robert W.
Enniss, Mrs. P.C. (Jane)
Enniss, Stephen Crosley
Erickson, Judy Lorraine
Gaines, Mrs. Alex P.
Grider, Susan Gray
Gunn, William Knox
Ireland, Mrs. Vera
Jennings, Mr. & Mrs. David C.
Kelly, Mrs. Betsy
Kennedy, Mrs. Frances Harris
Kennedy, Jane Harris
Kennedy, William Bean, Jr.
Kohn, Alan Earle
McClure, Donald A.
Neil, Mrs. Elizabeth M.
Neil, Elizabeth McClung
Neil, Marshall Banks, IV
Nix, Mary Evelyn
Oglesby, Richard Archer, Jr.
Pritchard, Mrs. Shirley
Richardson, Daniel Clyde
Ritchie, Catherine Cloe
Roberts, Ruby Lee
Russell, Caroline Ruth
Snyder, Mr. & Mrs. Robt. J.
Snyder, Susan Harriet
Stevens, Richard E., Jr.
Telford, John David
Thomas, Mr. & Mrs. Richard E.
Wheeler, Mr. & Mrs. Jas. Houston
Whiteside, Mr. & Mrs.Carl

1977

Brown, Mrs. Nancy Lowenkopf
Brunjes, Mr. & Mrs. Martin Edward
Burns, Beth
Burns, Mrs. Doris T.
Burns, Jon
Burns, Leah
Burns, Paul
Butts, David Stuart
Campbell, Thomas J.
Carlson, Mr. & Mrs. Dennis M.
Chalenor, Henrietta
Cook, Mr. & Mrs. Geo. T.
Counts, Louise
Force, Leanne
Good, Laura
Graham, Dr. Mildred W.
Hadley, Dr. Elizabeth Lime
Hammond, Mr. & Mrs. Larry H.
Hoskins, Mrs. Shirley H.
Jackson, Mrs. Ann King
Johnson, Mrs. Carolyn M.
Kennedy, Emily
Knox, Mr. & Mrs. William L.
Layne, Elizabeth
Linville, Wayne H.
Lloyd, Mr. & Mrs. Michael Hampton
Merritt, Mr. & Mrs. Dewey, Jr.
Overman, Mr. & Mrs. Thomas L.
Pervis, Ann
Purdon, Mr. & Mrs. Gerald R.
Purdon, Helen E.
Purdon, Jeffrey R.
Sanders, Michael
Schwartz, Mrs. Arthur
Stevens, Judy Lynne
Tate, Mr. & Mrs. Frank Carter
Taylor, Benjamin H., III
Taylor, John Hendricks
White, Mr. & Mrs. Jeff V.
Wilson, Dan

1978

Anglin, Mr. & Mrs. Homer E., Jr.
Bacon, Allan McLain
Bryan, Rebecca Lindsey
Cramer, Mr. & Mrs. Jeffrey D.
de La Rue, Mrs. Ann I.
Donham, Mr. & Mrs. Victor Reid
Ellis, Mary Ann
Fowlkes, Edward O.
Green, Rebecca D.
Hebert, Mr. & Mrs. Paul B.
Hightower, Mrs. Catherine S.
Huang, Mr. C.P.
Keaton, David Arthur
Keaton, Eric Nathaniel
Keaton, Mr. & Mrs. Jerry R.
Kyser, Julie
Lang, Jennifer Blair
Lehfeldt, Elizabeth Anne
Long, Mrs. Sherrill T.
Montgomery, Mr. & Mrs. William D.
Parsons, Annelee N.
Richardson, Anne Elizabeth
Savage, Donald Walter
Shipley, Elizabeth Claire
Sweat, Mrs. Peggy
Thurman, Martha Rebecca
Trottier, Ralph & Gay
Vepraskas, Mr. & Mrs. Marc
Webb, Beth

MEMBERS WHOSE YEAR OF JOINING IS UNKNOWN

Abbott, Albert
Abbott, Mrs. B.F.
Abbott, Mrs. Josephine
Abbott, Mrs. Kate C.
Ackerman, Mrs. Lena
Adams, Mrs. Clara K.
Adams, Mrs. John
Adams, Mrs. Mary K.
Akers, Annie Rosa
Akers, Mrs. Margie Morris
Akins, Mrs. M.
Alexander, Mrs. Eloise
Allen, Mrs. C.E.
Allen, Mrs. Elizabeth
Allen, Rotha Florence
Anderson, Mrs. A.A.
Anderson, Gracie L.
Appleyard, Mary
Arglin, Mrs. J.S.
Armstrong, Mrs. Mamie Frierson
Ash, Mrs. Manolia
Ash, T.J.
Askew, Mrs. Mary Woolf
Askew, Mrs. Mattie D.
Bain, M.D.
Baird, Mrs. Annie R.
Baird, Geraldine Alice
Baker, Mrs. R.M.
Bancker, Mrs. Nellie Black
Barfield, Mrs. Eva Abernathy
Barth, Alfred H.
Barth, Raimond Walter
Barth, Mrs. Rosalie Robinson
Barry, Mrs. Conkline
Barry, Conkline
Beatie, Mrs. Annie L.
Beem, Mrs. Maud M.
Bell, S.O.
Berkele, Mamie
Billingsly, Mrs. L.B.
Block, Ellen D.
Block, Frank C.
Block, Hamilton
Block, Mrs. Margaret
Boone, Mrs. Eliza H.
Bostrom, Mrs. Ella S.
Bostrom, Ernest A.
Boyd, Thomas M.
Brisendine, Miss Hattie
Brisendine, Mrs. Hattie
Brisendine, James M.
Brock, Mrs. Callie Robinson
Brooks, Mrs. J.B.
Brooks, Mrs. Matilda C.
Brown, Mrs. Bessie Young
Brown, Mrs. Ludie C.
Bruce, Cora

THE PEOPLE WHO STAYED (1858-1978)

Bryan, Florence Clair
Bryan, Mrs. Mary Russell
Bryant, Rountree
Buck, Mrs. A.E.
Bull, Mrs. Pearl Barron
Burruss, Mrs. Eddie Poel
Butler, Candler
Calhoun, Dr. A.W.
Calhoun, M.L., Jr.
Calhoun, Mrs. Mary Louise
Camp, Mrs. Maries
Cannon, Mrs. M.L.
Carlisle, Frederick
Carmichael, Mrs. Annie L.
Carmichael, C. Paschal
Carmichael, Lemuel R.
Carter, Mrs. Fannie I. Hooker
Cartledge, Mary
Chisholm, Mrs. Willie K.
Clarke, Mrs. Amanda S.
Clarke, John S.
Clarke, Logan
Clarke, Mrs. Mary Cartledge
Clarke, Walter
Clayton, Charles A.
Clayton, Mrs. Corinne H.
Clayton, Mrs. Felixina
Clayton, John M.
Clayton, Julia Adelaide
Clayton, Mary Rose
Cochran, Mrs. Lotta Clayton
Coffin, Mrs. Ida B.
Cole, Mrs. Kate Brantley
Colhaner, Willie J.
Collier, Mrs. Estelle Morgan
Cone, Mrs. Whittie Warner
Cone, William Warner
Connally, Mrs. Emma Calhoun
Cook, Mary Elizabeth
Cooper, Caroline
Corley, John Thomas
Corrie, Alexander
Corrie, Hazel
Corrie, Samuel W.
Corrie, Wallace
Cotton, Marion Leftwich
Cotton, William G.
Craig, Newton
Crawford, Mrs. Mary
Crist, Mrs. Flora Fain
Croft, George M.
Crusoe, Mrs. Annie S.
Cummings, F.A.
Cunningham, Miss Erin L.
Dabney, Tyree J.
Dargan, James T., Jr.
Dargan, Thelma M.
Davis, Mrs. Anna
Davis, Elizabeth
Davis, Jim Brown
Davis, Mrs. Rose
Dean, Mrs. Alice York
Dean, Lovic Marshall
Dennis, John H.
DeVore, Mrs. Estelle P.
DeVore, Kirk Le Masters
Dickert, Mrs. Annie Reed
Dickson, Mrs. Marie
Drier, Mrs. Susan
Dryman, Talmage Lamar
Dunlap, Mrs. John G.
Dunwody, Mamie
Ebbert, Mary R.
Edwards, Mrs. L.E.
Eickerhout, Mrs. Nellie R.
Elder, Mildred Love
Elgin, Mrs. Susan P.
Emery, Miss E.
Epps, George
Ervin, Mrs. Allie
Evans, Mrs. Annie Nelson
Evans, Mrs. Mary Lumslen
Evans, R.R.
Farr, Carrie
Farr, Lois
Fife, Mrs. Eva Miller
Fife, George
Finkell, Albert
Finkell, Mrs. Ella
Finkell, George D.
Fisher, Mrs. Ellen G.
Flemming, L.K.
Flemming, Mrs. L.K.
Force Mrs. Alice Logan
Fraser, Allie
Fraser, Marie
Frazier, Isaac Newton
Friesake, Mrs. Mamie C.
Frierson, Paul
Fuller, H. Walter
Fuller, Mrs. Mollie
Fulton, Mrs. India H.
Fuss, Albert L.
Gaines, Dr. Lewis M.
Gaines, Mary Eloise
Garrett, Mrs. Maude D.
Gilbert, Theodore
Gonzales, Mrs. Emma Bowie
Goodman, Mrs. Mary H.
Goodrum, Mrs. Agnes
Gowdy, Gussie
Gowdy, Mrs. Jennie Helmer
Grant, James L.
Grant, Caroline McIntyre
Grant, George M.
Grant, Henry W.
Grant, Mrs. L.P.
Grant, Nellie
Greene, Mrs. Anna R.
Greene, Archie S.
Greene, Ernest N.
Greene, Harriette L.
Greene, J.E.
Greene, Leslie C.
Greenlee, Gertrude N.
Gregory, Mrs. Emma
Griffin, Mrs. Nettie Wood
Grow, Myra
Grow, Steve
Hacklett, Coole
Hale, Mrs. Olive M.
Hall, Mrs. Martha T.
Hall, Mrs. Mary C.
Hall, Mrs. Nellie C.
Hardwick, R.W.
Harris, Mrs. Romo Barfield
Hayden, Mrs. Martha
Heard, Isaac
Heath, Eliza
Hendon, Mrs. Mattie
Hendrix, Annie
Hesterly, Anna
Heston, William Manry
Heston, William Reed
Hiett, Mrs. Lillie M.
Hightower, Mrs. Annie Myers
Hill, Delos Lemuel, Jr.
Hill, Mrs. Sallie C.
Hodnett, Mrs. Mary E.
Hodnett, Ruth
Holley, Mrs. Sara B.
Hooker, Carrie Victoria
Hopgood, Mrs. Annie Clarke
Howard, Mrs. Sarah R. Whitner
Howland, Mrs. Anne Wallace
Hubner, Mrs. Frank
Hudson, Mrs. Elvena G.
Hudson, Mrs. Myrtis Morgan
Hunter, James K.
Hunter, James K., Jr.
Hunter, Mrs. Vance
Hutchison, Mrs. Julian A.
Hyatt, Mrs. Carrie C.
Hyman, W.P.
Jackson, Evlene
Jackson, Mrs. Floyd Brewer
Jackson, Mamie Ethel
Jackson, Mrs. Sara
Jackson, Stonewall Jefferson
Jackson, Mrs. Stonewall M.
Jarvis, Mrs. Mary
Jawett, Simpson Y.
Jefferis, Dr. Francis
Jenkins, Nim
Johnson, Mrs. Annie Mae
Johnson, Mrs. Eleanor M.
Johnson, Mary I.
Jones, Azile
Jones, J.C.
Jones, James Logan
Jones, Mrs. Jessie Thornton
Jones, John A.
Jones, Mrs. Lillian Taylor
Jones, Mrs. Lou H.
Jones, Mrs. Mary C.
Jordan, Mrs. Annie M.
Joyner, Mrs. W.R.
Keeley, Maxwell M.
Kemp, Mrs. Frances E.
Kemp, Jehu C.
Kendrick, Mrs. Lula G.
Kendrick, Martha Frances
Kendrick, Mary Beulah
Kennedy, Mrs. Jane
Kennedy, Mrs. Mary Broughton
Kershaw, Mrs. Elizabeth W.
Ketner, James
Ketner, Richard
Ketron, Mrs. Nettie Lee C.
Kile, Mrs. Julia Harper
King, Mrs. Clara Belle R.
King, Clyde L., Jr.
King, James K.
Kingsberry, Mrs. Caroline F.
Kingsberry, Mrs. Laura J.
Kirby, Alton B.
Kirkpatrick, Maude
Lake, Mrs. Laura
Lambwright, Mrs. Lalla C.
Lawhorn, Mrs. Addie Stewart
Leach, Mrs. Ida Wingo
Leas, Julius Edwin
Leas, Mrs. Lula Eugenia

Logan, Prof. J.H.
Magbee, Mrs. Fannie P.
Magruder, Florence Edith
Magruder, Mrs. Mary Ramsey
Mallard, Mrs. Clara E.
Mallard, John L.
Mallard, John L., Jr.
Mallard, Mrs. Virignia E.
Mallard, Mrs. W.S.
Mallard, Wallace
Manahan, Mrs. Cynthia
Mann, Tilla L.
Manning, Mrs. Rosa Word
Marion, Robert F.
Marlin, Mrs. Kate Gowdy
Martin, Mrs. Rose
Mason, Albert Bellingrath
Mather, Elliot W.
Mathews, James T., Jr.
Maxey, Mrs. P.S.
Meader, Joseph J., Jr.
Meadow, Mrs. Mary E.
Meares, T.M.
Miller, James
Milner, James A.
Milner, Whitner
Mizzell, Mrs. Mamie
Montgomery, C.D., Jr.
Moore, Mrs. Hattie
Moore, Marion
Moore, Mrs. Thomas
Morgan, Claudia
Morgan, Dr. E.T.
Morgan, Herbert
Morgan, Jennie Anita
Mudge, Mrs. Annie
Mudge, Charles H.
Munger, Charles E.
Murphy, Mrs. Ella H.
Murphy, Dr. J.B.
Mynatt, Mrs. P.L.
McCay, Judge H.K.
McClaughry, Mrs. C.C.
McClaughry, Charles C.
McClaughry, Esther
McClaughry, Helen
McClaughry, Robert
McClelland, Grace
McClelland, Mrs. H.A.
McClelland, Minnie
McCoy, Catherine T.
McCrea, Mrs. Charlotte Hall
McDearmid, August
McDonald, Nellie E.
McGaughy, Bessie Estelle
McGaughy, Mrs. George W.
McGhee, Mrs. Mary J.
McIntire, Mrs. S. Louise
McKinley, Junia
McKoy, John J.
McLeod, Elizabeth
McLeod, James
McMasters, Lilly
McMillan, Cornelia Alfriend
McMillan, Mrs. Marie Alfriend
Nall, Mrs. L.C.
Neville, Charles R.
Neville, Joseph E.
Nichols, Kate
Nolan, Irene
Oglesby, Mrs. Susan Calhoun
O'Leary, Mrs. Bessie Marshall
Orme, A.J., Jr.
Orme, Callie J.
Orme, Mrs. Callie Jackson
Orme, Sarah C.
Orr, Mrs. Minnie
Ottley, Mrs. Passya
Page, Mrs. Louise
Parker, Mrs. Lelia
Parkhurst, Mrs. A.A.
Parkhurst, W.P.
Parkins, Isabel
Patrick, Margaret
Peacock, George T.
Pennington, Mrs. Annie B.
Perkins, Addie
Phillips, Mrs. Crawford
Pierce, John H.
Pierce, Maggie
Pierce, S.H.
Pike, Everett Hale
Pike, Mrs. Marion Corrie
Pinson, DeWitt
Pinson, Mrs. G.A.
Pinson, Mrs. P.A.
Pittman, Mrs. Nancy
Pittman, Mrs. Nannie
Plott, George F.
Porter, Mrs. Fannie L.
Porter, J.W.
Porter, J. Henry
Porter, Mrs. Katie Hook
Porter, William L.
Poss, Mrs. Martha Jane
Powers, Horace
Pritchard, Mrs. Katie M.
Rainey, Mrs. Ella
Rainey, Francis A.
Rainey, J. Thomas
Rainey, Ruth
Rainey, T.A.
Rainey, Mrs. T.A.
Ray, Ruby Felder
Redus, Attilee
Redus, Robert K.
Reed, Prentiss Bishop
Reid, Jessie S.
Rhoden, Mrs. Ethel Chaffin
Rigutti, Ferdinande
Ripley, Dr. E.C.
Ripley, Mrs. E.C.
Rivers, Mrs. Una Speery
Roberts, Mrs. Harry
Roberts, Mrs. Hattie
Roberts, Howard H.
Roberts, Mrs. Nancy E.
Robinson, Alice M.
Rogers, Mrs. Catherine C.
Rogers, Edith
Rosborough, Mrs. Anna C.
Rosborough, Caroline
Rosignol, Daisy M.
Rosignol, S.K.
Rosignol, Mrs. S.K.
Rushton, Margaret E.
Rustin, Mrs. Rainey Stout
Sanders, Mrs. Alice Fisk
Sawtell, Mrs. E.V.
Sawtell, Mary T.
Sawtell, Susie
Scattergood, Mrs. Eleanor H.
Schroeder, Augusta
Schwitzerlet, Mrs. Mary
Selby, Dorothy
Sharp, Mrs. Felix
Sharp, Mrs. Mattie Forbes
Smith, Mrs. Alice Coffin
Smith, Annie L.
Smith, Caleb Orion
Smith, Mrs. Cordelia
Smith, Mrs. Georgia E.
Smith, Hattie Lee
Smith, Horace Lacy
Smith, Mrs. Nannie Tuttle
Smith, Nellie Maude
Smith, Mrs. Sara Croft
Smith, Mrs. Sara Lane
Smith, Mrs. Sara Wyly
Smith, Mrs. Serena Butt
Smith, William Francis, III
Snead, Mrs. Lillian Z.
Spear, James O., Jr.
Spear, Mrs. Martha Cobb H.
Spencer, Mrs. Maria
Stephenson, Mrs. Lily May W.
Stevenson, Mrs. Eva
Stevenson, Clyde
Stevenson, Hazel
Stewart, Agnes M.
Stewart, Mrs. James H.
Stewart, Mrs. Mary Hooker
Stillman, Adra Lois
Stillman, Mrs. Laura
Stillman, Mrs. Mary
Stockdell, Mrs. Annie E.
Stokes, Mrs. W.F.
Stokes, William John
Stockton, Bobbie
Stockton, Ella
Stone, F.I.
Stone, F.J.
Stone, Mrs. Virginia Butler
Strickler, Mrs. Annie W.
Stull, Meade
Sturgean, Mrs. Lula V.
Swain, Mrs. Emma
Swain, John
Swift, Mattie R.
Taylor, Mrs. Bell Helmer
Taylor, Mrs. Lucy Bowie
Telford, Lee J.
Telford, Mrs. Maggie
Telford, Mary
Telford, W.L.
Thomas, Mrs. Mary York
Thompson, James Perrin
Thompson, Mrs. Janie Perrin
Thompson, Mrs. Irene Meridith
Thompson, Mrs. Lois Hodnett
Thompson, Mrs. Manise E.
Thompson, Mrs. Marx Perrin
Thompson, Mary Perrin
Thompson, R.C.
Thompson, W. Caldwell
Thornton, Mattie
Tickner, Mrs. Irving L.
Tidwell, Mrs. Marie Clio
Tillander, Leanus
Torrence, Mrs. Kate Clayton
Tracy, Mrs. Ray Griffith
Tucker, Mrs. Harriet A.
Tucker, William Armistead

THE PEOPLE WHO STAYED (1858-1978)

Twitchell, Mrs. Maude W.
Tye, Mrs. Carrie
Underwood, Mrs. Anna W.
Vaughn, Mrs. M.E.
Vawter, Thomas
Wallace, Mrs. Mary E.
Ward, Mrs. Leta Dallas
Weddell, Mrs. Lillian S.
Weeks, A.H.
Weeks, Caroline
Weeks, Miss Georgia
Weeks, Mabel
Weeks, Paul
Wells, Mrs. C. Florida
Wells, Mrs. Katie Cotton
Wells, William LaCoster
Wetmore, Charles H.
Whitlock, Mrs. Lelah
Whitner, Casper Simpson
Whitner, Charles F., Jr.
Whitner, Corrie S.
Whitner, Mrs. Emily Tichenor
Whitner, Henry Farrow
Whitner, John A., Jr.
Whitner, John Selby
Whitner, Mrs. Margaret Badger
Whitner, Thomas Cobb, Jr.
Wight, C.B.
Wilby, Mrs. Martha H.
Wilkinson, Mrs. Nannie
Willbrook, Mrs. Willie Pratte
Williams, Mrs. Addie C.
Williams, Mrs. Caroline C.
Williams, Mrs. Carrie
Williamson, Mrs. Jessie
Wilson, Mrs. Banna
Wilson, Mrs. Fannie Wallace
Wilson, Frank W.
Wilson, Mrs. Hattie
Wilson, Mrs. Iva E.
Wilson, J. Ross
Wilson, Mrs. J.W.
Wingo, Mrs. A.M.
Winn, Mrs. Lillie Van Epps
Wood, Mrs. Clara Morris
Wooding, Lillian
Wooding, N.J.
Woolf, Mrs. Ida P.
Wright, Mrs. Bertha L.
Wright, Mrs. Steve Catherine
Wyatt, M.
Yarborough, Mrs. Martha Stout
York, Fannie
York, Grady
York, John W.
York, Josiah C.
Young, Mrs. Eliza C.

DEACONS FROM 1858-1972

Rotation system started in 1961

1964 Abbott, George P., Sr.
1961 Alexander, J.E.
1912 Alexander, J. Harry
1961 Allen, R.L.
1970 Allen, Richard
1880 Anderson, Robert A.
1954 Ball, Samuel T.
1961 Bansley, J. David
1930 Bansley, John D., Jr.
1966 Bansley, Mrs. John D., Jr.
1943 Barbour, H. Wey
1964 Baria, Dr. William H.
1880 Barry, John A.
1962 Beachy, Robert C.
1870 Beatie, David A.
1945 Beatie, George L.
1958 Bellinger, Fred
1970 Bellinger, Mrs. Fred
1873 Block, Frank E.
1942 Boles, S.P.
1932 Bradshaw, J.A.
1962 Bradshaw, J.A., Jr.
1949 Bray, Hal W.
1957 Bright, Norris W.
1905 Brown, J.W.
1910 Brown, Paul F., Sr.
1938 Brown, Paul F., Jr.
1933 Brown, Dr. Samuel Y.
1966 Brown, Mrs. Samuel Y.
1961 Bryan, George W., Jr.
1969 Bryan, Dr. John A., Jr.
1923 Buchanan, William F.
1961 Burch, Marvin C.
1939 Butler, Ben
1964 Byington, Gerald A.
1938 Calkins, J.W.
1896 Campbell, J. Bulow
1933 Carlisle, Harry Lewis
1968 Carlisle, Mrs. Harry Lewis
1957 Carter, Frank E.
1957 Carver, Charles E.
1932 Clapp, M.G.
1962 Clark, Evert E.
1961 Clark, Jack C.
1873 Clarke, Thomas M.
1896 Clayton, Robert M.
1970 Cobb, Ike W.
1894 Cole, Fred W.
1958 Collins, A.W.
1930 Cook, Sam W.
1910 Cotton, W.W.
1970 Covington, Thomas, Jr.
1936 Cowan, R.E.
1943 Craig, Milton S.
1950 Crenshaw, Albert D.
1943 Crenshaw, John W.
1938 Crosland, W.A.
1930 Davis, A.O.
1962 Davis, Arthur O., Jr.
1896 Davis, Edwin D.
1943 DeFoor, Andy L.
1921 Dement, Dr. Robert L.
1949 Dendy, W. Clay
1967 Dennis, Dr. Brown W.
1903 Dickert, J.S.
1932 Dickson, James H.
1954 Dickson, James H., Jr.
1950 Dickson, Robert W.
1925 Dickson, Thomas C.
1959 Dorsey, George A.
1894 Eagan, John J.
1949 Eagan, William R.
1962 Edwards, Robert R.
1968 Eller, Lynn
1962 Ellison, Hairston M.
1870 Fain, John N.
1958 Fairleigh, George D.
1958 Fesperman, E.H.
1961 Fife, William M.
1913 Floding, W.E.
1947 Gaines, Alex P.
1912 Gaines, Dr. L.M.
1920 Gillespy, E.H.
1941 Glover, George Z.
1939 Graham, George
1969 Green, William O.
1950 Greene, Roy T.
1945 Greene, William Jeff, Jr.
1968 Guthrie, David
1967 Hacke, J. Richard
1894 Hale, Moses A.
1968 Hall, Richard W.
1939 Happoldt, Albert S.
1864 Harden, Dr. W.P.
1947 Heath, Gordon A.
1917 Heery, C.W.
1916 Heston, W.R.
1940 Hill, Hines L.
1933 Hills, Henry L.
1968 Hills, Mrs. Henry L.
1936 Hills, Richard A.
1912 Hodnett, A.W.
1949 Hollingsworth, J. Hope
1942 Hollingsworth, R.L.
1916 Howard, Whitner
1964 Hudson, Henry W.
1930 Huie, Ralph A.
1936 Humphries, W. Franklin
1950 Hunt, Paul W.
1965 Isaacs, Dr. James
1908 Jackson, Marion M.
1921 Johnston, Dr. Harry B.
1913 Jones, Dr. E.G.
1930 Jones, John Ashley
1958 Kane, Edward R.
1969 Kehrer, E.T.
1968 Kelley, Gordon B.
1903 Kirk, J.E.
1889 Kirkpatrick, John C.
1896 Knight, Lucian L.
1932 Knapp, John C.
1961 Kohn, Norman S.
1970 Kohn, Mrs. Norman S.
1925 Lake, Frank G.
1957 Large, Joseph W.
1935 Leach, R.L.
1962 Leftwich, Charles H.
1943 Lennard, Julius M., Jr.
1951 Lindsay, Lamar
1951 Logan, Joseph A.
1964 MacKay, Douglas A.
1916 MacLagan, R.W.
1933 MacRae, Douglas
1896 Martin, Charles J.
1969 Milner, I. Carl
1905 Milner, Willis J.
1880 Mitchell, Henry C.
1894 Montgomery, Charles D.
1917 Morrison, J.E.
1962 McClure, William J.
1970 McCord, Ned J., Jr.
1912 McCrea, T.H.
1943 McKee, J. Burruss
1968 McLeod, Marion E.
1900 McMillan, Garnett

Elders and Deacons, 1940

THE PEOPLE WHO STAYED (1858-1978)

1966 Neel, Richard
1968 Nelms, Frank D.
1938 Nessling, A.C.
1942 Newman, J.W.
1868 Newton, Charles S.
1964 Nix, John A.
1962 Oastler, Thomas W.
1957 O'Callaghan, Ben L.
1947 O'Callaghan, L.J.
1954 O'Callaghan, Richard H.
1918 O'Callaghan, W.J., Jr.
1955 Oglesby, M. Lamar
1951 Oglesby, Richard
1955 Ohl, Fred
1955 Palmer, Clarence
1934 Parker, O.J.
1868 Parkhurst, William F.
1970 Parnell, Albert H.
1864 Pease, P.P.
1942 Peddicord, Samuel R.
1868 Phillips, Henry T.
1880 Pinson, John L.
1958 Polk, James M.
1947 Radford, Garland S.
1947 Rand, Edgar O.
1929 Rand, F.L.
1945 Rayburn, F.T.
1968 Rebb, Otis M.
1966 Riddle, C.G., Jr.
1962 Robinson, Don C.
1858 Robinson, William P.
1964 Rogers, Frank W., Jr.
1943 Rogers, Kenneth
1964 Rogers, William G.
1941 Rumble, Douglas, Jr.
1889 Rushton, Robert E.
1925 Russey, George S.
1961 Savage, Walter H., Jr.
1964 Schaeffler, William A.
1964 Schneider, Guy H.
1962 Sharpe, B. Harold
1969 Shedd, Donald H.
1941 Shulenberger, J.H.
1966 Sims, C. William
1900 Simpson, O.F.
1955 Singleton, James F.
1935 Smith, B.H.
1921 Smith, Caleb O.
1900 Smith, Henry Lamar
1945 Smith, James D.
1936 Smith, L.N.
1946 Smith, Muggsy M.
1938 Smith, P.W.
1968 Sowell, C. Emmit
1946 Stalker, Ian
1964 Starnes, Robert A.
1966 Stephenson, Robert L.
1954 Stieglitz, Fred H.
1910 Stillman, Lowe
1905 Stokes, Charles A.
1900 Stone, F.I.
1942 Streater, Wallace F.
1945 Stribling, L.D.
1935 Strickler, G.B.
1915 Telford, J. Lee
1858 Thomas, George S.
1969 Thompson, Charles B.
1968 Thurman, C. Brown, Jr.
1949 Thurman, Charles B., Sr.
1955 Thurman, John K.
1917 Todd, Victor
1923 Tull, J.M.
1966 Turner, William M.
1929 Upchurch, Dr. W.A.
1939 Upchurch, Dr. W.E.
1896 Van Epps, Howard
1958 Veldhuis, J.A.
1970 Veldhuis, Mrs. J.A.
1964 Walker, Charles R.
1962 Wall, Hardy A.
1966 Walling, Robert H.
1917 Wardlaw, J.T.
1916 Way, E.L.
1935 West, Paul D.
1958 White, Robert E.
1864 Whitehead, Charles E.
1900 Whitner, Charles F.
1930 Whitner, Henry F.
1941 Whitner, Joseph
1954 Williams, Allen S.
1933 Willis, Eugene
1970 Wilson, Dan F.
1958 Wilson, Hugh A.
1941 Wilson, Robert E.
1945 Wilson, Sidney M.
1915 Winship, George, Jr.
1900 Woodruff, John W.
1939 Yarbrough, V. Jack
1939 York, Steele O.

ELDERS FROM 1858-1978

* indicates Elders for Life
Unicameral Rotation started in 1972

1968 *Alexander, Mrs. Victoria
1921 Alexander, J. Harry
1972 Allen, Richard
1974 Amos, Anthony
1977 Arnold, Frances Putman
1911 Axson, R.H.
1972 *Bansley, Grace Philips
1944 *Bansley, John D., Jr.
1972 *Barbour, H. Wey
1886 Barry, John A.
1859 Beach, John N.
1880 Beatie, David A.
1905 Beatie, W.D.
1968 *Bellinger, Frederick
1972 *Bellinger, Marie Parker
1977 Boggs, Wade H. III
1941 *Bradshaw, J.A., Jr.
1961 *Bray, Hal W.
1896 Brewster, Dr. T.F.
1913 Brown, J.W.
1971 *Brown, Marie Patterson
1939 Brown, Dr. Paul F., Jr.
1913 Brown, Dr. Paul F., Sr.
1946 Brown, Dr. Samuel Y.
1867 Brumby, A.V.
1966 Bryan, George W.
1972 Bryan, Dr. John A.
1977 Bryan, Robert F., Jr.
1912 Burruss, J.C.
1944 Butler, Ben
1900 Cameron, Benjamin H.
1903 Campbell, J. Bulow
1973 Caplan, I.L.
1937 Carlisle, Harry Lewis
1971 *Carlisle, Margaret Bansley
1967 Clark, Jack C.
1905 Clayton, Robert M.
1972 Cobb, Ike W.
1866 Cole, Moses
1972 Collins, A.W.
1975 Conklin, David
1918 Cotton, W.U.
1972 Covington, Thomas
1944 Crenshaw, John W.
1977 Daniel, Gayle Gellerstedt
1974 Daniel, Thomas R.
1974 Daniell, Winifred Griffith
1946 Davis, A.O., Sr.
1930 Dement, Dr. R.L.
1964 *Dendy, W. Clay
1971 Dennis, Dr. Brown W.
1968 Dickson, Dr. Robert W.
1930 Dickson, T.C.
1978 Dodd, Marcia
1903 Eagan, John J.
1977 Edenfield, Bruce M.
1972 Eller, Lynn
1880 Fain, John N.
1972 Fairleigh, George D.
1964 Fife, William M.
1918 Floding, W.E.
1955 *Gaines, Alex P.
1972 Gellerstedt, Larry L.
1968 *Glover, George Z.
1941 Graham, George
1977 Green, Trudy Curtis
1974 Green, William O.
1964 *Greene, Roy T.
1951 Greene, William J.
1977 Grider, Nancy Simon
1978 Griffith, Walter Kimball
1975 Hall, Richard
1962 *Happoldt, Albert S.
1939 Hansell, William A.
1928 Harvey, J.M.
1958 *Heath, Gordon A.
1925 Heston, W.R.
1972 Hills, Frances Oglesby
1951 *Hills, Henry L.
1975 Hollander, Kenneth A.
1944 Hollingsworth, R.L.
1933 Huie, R.A.
1977 Hunter, Ann Covington
1955 Jackson, James E.
1931 Jackson, Marion M.
1976 Johnson, Bettie McClintock
1973 Johnson, Walter
1928 Johnston, Dr. Harry
1934 Jones, John Ashley
1976 Jung, Jennifer
1913 Kendrick, W.S.
1896 Kendrick, Dr. W.S.
1977 Kimes, Martha Sanders
1901 Kingsbery, Edwin
1921 Kirk, J.E.
1896 Kirkpatrick, John C.
1934 Knapp, John C.
1976 Knight, Byron H.
1972 Kohn, Katherine Upchurch
1971 Kohn, Norman S.
1936 Lake, Frank G.
1925 Leadingham, Dr. R.S.
1977 Lehfeldt, Ann Ashford
1976 Lehfeldt, Martin
1949 Lennard, Julius M., Jr.
1975 Lewis, Bella Wilson
1880 Link, Dr. James A.
1858 Logan, Dr. Joseph P.
1972 Longbine, F. William
1886 Lumpkin, Prof. W.W.
1931 Maclagan, R.W.

Elders and deacons, 1958, in the semi-circular Sunday School assembly room, then used during the week by the baby clinic.

THE PEOPLE WHO STAYED (1858-1978)

1917 Maclean, Joseph
1975 MacRae, Annis Warner Phillips
1939 *MacRae, Douglas G.
1912 Martin, Charles J.
1972 Mathieson, Neil B.
1900 Montgomery, C.D.
1958 Montgomery, J. Howard
1936 Morrison, J.E.
1866 Murphy, Dr. John B.
1880 Mynatt, Pryor L.
1965 McClure, William J.
1873 McConnell, S.D.
1972 McCord, Ned J.
1977 McCord, Trip
1974 McCord, Virginia Parker
1978 McCreary, Fred R.
1972 McFarland, J. Edgar
1973 McLeod, Marion E.
1964 *McMahan, John H.
1905 McMillan, Garnett
1866 McNaught, William
1880 Newton, Charles S.
1972 Nix, John A.
1972 Oastler, Thomas W.
1972 O'Callaghan, Carolyn Winburn
1968 O'Callaghan, Richard H.
1930 O'Callaghan, W.J., Jr.
1971 Oglesby, M. Lamar
1968 Oglesby, Richard A.
1966 Oglesby, Stuart R., III
1961 Ohl, Fred
1963 *Palmer, Clarence E.
1896 Parkhurst, W.F.
1972 Parnell, Albert H.
1972 Parnell, Missy Satterfield
1861 Patton, Julius M.
1978 Pickens, John A.
1929 Rand, F.L.
1880 Rankin, Jessie W.
1972 Rebb, Otis M.
1858 Rhea, John Q.
1972 Robinson, Donald C.
1973 Robinson, Joseph L.
1960 *Rogers, Frank W., Sr.
1963 *Rogers, Kenneth
1896 Rushton, Robert E.
1972 Sanders, Walter L.
1975 Savage, Carleen Robinson
1973 Savage, Walter H.
1971 Schneider, Guy H.
1972 Schneider, Shirley Dunn
1900 Selby, J.W.
1972 Shipley, Norman B.
1936 Smith, C.O.
1949 *Smith, James D.
1886 Spencer, Samuel B.
1964 Stalker, Ian F.
1859 Stone, A.W.
1972 *Streater, Wallace F.
1949 *Strickler, G.B.
1976 Tate, John A.
1977 Telford, Sally Stoeling
1900 Thompson, James R.
1972 Thurman, John K.
1933 *Todd, Victor F.
1972 Turner, William M.
1975 Turoff, Lew W.
1951 *Upchurch, Dr. Wilborn E.
1977 Unwerth, Frederick von
1867 Van Epps, A.C.
1972 Veldhuis, Alice Laughlin
1972 Veldhuis, Jerry A.
1873 Wallace, Campbell
1920 Wardlaw, J.T.
1974 Weltner, Charles L.
1941 West, Paul D.
1924 Whitner, J.A.
1896 Whitner, John A.
1866 Whitner, John C.
1978 Wildman, James H.
1973 Wilson, Emily Ransone
1972 Wilson, Hugh A.
1951 Wilson, Robert E.
1973 Windsor, Clayton C.
1939 Willis, Eugene F.
1937 Winship, George Sr.
1955 *Yarbrough, V. Jack
1956 York, Steele A.

MINISTERS IN CENTRAL PRESBYTERIAN CHURCH

Alexander, John M.
Andres, Benjamin
Arnold, Ernest J.
Balof, Terre
Bonkovsky, Fred
Boyle, William P.
Burns, Hugh
Burroughs, Keith
Calhoun, Malcolm
Clarke, Thomas Erskine
Daughdrill, J.H.
Gear, Felix B.
Griffin, Robert B.
Gunn, George W.
Hightower, Ross
Holt, Jack
Huck, William
Hunter, Rodney J.
Hussel, Oscar
Johnson, Kermit
Jones, William C.
Kennedy, William B.
Lancaster, Lewis H.
Long, Tom
Loring, Edward
Morgan, Herbert
Myers, Robert L.
McClurg, Patricia
McDaniel, James M.
Nash, David William
Neil, Marshall B.
Nkonge, Julius
Patterson, Merle
Ray, Dr. Archie C.
Richards, J. McD.
Richardson, James T.
Richardson, Robert P.
Shriver, Donald W.
Smith, John Robert
Steinberg, Maurice
Taylor, B. Harrison
Taylor, Hubert V.
Telford, George
Tennis, Diane
Tippit, A.S.
Turner, Charles C.
Ward, Jack
Wilkinson, Doug
Wingard, George T.
Witherspoon, Eugene

MINISTERS FROM CENTRAL PRESBYTERIAN CHURCH

Beale, Joseph D.
Bland, Byron
Bray, Henry W. (Hal), Jr.
Brown, William C.
Cotts, John
Crosland, William A., Jr.
Crow, John M.
Deifell, Jey
Foley, Henry Thomas
Hahn, Carl Joseph, Jr.
Hammond, William E.
Horne, Robert Eugene
Lake, Julian
Leach, Susan Carolyn
Mobley, Lyman
McKee, Charles T.
Sutherland, Murphy
Taylor, Hubert V.
Tucker, Joyce
Whitner, John A.
Whitner, Joseph C.
Willson, Patrick James

MINISTERS TO CENTRAL PRESBYTERIAN CHURCH

PASTORS

Boggs, William E.
Davis, W.E.
Enniss, P.C.
Lacy, Ben R.
Leftwich, J.T.
Mallard, R.Q.
Ogden, Dunbar H.
Oglesby, Stuart R.
Porter, R.K.
Rice, Theron H.
Rogers, J.L.
Stair, Fred R.
Strickler, G.B.
Taylor, J. Randolph

ASSOCIATE PASTORS

Bacon, Steve
Buzard, Laura
Cook, Walter G.
Crook, James R.
Grider, Edgar M.
Holler, Z.N.
Rea, Robert J.
Smith, Harold C.

Central's beginnings were reported in the *Intelligencer,* Atlanta's first successful daily paper. R.R. and Whitehall Street, 1860.

Parents Trip and Linda McCord, Elder/Grandmother Carleen Savage, Pastors Steve Bacon and P.C. Enniss. Being baptized is daughter Larkin, through Linda a fourth, and through Trip a third generation Centralite.

BIBLIOGRAPHY

Allen, Ivan, Jr., *Mayor: Notes on the Sixties*, New York, Simon and Schuster, 1971.

Bell, Piromis H., "The Calico House", *Atlanta Historical Bulletin*, Vol. I, No. 6, January, 1932.

Berry, Carrie, diary, 1864, *Typescript*, Atlanta Historical Society.

Brine, Florence W., "Central Presbyterian Church", *Atlanta Historical Bulletin*, Vol. III, No. 14, July, 1938.

Calhoun, James M., *Affidavit as to Facts in Regard to Surrender of Atlanta*, 1864, *Typescript*, Atlanta Historical Society.

Carter, Samuel, III., *The Siege of Atlanta, 1864*, New York, St. Martim's Press, 1973.

Central Presbyterian Church (1858-1978), records, official and unofficial, in archives of the Atlanta Historical Society as follows:

Extant minutes of Session, 1858-1970, with minutes of congregational meetings and annual reports.

Extant issues of the *Weekly* beginning in 1900.

Published brochures of Central Church.

Collected photographs.

Crane, Sara Clayton, personal reminiscences, 1861-1864, *Typescript*, Atlanta Historical Society.

Eagan, John J., private collection, 1865-1940, Atlanta Historical Society.

Files of Atlanta newspapers, Atlanta Historical Society, selected issues of:

Atlanta Constitution

Atlanta Evening Capitol

Atlanta Georgian

Atlanta Journal

Daily Intelligencer

Georgia Temperance Crusader

Files of Atlanta photographs, Atlanta Historical Society.

Flint River Presbytery, minutes, 1857-1864, Historical Foundation, Montreat, N.C.

Fries, Adelaide L., "The Elizabeth Sterchi Letters", *Atlanta Historical Bulletin*, Vol. V., No. 21, April, 1940.

Garrett, Franklin M., *Atlanta and Environs*, Vols. I and II, Atlanta, University of Georgia Press, 1969.

Garrett, Franklin M., *Yesterday's Atlanta*, Miami, E.E. Seemann Publishing, Inc., 1974.

Grant, Lemuel P., private papers, 1840-1864, Atlanta Historical Society.

Hoehling, Adopph A., *Last Train from Atlanta*, New York, Thomas Yoseloff, 1959.

Isham, John, journal, 1870's, Atlanta, Historical Society.

Kurtz, Wilbur G., paintings of early Atlanta, photographed copies, Atlanta Historical Society.

Martin, Thomas H., *Atlanta and its Buildings*, two volumes, Atlanta, Century Memorial Publishing Company, 1902.

McCallie, Elizabeth H., "Atlanta in the 1850's", *Atlanta Historical Bulletin*, Vol. VIII, No. 33, October, 1948.

Nesbitt, Martha Tovell, *The Social Gospel in Atlanta: 1900-1920*, unpublished dissertation manuscript, 1975, Atlanta Historical Society.

Oglesby, Stuart R., private collection, 1915-1975, Atlanta Historical Society.

Richards, Samuel P., diary, Atlanta Historical Society.

Sibley, Celestine, *Peachtree City, U.S.A.*, New York, Doubleday, 1963.

Speer, Robert E., *John J. Eagan — A Memoir*, privately printed, 1939.

Talmage, Franklin C., *The Story of the Presbytery of Atlanta*, Atlanta, Foote and Davies, 1960.

Miss Gussie Fraser in 1923, the year she left for forty years service in China, sponsored by the Young Women's Missionary Society of Central Church. She is representative of Central's participation in world mission enterprises.

In 1858, Central member, Col. Lemuel P. Grant built his residence in the now Grant Park area. In 1859, he signed the original deed for the land on which Central still stands.

INDEX

Cafeteria style of serving present-day meals — Wednesday evenings and Sunday noon.